DISABLED PEOF[...]
AND WEL[...]

Is employment eally
the answei ?

Edited by Chris Grover and Linda Piggott

First published in Great Britain in 2015 by

Policy Press
University of Bristol
1-9 Old Park Hill
Bristol
BS2 8BB
UK
t: +44 (0)117 954 5940
pp-info@bristol.ac.uk
www.policypress.co.uk

North America office:
Policy Press
c/o The University of Chicago Press
1427 East 60th Street
Chicago, IL 60637, USA
t: +1 773 702 7700
f: +1 773-702-9756
sales@press.uchicago.edu
www.press.uchicago.edu

British Library Cataloguing in Publication Data
A catalogue record for this book is available from the British Library

Library of Congress Cataloging-in-Publication Data
A catalog record for this book has been requested

ISBN 978-1-4473-1833-0 paperback
ISBN 978-1-4473-1832-3 hardcover

Cover design by Robiin Hawes
Front cover image: www.alamy.com
Printed and bound in Great Britain by CMP, Poole
Policy Press uses environmentally responsible print partners.

For
Tom and Emma
Matthew and Robert

Contents

Contents

List of tables and figures

Tables

Figures

List of abbreviations

ACA	Affordable Care Act
ADA	Americans with Disabilities Act
ADL	anti-discrimination legislation
AFDC	Aid to Families with Dependent Children
ALMP	active labour market policy
BSL	British Sign Language
DAB	Disability Assessment Board
DDA	Disability Discrimination Act
DHH	deaf or hard of hearing
DHSSPS	Department of Health, Social Services and Public Safety
DWP	Department for Work and Pensions
EN	Employer Network
ESA	Employment and Support Allowance
EU	European Union
GDP	Gross Domestic Product
GP	general practitioner
IB	Incapacity Benefit
IWSC	Inner West Skills Centre
IWSP	In Work Support Project
JSA	Jobseeker's Allowance
KRUS	Agricultural Social Insurance Fund
LBR	*LokalBeskaeftelses Rad* (local employment committee)
NDDP	New Deal for Disabled People
NDIS	National Disability Insurance Scheme
NGO	non-governmental organisation
NHS	National Health Service
NICE	National Institute for Health and Care Excellence
npn	no page number
NWRN	National Welfare Rights Network
OECD	Organisation for Economic Co-operation and Development
PA	personal assistant
PLN	Polish Zloty
PRWORA	Personal Responsibility and Work Opportunity Reconciliation Act 1996
PtW	Pathways to Work
SFRDP	State Fund for Rehabilitation of Disabled Persons
SG	support group

SII	Social Insurance Institution
SIMD	Scottish Index of Multiple Deprivation
SSDI	Social Security Disability Insurance
SSI	Supplemental Security Income
TTW	Ticket To Work
UI	unemployment insurance
UK	United Kingdom
UN	United Nations
UNCRPD	United Nations' *Convention on the rights of persons with disabilities*
UPIAS	Union of Physically Impaired Against Segregation
US	United States
VAE	Vocational Activity Enterprise
VAS	Visual Analogue Scale
WCA	Work Capability Assessment
WP	Work Programme
WRAG	work-related activity group

Notes on contributors

Clare Bambra is a Professor of Public Health Geography at Durham University, UK. Her research focuses on the social and political determinants of public health and health inequalities, with a particular focus on welfare and labour markets. She is author of *Work, worklessness and the political economy of health* (Oxford University Press, 2011). She holds a Leverhulme Research Leadership Award, which investigates health inequalities in an age of austerity. She is the health inequalities lead of Fuse: The Centre for Translational Research in Public Health (funded by the Medical Research Council) and she is a member of the School for Public Health Research (funded by the National Institute for Health Research).

David Etherington is a Principal Researcher in the Centre for Enterprise and Economic and Development Research at Middlesex University, UK. He has been involved in developing research on comparative welfare and active labour market policy with a specific interest in the Danish and Nordic models. Other research interests include employment and skills policy, economic governance and social inclusion. David has undertaken research for the Joseph Rowntree Foundation, the Economic and Social Research Council, the Department for Work and Pensions, the Department for Business, Innovation & Skills and the European Commission. He has published in international peer-reviewed journals, including *Environment and Planning A*, the *Journal of European Social Policy* and *Work, Employment & Society*. David is currently working on a research project on welfare reform and benefit conditionality in the UK.

Deborah Fenney is a postgraduate researcher in the School of Sociology and Social Policy at the University of Leeds, UK. Her doctoral research explores disabled people's experiences of sustainable lifestyles through the concepts of 'environmental justice' and 'environmental citizenship'. Her research interests also include environmental and disability policy. Deborah's recent publications include 'Exceptions to the green rule? A literature investigation into the overlaps between the academic and UK policy fields of disability and the environment' (*Local Environment*, 2011).

Mariela Fordyce is a Research Fellow in the Centre for Research in Education, Inclusion and Diversity at the University of Edinburgh, UK. She has worked with children with special educational needs, and since gaining a PhD in special education from Hiroshima University in Japan she has published on issues related to deaf literacy and post-school outcomes of young people who are deaf or hard of hearing.

Kayleigh Garthwaite is a Postdoctoral Research Associate in the Department of Geography at Durham University, UK. She has been involved in a range of research projects around poverty, social exclusion, chronic illness, disability, health inequalities and worklessness. Currently, Kayleigh is working on a five-year project involving an urban ethnography of health inequalities in the borough of Stockton-on-Tees, UK. The project is examining how health inequalities are embodied in lived experiences. She is also co-author of *Poverty and insecurity: Life in low-pay, no-pay Britain* (Policy Press, 2012).

Robert Gould is a doctoral candidate in the Department of Disability and Human Development at the University of Illinois at Chicago, USA. He also works as the project coordinator of the ADA National Network Knowledge Translation Center systematic review of the Americans with Disabilities Act (ADA). His work and dissertation both explore the promise of disability rights in the context of the United States. His dissertation includes an evidence-based review of the ADA's progress towards achieving its goal of equal opportunity for disabled people. His broader research interests include social policy and evaluation, employment and vocational rehabilitation, and theories of rights and social justice as they pertain to disabled people. His past research and publications relate to his experience coordinating a state-wide evaluation of the state's managed healthcare programme for disabled people, and conducting a series of policy analyses of international trends in welfare policies, including a comparative study of liberal welfare-to-work programmes. He is currently the assistant to the editors of the forthcoming volume *Disability in American life: An encyclopedia of policies, concepts, and controversies* (ABC-CLIO). He intends to graduate with his PhD in disability studies from the University of Illinois at Chicago in 2015.

Chris Grover is a Senior Lecturer in Social Policy in the Law School at Lancaster University, UK. His research interests are in the political economy of social security policy. His recent work focuses on income replacement benefits for disabled people and 'special expenses' policy, and he is currently writing a book about state responses to low wages.

Edward Hall is a Senior Lecturer in Human Geography at the University of Dundee, UK. He has undertaken a series of research projects on the social geographies of disability, with a particular focus on learning disability. The projects have examined the positions and experiences of disabled people in employment; the social exclusion and inclusion of learning disabled people; the 'personalisation' of social care for disabled people; and the potential of creative arts to develop belonging for learning disabled people. These projects have been funded by the Economic and Social Research Council (ESRC), the Nuffield Foundation and the Scottish Government. Edward has published widely in leading journals, including *Environment and Planning A*, *Geoforum*, *Social & Cultural Geography* and *Disability & Society*, and co-edited, with Vera Chouinard and Robert Wilton, *Towards enabling geographies: Disabled bodies and minds in society and space* (Ashgate, 2010). In 2012–13 he coordinated an ESRC Seminar Series entitled 'Rethinking Learning Disability', bringing together academics from a range of disciplines, learning disabled people, social care practitioners and policy makers. His current research focuses on the experiences of disabled people of power outages in extreme weather events, and innovations in social care provision in a context of austerity.

Dan Heap is a PhD student and Senior Tutor in Social Policy at the University of Edinburgh, UK. His research focuses on active labour market policy for sick and disabled working-age benefit claimants in a cross-national perspective, with a focus on Britain and Denmark. His current projects are focused on establishing a way of measuring the institutionalisation of back-to-work support for such groups and on conceptualising the balance between increased benefit conditionality and better support.

Jo Ingold is a Lecturer in Human Resource Management and Public Policy at the University of Leeds, UK. She has previously worked in the voluntary sector and held posts in the Department for Work and Pensions and the Department for Education and Skills. Her research interests include active labour market programmes in comparative context, the intersection of care, work and welfare, and policy learning between countries. She has published in journals such as *Work, Employment & Society* and the *Journal of European Social Policy*. Jo is currently leading an ESRC Future Leaders project comparing employer engagement in active labour market programmes in Denmark and the UK.

Alan Morris is an Associate Professor and a researcher in the Australian Centre of Excellence for Local Government at the University of Technology, Sydney, Australia. His main areas of research are urban and housing studies, marginality and social policy. He has published extensively in peer-reviewed journals in Australia, South Africa, the

UK and the United States. He was recently awarded an Australian Research Council grant to investigate the circumstances of long-term private renters.

Randall Owen is a Research Assistant Professor in the Department of Disability and Human Development (DHD) at the University of Illinois at Chicago, USA. He earned a PhD in disability studies from DHD in 2011, and his dissertation focused on comparative policy analysis of welfare-to-work reforms in Australia, the United States and the UK. Randall is a mixed-methods researcher, with substantial experience conducting and analysing both focus groups and surveys. His research interests include healthcare policies and disparities, employment policies and practices, disability/human rights, the impacts of neoliberalism, and comparative analysis. The overarching theme of Randall's research and scholarship is the impact that policy reforms have on disabled people's lived experiences. He has published widely on the topic of rights and welfare to work, including articles in *Disability & Society, Disability Studies Quarterly* and the *Journal of Vocational Rehabilitation*. His current research projects focus on recent reforms to the Medicaid programme, focusing on the transition to Medicaid Managed Care for disabled people. These interests fuel the guest lectures Randall gives, as well as the graduate-level Introduction to Disability Policy course he teaches.

Sarah Parker Harris (formally Sarah Parker) is an Associate Professor in the Department of Disability and Human Development at the University of Illinois at Chicago, USA. She received her PhD in sociology and social policy from the University of Sydney in Australia, and has worked in social policy research, primarily relating to disability policies and programmes, economic and social inequalities and labour market and income support policies. She is experienced in mixed-method systematic reviews, comparative policy analysis, critical discourse analysis, programme evaluation and qualitative research design and analysis. Sarah has published and presented widely in areas of disability policy and law, social entrepreneurship, welfare-to-work and international human rights, and is co-author of *Disability through the lifecourse* (SAGE Publications, 2012) and co-editor of the forthcoming volume, *Disability in American life: An encyclopedia of policies, concepts, and controversies* (ABC-CLIO). Her research focuses on comparative and national disability policies and legislation, employment and entrepreneurship, human rights, theories of social justice and citizenship, and systematic review methodology of social policy. Current research grants include a five-year systematic review of the Americans with Disabilities Act, and an interdisciplinary pilot study that examines social entrepreneurship as a pathway to employment for disabled people. She teaches graduate courses in theories and perspectives of disability studies, and disability policies and legislation.

Ruth Patrick is a Postgraduate Researcher in the School of Sociology and Social Policy at the University of Leeds, UK. Her doctoral research explores the lived experiences of welfare reform in Britain and her research interests encompass social security, disability, citizenship and qualitative longitudinal research methods. She is a columnist for *Disability Now*, and was the research lead on the animated film project 'Dole Animators' (see www.doleanimators.org). Ruth's recent publications focus on welfare reform and the valorisation of work, for example: 'Is work really the best form of welfare?', in M. Harrison and T. Sanders (eds) *Social policies and social control: New perspectives on the 'not-so-big society'* (Policy Press, 2014) and 'All in it together? Disabled people, the coalition and welfare to work' (*Journal of Poverty and Social Justice*, 2012).

Linda Piggott is a former Lecturer in the Law School at Lancaster University, UK. She has a background in disability and social policy. Following the social model of disability, her research interests are related to barriers to education and employment faced by disabled people, produced by discriminatory attitudes and practices in education settings and in the workplace. Linda has recently retired.

Sheila Riddell is a Director of the Centre for Research in Education, Inclusion and Diversity at the University of Edinburgh, UK. She was previously Director of the Strathclyde Centre for Disability Research at the University of Glasgow. She is also a Visiting Professor at the University of Gothenburg, Sweden. Sheila's research interests focus on issues of social justice and equality in the fields of education, training, employment and social care.

Alan Roulstone is a Professor of Disability Studies at the University of Leeds, UK. He has also held senior posts at De Montfort, Northumbria and Sunderland universities. He has led or been involved in a range of research projects around independent living, disablist hate crime, transitions to work and adulthood, new technologies, older people and disability law. Funders of his work have included the Department of Health, the Economic and Social Research Council, the European Commission, the Equality and Human Rights Commission, the Joseph Rowntree Foundation, regional development agencies, the Social Care Institute for Excellence, The Leverhulme Trust and UNESCO.

Karen Soldatic is an international Researcher in Disability Studies at the University of New South Wales, Sydney, Australia and was recently recognised for her research on changing international disability policy regimes with a British Academy International Visiting Fellowship. Karen is also an Adjunct Research Fellow in the Centre of Human Rights Education at Curtin University, Perth, Australia where she works with colleagues on issues of disability, migration and rights realisation at the transnational scale.

Bruce Stafford is Head of School and Professor of Public Policy at the School of Sociology and Social Policy, Nottingham, UK. He has over 30 years' experience of applied public and social research, with a focus on policy evaluation and social security (notably, welfare to work, the delivery of welfare services and disability issues). He has been involved with several disability-related research and evaluation studies. Bruce led an international consortium evaluating the New Deal for Disabled People. In addition, he has undertaken reviews of the factors affecting the employment retention of disabled people and of the definition of disability from an employer's perspective; and conducted research on employers' and service providers' responses to the Disability Discrimination Act 1995 and the Equality Act 2010. His research has also included large-scale surveys on the prevalence, experiences and views of disabled people. Currently, he is an International Expert for the large-scale evaluation of the National Disability Insurance Scheme being led by Flinders University, Australia.

Monika Struck-Peregończyk is a Lecturer in the Department of Social Sciences at the University of Information Technology and Management in Rzeszów, Poland. She completed her doctoral thesis on the situation of young disabled people in the labour market in Poland in 2014 at the Institute of Social Policy of the University of Warsaw. Her research interests are centred around contemporary social policy issues, with special reference to the situation of disabled people.

Jon Warren is a sociologist who is currently Senior Research Associate in Health Inequalities in the Department of Geography at Durham University, UK. His research interests are centred on work, employment, the work–life interface and the industrial history of the North East of England. Jon is involved with methodologically innovative research and is currently involved with projects using Qualitative Comparative Analysis (QCA) and visual methods. He has published work in the fields of disability studies, public health policy and the sociology of work. Jon was previously part of the School of

Applied Social Sciences at Durham where he taught sociology and social work.

Shaun Wilson is Senior Lecturer in the Department of Sociology at Macquarie University, Australia. His research covers areas of political sociology, social policy and the sociology of work and employment. At present, Shaun is interested in the interaction between reforms to social policy and rising inequality, precarious employment, and the potentials for the redesign of social security systems given low growth, unemployment and rising inequality. Shaun's research has been published in journals, including *the British Journal of Sociology*, *Work, Employment & Society*, the *British Journal of Industrial Relations* and *Policy & Politics*. Shaun teaches courses on modernity, social policy and social movements at Macquarie.

Robert Wilton is a Professor in the School of Geography and Earth Sciences at McMaster University in Hamilton, Ontario, Canada. He is a broadly trained social geographer whose primary research interest over the last two decades has been the problems of social and spatial exclusion confronting people living with disabilities, chronic illness, mental ill-health and, most recently, alcoholism and addiction. His work has explored the problem of social exclusion in relation to paid employment, neighbourhoods and housing, and income supports. His current research is focused on mental health and employment in the social economy, and learning disabled people's experiences of urban space.

Sarah Woodin is a Research Fellow at the University of Leeds, UK working on a wide range of issues connected to disability, employment and independent living in its broadest sense. She previously worked for many years as a practitioner to develop leadership, policy and practice in supported employment in the UK at local and national levels, including the coordination of the national TSI (training in systematic instruction) network. She is currently one of the coordinators for the British Sociological Association Study Group on Disability and is working on several international projects, which include research on disability equality and transitions to work for young disabled people.

Acknowledgements

We would like to thank the Centre for Disability Research at Lancaster University, UK for funding a symposium at Lancaster in 2012 that provided the impetus for this book and for funding our attendance at various European and Nordic conferences. We would also like to thank colleagues, notably Hannah Morgan and Bob Sapey, of the former Department of Applied Social Science at Lancaster University who were always interested in and supportive of our work, and who were generous with suggested reading and the loan of books. Thanks also to Alan Roulstone who helped us to focus the proposal for the book. Finally, we would like to thank all of our contributors who made editing the book a pleasure. Their patience with our various requests for developing chapters was greatly appreciated.

Chris Grover and Linda Piggott

ONE

Disabled people, work and welfare

Chris Grover and Linda Piggott

Encouraged by national and international pressures, there have been attempts in many countries in recent decades to increase the employment rates of disabled people. In Britain, for example, Labour governments between 1997 and 2010 developed several policies with such aims. These policies have been extended since 2010 by Britain's coalition government. The British example is instructive because it demonstrates the range of often contradictory considerations – economic, moral and social – that have framed various governments' desire to increase the participation of disabled people in wage work. These include:

- a concern with tackling the social exclusion – defined as exclusion from wage work – of disabled people;
- a concern with the human rights of disabled people – that facilitating access to paid employment is an important way in which commitments to human rights can be addressed;
- a concern with the numbers of people receiving out-of-work benefits, including disability benefits, because of the alleged effects that such benefits have on recipients' motivation for paid work and their wider attitudes (the so-called 'dependency culture');
- a concern with the intergenerational transmission of wage worklessness from disabled people to their offspring;
- the economic need to increase the number of people competing for wage work through what has been referred to as the 'effective labour supply' and the reserve army of labour to constrain wage inflation;
- economic redistribution – for example to tackle child and older people's poverty;
- a reorientation of welfare benefit support for disabled people that has emphasised a contractual, rather than rights-based, approach and which as a consequence has increased the expectation that in order to receive such support, individuals will have to act in a prosocial manner, most notably through attempts to (re)enter wage work at the earliest opportunity;

- a desire to save money, particularly but not exclusively after the financial crash of 2008 and the ensuing drive for austerity (see, for example, Secretary of State for Social Security and Minister for Welfare Reform, 1998; Secretary of State for Work and Pensions, 2006, 2008a, 2008b, 2010a, 2010b; for discussion, see Piggott and Grover, 2009; Bambra and Smith, 2010; Grover and Piggott, 2010, 2013; Houston and Lindsay, 2010; Deacon and Patrick, 2011; Garthwaite, 2011; Patrick et al, 2011; Lindsay and Houston, 2013).

Such issues, however, are not unique to Britain. In various configurations they have been demonstrated across the developed world – see, for example, Soldatic and Pini (2009, 2012) and Lantz and Marston (2012) on Australia; Caswell and Bendix Kleif (2013) on Denmark; Lunt and Horsfall (2013) on New Zealand; Ulmetsig (2013) on Sweden and van Berkel (2013) on the Netherlands. Furthermore, and encouraged through the work of supranational organisations (OECD, 2003, 2009; IMF, 2004, 2011a, 2011b), welfare benefit policies for disabled people have been problematised.

As Alan Roulstone highlights in Chapter Fourteen of this volume, the desire to increase the employment rate of disabled people produces a number of paradoxes. For example, Roulstone points to the fact that in recent years much effort has gone into incorporating disabled people into an economic system that they were 'designed out' of in earlier years (see, for instance, Chapters Four, Five and Eleven), and that while policies such as anti-discrimination legislation and reasonable adjustments might be welcomed, they are limited because they focus entirely on (and it could be argued they entrench) the belief that wage labour is an activity that all disabled people should engage with. There are other paradoxes that frame policy developments to increase the labour market participation of disabled people, most notably that their demands and those of the disabled people's movement for their increased participation in paid employment have, at least in part, been used to justify the retrenching of out-of-work disability benefits (Piggott and Grover, 2009). This retrenching has included:

- making out-of-work (or income replacement) disability benefits more difficult to claim by developing new tests of incapacity to work, thereby diverting people to unemployment-related benefits (essentially redrawing what Stone, 1984, calls the disability category);
- eroding the absolute value of out-of-work disability benefits and their relative value to unemployment benefits;

- increasing conditionality so that all, except those deemed the most disabled (for example, in Britain those deemed to 'have a severe limitation which creates a significant disability in relation to the labour market, regardless of any adaptation they may make or support with which they may be provided'; DWP, 2009, p 8), have to make efforts to hasten their (re)entry into wage work;
- increasing sanctioning, most notably the threat, and actual, withdrawal of income replacement benefits for those people who are adjudged not to have made suitable efforts to return to work.

Given the path dependency of welfare systems, it is not the case that all countries, even those that we focus on in *Disabled people, work and welfare*, have developed all these approaches, but, nevertheless, many have developed some (or all) of them over recent decades, or are currently discussing ways of doing so. In this context, while the detail of policy developments varies between countries, it is also the case that in many countries in recent years, it has become more difficult for disabled people to claim income replacement benefits when they are not in wage work. Indeed, in many countries it is disabled people who seem to be the main targets of welfare 'reform' and cost savings (see, for instance, Chapter Three of this volume on Australia). In Britain, for example, it has been estimated that between 2013/14 and 2017/18, disabled people will lose £28 billion of their collective benefit income (Demos, 2013). The consequence is that disabled people in many countries face an economically uncertain future and the consequences of this (for example, increased rates of poverty, greater levels of exclusion, increased isolation, and poorer physical and mental health).

The approach of *Disabled people, work and welfare*

The origins of *Disabled people, work and welfare* were in a symposium hosted by Lancaster University's Centre for Disability Research in 2012. The symposium was entitled 'Is work fit for disabled people?' and was intended to address some of the issues that the mainstream social administrative approaches at the time did not really engage with. Such approaches were particularly concerned with whether disabled people were fit for wage work and what needed to be done on the demand and supply sides to make labour markets fit to employ disabled people (see, for example, Beatty et al, 2009; Houston and Lindsay, 2010; Kemp and Davidson, 2010; Lindsay and Dutton, 2010). For the editors of *Disabled people, work and welfare*, such approaches left unanswered important questions, for they lacked engagement with concerns raised by disability studies scholars who had been questioning the nature of wage work and its relationship to disabled people for a number of years (see, for example, Abberley, 1996a, 1996b; Oliver and Barnes, 1998; Roulstone, 2000, 2002; Taylor, 2004; Barnes and Mercer, 2005; Roulstone and Barnes, 2005).

While we appreciate the importance of social administrative-type analysis and arguments and, indeed, *Disabled people, work and welfare* engages with these, we also thought that there was a need to critically engage with the notion that wage work is an activity that disabled people (Piggott and Grover, 2009; Grover and Piggott, 2013) and non-disabled people (Grover and Piggott, 2013) should be forced to engage with on the threat of impoverishment. This concern was essentially driven by the social model of disability's emphasis on the social basis of disabled people's disadvantage and oppression, rather than their being located in the functional impairments of disabled people (for example, Finkelstein, 1980; Gleeson, 1999; Oliver, 2009). If the basis of disabled people's exclusion from wage work is misunderstood as merely being a consequence of their individual characteristics and capabilities, the result, at least in Britain, has been poorly administered and targeted welfare benefits (North Lancashire Citizens Advice Bureau, 2012; Pearlman et al, 2012) and the very poor treatment of disabled people in the process of determining the disability category for the purposes of out-of-work benefits (We Are Spartacus, 2012, 2013).[1] In this context, therefore, *Disabled people, work and welfare*:

- critically engages with dominant discourses and policy developments for disabled people that are focused on getting them into wage work;
- critically questions the institution of wage work through sociological and philosophical approaches which suggest that alternatives are available;
- develops the knowledge of social policy approaches taken in several countries to address wage worklessness among disabled people, the ideas that inform these approaches and the impacts of the policies.

Understanding disabled people, work and welfare

Disabled people, work and welfare brings together a group of academics at various points in their careers, from various countries and various disciplines. While the book focuses predominantly on Britain, relationships between work, welfare and disabled people in other European nations are also examined (Poland in Chapter Six and

Denmark in Chapter Eight). Australia (Chapter Three) and North America (the United States [US]; in Chapter Seven and Canada in Chapter Twelve) are also represented in the book. Constituent countries of Britain are also focused on. Chapter Nine, for example, focuses on the experiences of young deaf and hard of hearing people in Scotland of accessing and doing wage work, while Chapter Eleven discusses an employment support programme in the North of England.

The academic disciplines of disability studies, public health, social policy and sociology are represented in a multidisciplinary approach to understanding employment and welfare benefit policies as they relate to disabled people. While each chapter could be read as an analysis of the relationships between work, welfare and disability in the country on which it focuses, we hope that the book will be read as a whole. This will help to demonstrate the similarities and differences between the countries examined in their attempts to address a range of issues related to disabled people, work and welfare that affects them all.

Work and disabled people

> Work occupies a substantial proportion of most people's lives and has often been taken as a symbol of personal value: work provides status, economic reward, a demonstration of religious faith and means to realize self-potential. But work also embodies the opposite evaluations: labour can be back-breaking and mentally incapacitating; labour camps are punishment centres; work is a punishment for original sin and something we would rather avoid. (Grint, 2005, p 1)

As Grint's comments suggest, defining what 'work' is is complex. For example, he criticises Arendt's (1958) distinction between 'labour' ('bodily activity designed to ensure survival in which the results are consumed immediately'; Grint, 2005, p 7) and 'work' ('activity undertaken with our hands which gives objectivity to the world'; Grint, 2005, p 7) as lacking relevance to both industrial and pre-industrial societies. 'Work' has also been seen as having transformative capacity, an activity that alters nature. In many ways, this approach is taken in radical political economy where work is recognised as an interaction between individuals and nature, and wage work is recognised as a commodified version of that activity (for a discussion in relation to disabled people, see Abberley, 1996a, 1996b). Such distinctions are problematic because, for example, it is not easy to delineate which activities might be considered as not helping to transform nature (Grint, 2005). Grint

(2005) argues that 'work' should be understood as a construct of often competing discourses. Those competing discourses, however, lead to different material expressions and consequences affecting those people who might be considered to be 'workers' or 'workless'.

In *Disabled people, work and welfare*, we are concerned with what, at least in a party-political and policy sense, might be described as a hegemonic discourse that equates work with wage work and/or other kinds of paid employment (for example self-employment). It is not that all the authors in this volume agree with the prominence of wage work in policy terms (see, for example, Chapters Twelve to Fourteen), but in policy terms it is wage work that is *the* concern. Recent policy developments, for example – such as the introduction of Employment and Support Allowance (ESA) in Britain, the shifting of disabled people from Disability Pension to Newstart in Australia (Chapter Three) and the increasing conditionality within the Danish welfare system (Chapter Eight), have all been aimed at 'incentivising' (according to economic liberals) or 'forcing' (according to social liberals) disabled people into paid employment.

It is not the case that wage work is unknown to disabled people. It was estimated in the United Kingdom (UK), that in 2012 just under a half (46.3%) of disabled people were in wage work, although some disabled people, for instance learning disabled people, are particularly disadvantaged in terms of employment (see Chapter Ten). What this means, however, is that the majority (53.7%) of disabled people were not in wage work. Moreover, the figures compare poorly with those for non-disabled people, of whom three quarters (76.4%) were in wage work.[2] In the UK there is, then, an 'employment gap' of 31.1 percentage points between disabled and non-disabled people. However, the UK is not unique in this regard. Across the countries of the Organisation for Economic Co-operation and Development, for instance, in the mid-2000s a little over half of disabled people were employed compared with over 70% of non-disabled people (OECD, 2010). In Britain, however, between 1998 and 2012 the proportion of disabled people in employment increased by 10 percentage points. The reasons for this relate to the economic expansion experienced in Britain between the late 1980s and the 2008 financial crash, supporting the evidence which suggests that disabled people are more likely to be employed when labour markets are tight (Beatty et al, 2000; Beatty and Fothergill, 2002, 2005, 2013).

The number of people in employment, however, is a crude measure of the success or otherwise of policies that are supposed to help address the disadvantages that disabled people face. Equally important are the nature of employment that disabled people are in and, particularly relevant to contemporary debates about employment, whether it protects them from poverty and social exclusion. There are several reasons to assume that it does not.

First, disabled people in Britain are more likely to be in part-time employment compared with non-disabled people. In 2011, for example, a third (33.8%) of disabled people compared with a quarter (24.7%) of non-disabled people worked part time. This observation can be interpreted as being positive. As Jones (cited in Meager and Hill, 2005, p 16) notes: 'Evidence from the Labour Force Survey suggests that part-time employment provides an important way of accommodating a work-limiting disability rather than reflecting marginalisation of the disabled by employers.' However, part-time employment is also problematic because it is less well paid compared with full-time employment. For example, the median hourly wage for part-time employees in the UK is less than two thirds that of full-time employees (£8.29 compared with £13.03 in April 2013, respectively) (ONS, 2013, table 3). Moreover, wage data suggest that disabled people are, on average, likely to receive lower wages than non-disabled people. In 2005, for instance, people with a work-limiting disability earned 13.2% less per hour than non-disabled people (£9.55 compared with £10.81 per hour, respectively) (Meager and Hill, 2005, table 29, UK figures).

Second, evidence suggests that the 'low pay, no pay cycle', whereby people move between periods of no and poorly paid wage work, is exacerbated by poor health (Kemp and Davidson, 2010). It is known, for instance, that people who claim ESA in Britain tend to be disadvantaged in labour markets because they tend to be in non-standard or 'bad jobs' (for example, Davidson and Kemp, 2008; Kemp and Davidson, 2010). These are jobs denoted by poor terms and conditions, such as low pay, little access to occupational sick pay and pensions, and no recognised career or promotion ladder (Davidson and Kemp, 2008, p 225).

Productivity and barriers to wage work

As we have noted, disabled people are disadvantaged in wage work in terms of the proportion in work, the proportion who work part time and the level of their wages compared with non-disabled people. There are various ways of explaining these observations, but for the purposes of *Disabled people, work and welfare* the focus is on social explanations of such disadvantage, even though in policy terms that disadvantage is predominantly individualised as a supply-side problem (a problem of disabled people's attitudes, character, skills and potential economic contribution).

The issue relates to the social reaction to disabled people and the barriers – for instance, the physical environment, the rhythms and patterns of wage work and the attitudes of employers and co-workers to hiring and working with disabled people – that this creates for disabled people in accessing wage work. As we have noted, such arguments are drawn from the social model of disability and while a great deal has been written about the barriers to wage work faced by disabled people, it has recently been argued by Oliver (2013, p 1025) that the 'social model has ... barely made a dent in the employment system because, although it has identified many of the disabling barriers in the international labour market and with the behaviour of employers, the solutions offered have usually been based on an individual model of disability'. We see this in many social welfare systems where the focus is on functional capability to do wage work and on rehabilitating those disabled people whose capabilities are deemed to be outwith of labour markets. The focus on capability for wage work is often used, as noted below in our discussion of conditionality, to threaten the impoverishment of disabled people.

For the social model of disability, however, it is argued (although this is denied – see Oliver, 2009) that there are difficulties with dealing with the effects (for instance the pain and limitations) that particular impairments – 'variations in the structure, function and workings of bodies which, in Western culture, are medically defined as significant abnormalities or pathologies' (Thomas, 2007, p 8) – might bring. For *Disabled people, work and welfare* the relationship between disability and impairment is most important when the reasons for the disadvantaged labour market provision of disabled people are considered.

As we have noted, the thrust of the social model of disability is that disabled people are disadvantaged by socially embedded barriers. In employment terms, however, the explanation of why disabled people are disadvantaged is complex because of the individual attributes and social structures and processes that help to explain people's location in labour markets; in other words, how far the labour market position of disabled people reflects 'their skill, qualifications, work experience and any occupational or sectoral segregation which exists, and how far it reflects discriminatory behaviour on the part of employers' (Meager and Hill, 2005, p 27). Of course, many of the so-called individual characteristics (for example, skills, qualifications and work experience) are also socially embedded (see, for example, Chapter Nine). The evidence suggests that the employment and wage disadvantage faced by disabled people is, at least in part, explained by employer discrimination.

That discrimination, however, is arguably located within the economic imperatives of capitalism. For instance, in a quantitative study of employer attitudes to disabled people, Davidson (2011) found that one of the concerns that brought 'uncertainties' to employing disabled people was potential risks to productivity and, therefore, profitability. In this sense, impairment can be understood in a social sense. This is a point that Abberley (1996a, 1996b) makes. For Abberley, there is little doubt that the oppression and disadvantage that disabled people face was, historically, located in a form of production that in Roulstone's terms (Chapter Fourteen, this volume) 'designed disabled people out'. However, locating concerns with wage work within the preventative and curing characteristics of mainstream medicine, Abberley argues that there will always be disabled people who are not as productive in an economic sense as non-disabled people (see also Barnes, 1999, 2000). While, as we have noted, Abberley does not deny that materialist understandings provide a useful explanation of the antecedents of disabled people's disadvantage, he problematises the argument that the solution to this will be in greater access to wage work. This is because such a solution will only be 'insofar as there is a happy conjunction between an individual's impairment, technology and socially-valued activity' (Abberley, 1996a, p 14). He therefore sees the need for an alternative that 'rejects work as crucially definitional of social membership' (Abberley, 1996a, p 14). While he does not reject the need for policies to support disabled people into paid work, he does not see such work as being the enabling activity that many do.

Conditionality: enforcing labour discipline

As we have noted, in recent years more has been demanded of disabled people claiming income replacement benefits to hasten their (re)entry into wage work in Britain and other nations. In many senses, this has been part of a wider trend in welfare systems towards the re-commodification of paid employment (see Streeck, 2007). Conditionality has been central to this process (Grover, 2012). As Dwyer (2004, p 269) notes, a 'principle of conditionality holds that eligibility to certain basic, publicly provided, welfare entitlements should be dependent on an individual first agreeing to meet particular compulsory duties or patterns of behaviour'.

In the case of developments in welfare and (wage) work policies for disabled people in Britain, such a view was reflected in the Green

Paper which announced the then Labour government's intention to introduce ESA. It noted, for instance, that ESA would be:

> paid to most people in return for undertaking work-related interviews, agreeing an action plan and, as resources allow, participating in some form of work-related activity. If benefit claimants do not fulfil these agreed responsibilities the ... benefit will be reduced in a series of slices ultimately to the level of Jobseeker's Allowance.[3] (Secretary of State for Work and Pensions, 2006, p 4)

An approach to welfare policy premised upon the enforcement of conditionality, according to Deacon (2002, 2004a, 2004b; see also Chapter Two, this volume), can be justified through at least three broad approaches:

- the contractualist;
- the paternalistic;
- the mutualist.

Deacon (2004b, p 915) argues that the *contractualist* justification for welfare conditionality was the most visible during the years of New Labour governments in the 1990s and 2000s in Britain and 'rests upon the argument that it is reasonable to use welfare to enforce obligations where this is part of a broader contract between government and claimants. If the government keeps its part of the bargain, then the claimants should keep theirs'. In the case of income replacement benefits for disabled people, the provision of the benefit and 'support' services to help them (re)enter paid work are considered by the state to be its side of the contract and, hence, it expects disabled people to engage with the services provided as their side of the welfare contract.

The basic premise of the *paternalistic* justification is that conditionality is in the interests of the recipients of state benefits or services and is most closely associated with the American political scientist, Lawrence Mead (1992; Patrick et al, 2011). We can see this in regard to the increasing conditionality being applied to the income replacement benefits for disabled people. The argument, at least in part, is that long-term benefit 'dependency' erodes either the self-confidence or aspiration, or both, of disabled people not in wage work so that they are unable to take on a job. As a consequence, and like any other wage workless person, they require a combination of "'help and hassle", reinforced by sanctions for those who do not co-operate' in order to get them into work (Deacon, 1997, p xiv).

The *mutualist* justification for conditionality is associated with communitarians and is premised upon the idea that responsibilities 'arise from social involvements or commitments. Our lives touch others in many ways, for good or ill, and we are accountable for the consequences' (Selznick, 1998, p 62). In terms of applying conditions to benefits for disabled people, we can point to welfare policies as being one of many arenas in which the lives of individuals affect others because, for example, they have to be paid through collectivised forms of revenue (taxation). Because of this, for example, it should be expected that disabled people should make efforts to reduce the financial cost they present to taxpayers. Generally speaking, this takes the form of the expectation that such people prepare themselves for wage work. Any arguments that they should not do so because of the barriers that they face in attempting to secure paid work, would not be countenanced in the mutualist approach. This is because the responsibility to prepare for, and eventually seek, paid work is held to exist independently of their likely success in securing paid work.

There are, however, also powerful arguments that critique the idea that the responsibilities conferred upon individuals needing access to state-sponsored welfare policies should be enforced through conditionality. Deacon (2004, p 913) points to two of these: first, that conditionality 'rests upon a false analysis of the problems it seeks to remedy' and, second, that 'the effect of imposing behavioural conditions will be to worsen rather than eliminate the problem'. In the first instance, it could be argued, for example, that the imposition of conditionality in ESA is premised upon the mistaken assumption that people are disabled by their impairment, rather than the structures of capitalism that privilege the non-disabled over the disabled body (Oliver, 1990; Thomas, 2007). In the second instance, we might point to arguments which suggest that the imposition of conditionality in benefits for disabled people, rather than encouraging a return to work, will have the opposite effect, for example by exacerbating impairments related to mental health (see Mitchell and Woodfield, 2008; Hudson et al, 2009; NACAB, 2009).

A third set of issues is essentially pragmatic in nature and relates to the effectiveness of conditionality in helping wage workless people compete for, and take, wage work. The evidence for increased conditionality having a substantial impact on bettering the employment position of disabled people is not particularly convincing (see Chapters Four and Five, this volume). So, for example, in their review of evidence from around the world, Griggs and Evans (2010, p 5) found that sanctions linked to employment-related conditionality 'strongly reduce benefit use and raise exits from benefits'. However, they also note that exits from benefit receipt are not the only measure of the success of conditionality and sanctions. In contrast, on other measures, there are worrying trends. In particular, conditionality and sanctions have 'generally unfavourable effects on longer-term outcomes (earnings over time, child welfare, job quality) and spill-over effects (i.e. crime rates)' (Griggs and Evans, 2010, p 5). In other words, the use of conditionality and sanctions may encourage people to leave benefits, but at the expense of the longevity and quality of jobs they are able to access. These findings are consistent with what we have seen described as the 'low pay, no pay cycle'.

Outline of the book

Chapters Two and Three (Part One) focus on the ways in which disability benefit receipt in Britain and Australia has reflected and helped to constitute the shift in both countries to make disabled people do more to enter wage work. They demonstrate the increasingly work-related conditional nature of disability benefits, and discuss political and intellectual ways of understanding the application of conditionality to out-of-work benefits for disabled people. In Chapter Two, for example, Ruth Patrick and Deborah Fenney discuss the relationships between welfare conditionality and disabled people in Britain. The chapter examines a small-scale study by the authors into attitudes towards conditionality of both disabled and non-disabled people. Their research suggests that disabled and non-disabled participants did not agree on the appropriateness of sanctions for disability benefit recipients, with the latter, for example, pointing to the potential of conditionality to exacerbate impairment while ignoring the barriers that disabled people face in accessing paid work. Drawing on the work of White (2003), Patrick and Fenney conclude that welfare conditionality in Britain is currently incompatible with social justice.

Chapter Three sees Alan Morris, Shaun Wilson and Karen Soldatic focus on the tightening of eligibility rules for disability benefits in Australia over recent years. They examine the political and policy basis for these changes and highlight how they are designed to shift people onto Newstart (Australia's unemployment benefit). The chapter then goes on to consider a qualitative research project carried out by the authors which focused on the lived experience of Newstart recipients experiences which the authors argue sre denoted by a life of 'hard yakka'. The effect of disability benefits policy in Australia has involved, the authors suggest, a subversion of the disability movement's claims for decent work through a policy framework mainly interested in 'jobs' and 'partial ability to work' as mechanisms to reduce benefit levels and availability for disabled people.

Chapters Four to Eight (Part Two) focus on aspects of policies in various countries that are supposed to support disabled people in accessing paid employment. The chapters take a critical approach to those policies, highlighting issues that arise because of economic, ideological, political and policy problems in designing work and welfare policies for disabled people. For instance, in Chapter Four, Bruce Stafford examines market-based programmes that seek to assist disabled people in receipt of income replacement benefits to move towards or into paid work in Britain. He provides an overview of past wage work-related (the New Deal for Disabled People and Pathways to Work) and, by drawing on the ideas of adverse selection and moral hazard, he argues that disabled people are among the least well served by marketised employment service programmes. In Chapter Five, Dan Heap extends this theme in his focus on the Work Programme in Britain. Using data from interviews with current and former government officials, he finds that the current system of employment support is often unable to meet the needs of disabled claimants. He concludes that the justification – that more employment support for disabled people would be provided – for the more controversial aspects of welfare reform has not been met because of the failure of previous specialist employment services, changed labour market conditions and the inability of the Work Programme to provide the specialist and sustained support that disabled claimants require in accessing wage work.

In Chapter Six, Monika Struck-Peregończyk examines changes in disability employment policy in Poland since 1991. She suggests that, despite these changes, employers are reluctant to take on disabled workers, fearing lower productivity and higher costs. Many disabled people in Poland, therefore, endure low-paid, low-skill and low-status employment. This puts families with a disabled member at higher risk of poverty because, Struck-Peregończyk argues, employment policies for disabled people in Poland remain ineffective.

Chapter Seven focuses on the US. Randall Owen, Robert Gould and Sarah Parker Harris indicate in this chapter that in the US, market-based solutions are preferred to publicly funded systems of welfare, so that individuals have responsibility for their own welfare. The chapter uses competing discourses – neoliberalism and rights – to understand how recent reforms (the Ticket to Work and Work Incentives Improvement Act 1999 and the Patient Protection and Affordable Care Act 2010) relate to disabled people. They argue that the Patient Protection and Affordable Care Act 2010 in particular has added a complex layer to welfare eligibility, but also provides the possibility of expanding the employment of disabled people who traditionally had to choose between holding out for wage work that either had employer-sponsored healthcare or was so poorly paid that it allowed access to Medicaid.

In Chapter Eight, David Etherington and Jo Ingold examine active labour market policies in Denmark over the last 15 or so years. In particular, they focus on the influence of social dialogue and suggest that in the Danish model it has been important in supporting disabled people to enter and remain in paid work. However, Etherington and Ingold argue that social dialogue has been compromised by the shift towards workfarist policies in Denmark. They conclude that while the move towards co-production is important in incorporating the voice of disabled people, the availability of quality, sustainable jobs for disabled people in difficult labour market conditions remains a challenge.

Chapters Nine to Eleven (Part Three) focus on various issues related to disabled people accessing and keeping paid employment. In Chapter Nine, Mariela Fordyce and Sheila Riddell examine their research with young deaf and hard of hearing people in Scotland. Their research found that experience of discrimination in recruitment made some young people fearful of disclosing their impairment, while success in employment could depend on finding work through family, friends and wider social networks. Jobseekers with high socioeconomic status often depended on this to facilitate entry into professions via internships and work experience, meaning that young people from less privileged backgrounds were doubly disadvantaged by disabling barriers and less advantaged social networks.

In Chapter Ten, Sarah Woodin indicates that in Britain learning disabled people value the opportunity to work, but that they risk exploitation and increased competition for satisfying work. Learning disabled people tend to have an employment rate that is lower than disabled people generally and, in the main, the work they do tends to be relatively low skilled. Current working practices, such as zero hours contracts, may have further disadvantaged learning disabled employees. Woodin argues that where workplaces do manage to offer the conditions needed by learning disabled people, there is evidence that they hold down challenging and interesting jobs.

In Chapter Eleven, Jon Warren, Kayleigh Garthwaite and Clare Bambra examine what happens to people in England after they enter employment and what challenges they can face in retaining it. They examine these issues through an evaluation of an in-work support service in the North of England and demonstrate the intertwined issues that disabled people face in maintaining their employment status. The authors suggest that the almost exclusive focus on employability in employment support programmes is misplaced and that it would helpful if they assisted with job retention by tackling health and debt issues, low levels of confidence and working arrangements.

Chapters Twelve to Fourteen (Part Four) examine empirical and theoretical work in order to question whether wage work in the open market is the only way that the contribution and social inclusion of disabled people should be understood. In Chapter Twelve, Edward Hall and Robert Wilton consider the hardening of attitudes in relation to welfare payments and the perceived inactivity of disabled people. Drawing on research from Canada and Britain, they examine whether there are potential alternatives for disabled people to working in the open market. In the case of Canada, they focus on the potential of social enterprises to offer flexible and accommodating conditions of employment and, in the case of Britain, participation in volunteering and the creative arts as a means of enabling disabled people to challenge dominant assumptions about their place in society.

Chapter Thirteen sees Chris Grover and Linda Piggott explore the ideas of the right to work and the right not to work. They argue that by its nature, wage work is exploitative and disabling, and that the current thrust of policies to oblige disabled people to work is problematic because not only do the policies privilege one activity (wage work) over other activities that people might choose to do, they also remove one of the central demands – for control and choice over their lives – of the disabled people's movement. In this context, and following Taylor (2004), Grover and Piggott argue that a right not to work is as defensible as a right to work.

In Chapter Fourteen, Alan Roulstone explores current developments in work and welfare policies for disabled people by focusing on longer-run developments in the ways that work has been defined. He argues that with industrialisation, work became associated with wage work, a narrowly defined parameter for productive capacity that only values certain forms of work and productivity. In contrast, Roulstone suggests that a humane society has to acknowledge diversity in all its forms and foster a critique of narrowly defined systems that value only certain forms of work and productivity.

Chris Grover and Linda Piggott draw together themes from Parts One to Four of *Disabled people, work and welfare* in the conclusion to the book – Part Five (Chapter Fifteen). This chapter focuses on three issues:

- the nature of wage work as a social process;
- the difficulties for disabled people that come from the policy push to commodify their labour power;
- the difficulties there are in the claim that wage work provides for disabled people a secure income that is above the poverty level.

Notes

[1] For example, the number of appeals against ESA decisions increased by 67% (from 279,000 to 465,500) between 2009/10 and 2012/13, while the number of disposals (that is, the number of appeals that actually got to a tribunal) increased by 280% (from 70,535 to 268,157) over the same period (www.publications.parliament.uk/pa/cm201314/cmhansrd/cm130717/text/130717w0002.htm). Furthermore, a substantial proportion (43% in the quarter from July to September 2013) of appeals against ESA decisions was found in favour of the applicant (Ministry of Justice, 2013).

[2] Figures on employment rates are from http://odi.dwp.gov.uk/disability-statistics-and-research/disability-facts-and-figures.php#imp

[3] Jobseeker's Allowance is the main out-of-work benefit for people administratively defined as unemployed in Britain.

References

Abberley, P. (1996a) 'The significance of work for the citizenship of disabled people', paper presented at University College Dublin, 15 April, http://disability-studies.leeds.ac.uk/files/library/Abberley-sigofwork.pdf

Abberley, P. (1996b) 'Work, utopia and impairment', in L. Barton (ed) *Disability and society: Emerging issues and insights*, London: Longman, pp 61-79.

Bambra, C. and Smith, K. (2010) 'No longer deserving? Sickness benefit reform and the politics of (ill) health', *Critical Public Health*, 20(1), pp 71-83.

Barnes, C. (1999) 'A working social model? Disability and work in the 21st century', paper presented at the Disability Studies Conference and Seminar, Edinburgh, 9 December.

Barnes, C. (2000) 'A working social model? Disability, work and disability politics in the 21st century', *Critical Social Policy*, 20(4), pp 441-57.

Barnes, C. and Mercer, G. (2005) 'Disability, work, and welfare: challenging the social exclusion of disabled people', *Work, Employment & Society*, 19(3), pp 527-45.

Beatty, C. and Fothergill, S. (2002) 'Hidden unemployment among men: a case study', *Regional Studies*, 34(7), pp 617-30.

Beatty, C. and Fothergill, S. (2005) 'The diversion from "unemployment" to "sickness" across British regions and districts', *Regional Studies*, 39(7), pp 837-54.

Beatty, C. and Fothergill, S. (2013) 'Disability benefits in the UK: an issue of health or jobs?', in C. Lindsay and D. Houston (eds) *Disability benefits, welfare reform and employment policy*, Basingstoke: Palgrave Macmillan, pp 15-32.

Beatty, C., Fothergill, S. and Macmillan, R. (2000) 'A theory of employment, unemployment and sickness', *Regional Studies*, 34(7), pp 617-30.

Beatty, T., Fothergill, S., Houston, D., Powell, R. and Sissons, P. (2009) 'A gendered theory of employment, unemployment and sickness', *Environment and Planning C: Government and Policy*, 27(6), pp 958-74.

Caswell, D. and Bendix Kleif, H. (2013) 'Disability pensions and active labor market policy', *Journal of Social Service Research*, 39(4), pp 572-84.

Davidson, J. (2011) *A qualitative study exploring employers' recruitment behaviour and decisions: Small and medium size employers*, Research Report 754, London, DWP.

Davidson, J. and Kemp, P. (2008) 'Sickness benefits in a polarised labour market', *Benefits*, 16(3), pp 225-33.

Deacon, A. (ed) (1997) *From welfare to work: Lesson from America*, Choice in Welfare no. 39, London: Institute for Economic Affairs' Health and Welfare Unit.

Deacon, A. (2002) *Perspectives on welfare: Ideas, ideologies and policy debates*, Buckingham: Open University Press.

Deacon, A. (2004a) 'Justifying conditionality: the case of anti-social tenants', *Housing Studies*, 19(6), pp 911-26.

Deacon, A. (2004b) 'Can conditionality be justified?', in P. Collins and A. Rossiter (eds) *On condition*, London: The Social Market Foundation, pp 38-56.

Deacon, A. and Patrick, R. (2011) 'A new welfare settlement? The coalition government and welfare to work', in H. Bochel (ed) *The Conservative Party and social policy*, Bristol: Policy Press.

Demos (2013) 'Disabled people set to lose £28.3bn of support', www.demos.co.uk/press_releases/destinationunknownapril2013

DWP (Department for Work and Pensions) (2009) *Work Capability Assessment internal review*, Report of the working group commissioned by the Department for Work and Pensions, London: DWP.

Dwyer, P. (2004) 'Creeping conditionality in the UK: from welfare rights to conditional entitlements?', *Canadian Journal of Sociology*, 29(2), pp 265-87.

Finkelstein, V. (1980) *Attitudes and disabled people: Issues for discussion*, New York, NY: International Exchange of Information in Rehabilitation.

Garthwaite, K. (2011) '"The language of shirkers and scroungers?" Talking about illness, disability and coalition welfare reform', *Disability & Society*, 26(3), pp 369-72.

Gleeson, B. (1999) *Geographies of disability*, London: Routledge.

Griggs, J. and Evans, M. (2010) *Sanctions within conditional benefit systems: A review of the evidence*, York: Joseph Rowntree Foundation.

Grint, K. (2005) *Sociology of work: An introduction* (3rd edn), Cambridge: Polity.

Grover, C. (2012) '"Personalised conditionality": observations on active proletarianisation in late Modern Britain', *Capital and Class*, 36(2), pp 283-301.

Grover, C. and Piggott, L. (2010) 'From Incapacity Benefit to Employment and Support Allowance: social sorting, sick and impaired people and social security', *Policy Studies*, 31(2), pp 265-82.

Grover, C. and Piggott, L. (2013) 'A right not to work and disabled people', *Social and Public Policy Review*, 7(1), www.uppress.co.uk/SocialPublicPolicy2013/Grover.pdf

Houston, D. and Lindsay, C. (2010) 'Fit for work? Health, employability and challenges for the UK welfare reform agenda', *Policy Studies*, 31(2), pp 133-42.

Hudson, M., Ray, K., Vegeris, S. and Brooks, S. (2009) *People with mental health conditions and Pathways to Work*, DWP Research Report 593, London: Department for Work and Pensions.

IMF (International Monetary Fund) (2004) *Australia: Selected issues*, IMF Country Report no. 04/354, Washington, DC: IMF.

IMF (2011a) *The challenge of public pension reform in advanced and emerging economies*, Washington, DC: IMF.

IMF (2011b) *Australia: Selected issues*, IMF Country Report no. 11/301, Washington, DC: IMF.

Kemp, P. and Davidson, J. (2010) 'Employability trajectories among new claimants of incapacity benefits', *Policy Studies*, 31(2), pp 203-21.

Lantz, S. and Marston, G. (2012) 'Policy, citizenship and governance: the case of disability and employment policy in Australia', *Disability & Society*, 27(6), pp 853-67.

Lindsay, C. and Dutton, M. (2010) 'Employability through health? Partnership-based governance and the delivery of Pathways to Work condition management services', *Policy Studies*, 31(2), pp 245-64.

Lindsay, C. and Houston, D. (2013) 'Fit for work? Representations and explanations of the disability benefits "crisis" in the UK and beyond', in C. Lindsay and D. Houston (eds) *Disability benefits, welfare reform and employment policy*, Basingstoke: Palgrave Macmillan, pp 1-14.

Lunt, N. and Horsfall, D. (2013) 'New Zealand's reform of Sickness Benefit and Invalid's Benefit', in C. Lindsay and D. Houston (eds) *Disability benefits, welfare reform and employment policy*, Basingstoke: Palgrave Macmillan, pp 216-32.

Mead, L. (1992) *The new politics of poverty: The nonworking poor in America*, New York, NY: Basic Books.

Meager, N. and Hill, D. (2005) *The labour market participation and employment of disabled people in the UK*, Working Paper 1, Brighton: Institute for Employment Studies.

Ministry of Justice (2013) *Tribunals Statistics Quarterly July to September 2013: Includes SEND information for the academic year 2012/13*, London: Ministry of Justice.

Mitchell, M. and Woodfield, K. (2008) *Qualitative research exploring the Pathways to Work sanction regime*, Research Report no. 475, London: Department for Work and Pensions.

NACAB (National Association of Citizens Advice Bureaux) (2009) *Response to the Work and Pensions Committee inquiry: decision making and appeals in the benefits system*, London: NACAB.

North Lancashire Citizens Advice Bureau (2012) *Fitness for work test? Not fit for purpose*, Social Policy Report, Morecambe, North Lancashire Citizens Advice Bureau.

OECD (Organisation for Economic Co-operation and Development) (2003) *Disability programmes in need of reform*, Paris: OECD.

OECD (2009) *Sickness, disability and work: Keeping on track in the economic downturn*, Paris: OECD.

OECD (2010) *Sickness, disability and work: Breaking the barriers. Canada: Opportunities for collaboration*, Paris: OECD.

Oliver, M. (1990) *The politics of disablement*, Basingstoke: Macmillan.

Oliver, M. (2009) *Understanding disability: From theory to practice* (2nd edn), Basingstoke: Palgrave Macmillan.

Oliver, M. (2013) 'The social model of disability: thirty years on', *Disability & Society*, 28(7), pp 1024-6.

Oliver, M. and Barnes, C. (1998) *Disabled people and social policy: From exclusion to inclusion*, London: Longman.

ONS (Office for National Statistics) (2013) *Annual Survey of Hours and Earnings, 2013: Provisional results*, London: ONS.

Patrick, R., Mead, L., Gregg, P. and Seebohm, P. (2011) 'The wrong prescription: disabled people and welfare conditionality', *Policy & Politics*, 39(2), pp 275-91.

Pearlman, V., Royston, S. and Silk, C. (2012) *Right first time? An indicative study of the accuracy of ESA work capability assessment reports*, London, Citizens Advice.

Piggott, L. and Grover, C. (2009) 'Retrenching Incapacity Benefit: Employment Support Allowance and paid work', *Social Policy and Society*, 8(2), pp 1-12.

Roulstone, A. (2000) 'Disability, dependency and the New Deal for Disabled People', *Disability & Society*, 15(3), pp 427-43.

Roulstone, A. (2002) 'Disabling presents, enabling futures? How does the changing nature of capitalism impact on the disabled worker and jobseeker', *Disability & Society*, 17(6), pp 627-42.

Roulstone, A. and Barnes, C. (eds) (2005) *Working futures? Disabled people, policy and social inclusion*, Bristol: Policy Press

Secretary of State for Social Security and Minister for Welfare Reform (1998) *New ambitions for our country: A new contract for welfare*, Cm 3805, London: The Stationery Office.

Secretary of State for Work and Pensions (2006) *A new deal for welfare: Empowering people to work*, Cm 6730, London: The Stationery Office.

Secretary of State for Work and Pensions (2008a) *No one written off: Reforming welfare to reward responsibility*, Cm 7363, Norwich: The Stationery Office.

Secretary of State for Work and Pensions (2008b) *Raising expectations and increasing support: Reforming welfare for the future*, Cm 7506, Norwich: The Stationery Office.

Secretary of State for Work and Pensions (2010a) *21st century welfare*, Cm 7913, Norwich: The Stationery Office.

Secretary of State for Work and Pensions (2010b) *Universal Credit: Welfare that works*, Cm 7957, Norwich: The Stationery Office.

Selznick, P. (1998) 'Social justice: a communitarian perspective', in A. Etzioni (ed) *The essential communitarian reader*, Oxford: Rowman & Littlefield, pp 61-72.

Soldatic, K. and Pini, B. (2009) 'The three Ds of welfare reform: disability, disgust and deservingness', *Australian Journal of Human Rights*, 15(1), pp 76-94.

Soldatic, K. and Pini, B. (2012) 'Continuity or change: disability policy and the Rudd government', *Social Policy & Society*, 11(2), pp 183-96.

Stone, D. (1984) *The disabled state*, Basingstoke: Macmillan.

Streeck, W. (2007) '"Globalization": nothing new under the sun', *Socio-Economic Review*, 5(3), pp 537-47.

Taylor, S. (2004) 'The right not to work: power and disability', *Monthly Review*, 55(1), http://monthlyreview.org/2004/03/01/the-right-not-to-work-power-and-disability

Thomas, C. (2007) *Sociologies of disability and illness: Contested ideas in disability studies and medical sociology*, Basingstoke: Palgrave Macmillan.

Ulmetsig, R. (2013) 'Incapacity benefits – change and continuity in the Swedish welfare state', in C. Lindsay and D. Houston (eds) *Disability benefits, welfare reform and employment policy*, Basingstoke: Palgrave Macmillan, pp 178-98.

van Berkel, R. (2013) 'From Dutch disease to Dutch fitness? Two decades of disability crisis in the Netherlands', in C. Lindsay and D. Houston (eds) *Disability benefits, welfare reform and employment policy*, Basingstoke: Palgrave Macmillan, pp 199-215.

We are Spartacus (2012) *The people's review of the Work Capability Assessment*, We are Spartacus.

We are Spartacus (2013) *The people's review of the Work Capability Assessment: Further evidence*, We are Spartacus.

White, S. (2003) *The civic minimum*, Oxford: Oxford University Press.

Part One
Changing constructions of disability and welfare

Disabled people, conditionality and a civic minimum in Britain: reflections from qualitative research

Ruth Patrick and Deborah Fenney

Introduction

Across countries of the Organisation for Economic Co-operation and Development (OECD), there is now a marked reliance on measures that employ welfare conditionality in an effort to support and encourage people on out-of-work benefits to enter (or return to) paid employment (Gilbert and Besharov, 2011). Welfare conditionality refers to the attaching of behavioural conditions to benefit receipt, and has long been a marked feature of welfare state regimes (Deacon, 2002).

In Britain, under first New Labour governments and then the coalition government, the reach of conditionality has been considerably extended, with Dwyer (2008) characterising what has emerged as a 'conditional welfare state', where conditionality is accepted and embraced by all three main political parties. A particularly important policy development in this regard was the introduction of Employment and Support Allowance (ESA) in 2008. Following its introduction, many disabled people have been subject to work-related conditionality.

While the theoretical defences and government rhetoric around conditionality have been extensively interrogated from a number of standpoints (Dean, 2002; Deacon, 2004a; Dwyer, 2004; Wright, 2011), what has been lacking, with the notable exception of Dwyer (2000), is any consideration of how citizens themselves, and disabled people in particular, interpret conditionality. Drawing on qualitative research conducted with both disabled and non-disabled individuals, this chapter explores attitudes to the applicability of welfare conditionality to disabled people. The chapter starts with a review of the relevant policy and theoretical context, before outlining the methods employed to generate the qualitative data discussed in the chapter. Findings from the study are then outlined, with a focus on how far and in what ways various defences of conditionality for disabled people were utilised by the research participants. The chapter argues that, while enforcing work-related conditionality on disabled people is problematic, it could perhaps be justifiably applied in conjunction with Stuart White's (2003) notion of a 'civic minimum'. However, the chapter also argues that currently in Britain there is what might be described as a 'civic minimum deficit'; a gap between the status quo and what would be needed for a 'civic minimum' to be in place, a vital precondition to conditionality being more justly employed.

Policy context: a 'principle of conditionality' and the Employment and Support Allowance

In Britain, the 'principle of conditionality' in welfare (Dwyer, 2004, p 266) was entrenched by New Labour governments' (1997–2010) welfare reforms that were framed by a rhetoric of 'no rights without responsibilities' (Giddens, 1998, p 65). Defined as 'the principle that entitlement to benefits should be conditional on satisfying certain conditions' (Stanley and Lohde, 2004, p 1), theorists in the United States (US) such as Lawrence Mead (1992, 1997, 2011) have defended conditionality as a central issue of reciprocity, without which those in receipt of benefits cannot be seen as equal citizens. For disabled people, conditionality is most visible in the ESA regime. Introduced in 2008 as a replacement for Incapacity Benefit (IB), ESA is the latest earnings replacement benefit in Britain for those who are unable to work due to illness or disability (Burchardt, 1999).

There are two main ways in which disabled people face increased conditionality via ESA. First, some disabled people who would previously have been eligible for IB do not meet the stricter qualifying criteria for ESA and will now be receiving Jobseeker's Allowance (JSA) – Britain's primary benefit for unemployed people – and, therefore, face even greater conditionality than had their ESA application been successful (Piggott and Grover, 2009).

Second, applicants who meet eligibility thresholds for ESA are considered to have 'limited capability for work' and are placed in one of two groups – the 'work-related activity group' (WRAG) or the 'support group' (SG) – based on their adjudged capability to do paid work-related activity. Those who are assessed as having the capability of doing work-related activity to hasten their re-entry into employment are placed in the WRAG, while those deemed to not have such capability are placed in the SG. For our purposes, the most important of these two groups is the WRAG, as people in it are subject to work-related conditions (those in the SG are exempt from such conditions).

The Westminster coalition government, formed in 2010, has continued with ESA and has overseen the migration of existing IB claimants onto ESA. Iain Duncan Smith, the-then Conservative Work and Pensions Secretary, declared his support for conditionality, arguing that: 'it is only right that if we are helping people to get back into work, then we also have a right to expect that those we support are ready and willing to take on work if it is offered' (DWP, 2010). In its commitment to conditionality, coalition policy represents a clear continuation of New Labour's approach to welfare reform (Deacon and Patrick, 2011). However, the coalition government has increased the conditionality that frames ESA, an extension of New Labour's original plans (DWP, 2008; Patrick, 2012).

For all ESA claimants, the Welfare Reform Act 2012 introduced a 'claimant commitment' clause as part of its basic eligibility criteria, although in practice those who qualify for the SG would not be subject to conditionality regarding its 'work-related requirements' (Dwyer and Wright, 2014). This entrenched the idea of individual responsibilities and conditionality. For those in the WRAG, conditionality has been further extended from New Labour's original work-focused interviews and training to include the possibility of work experience and/or work placements. Sanctions have increased, while the amount of benefit income that can be withheld for deemed non-compliance has also risen (DWP, 2012). Over 19,000 adverse sanction decisions were made against ESA claimants between December 2012 and September 2013, the latest period for which statistics are currently available (DWP, 2014). As yet there is little research evidence available about the impact that these sanctions are having on disabled people. However, research into the effects of sanctions more generally suggests that they do not necessarily lead to improved employment outcomes and at the same time carry a real risk of destitution (Homeless Watch, 2013; Miscampbell, 2014; see also Chapter One, this volume). Despite this, the coalition government remains committed to welfare reforms premised upon welfare conditionality.

Justifying conditionality

Whether by government or by academics, the three justifications most often employed to justify conditionality are mutualism, paternalism and/or contractualism (Deacon, 2004a, 2004b, 2005). The *mutualist* justification is heavily influenced by the work of communitarians, such as Etzioni (1997), Selznick (2002) and Sacks (2008), and centres on the notion that individuals have obligations towards one another that arise independently from the actions of government (Deacon, 2004b, 2005). Thus, conditionality is simply upholding and instilling personal responsibility, an essential pillar of a functioning and well-ordered society.

The *paternalist* justification suggests that conditionality is an exercise of power and compulsion, which, where appropriately employed, actually operates to further the affected individual's own interests (Mead, 1992, 1997; Driver, 2004). The paternalist standpoint is grounded in three central ideas:

- that poor people not in paid work lack competence;
- that paid work is good for the self;
- that compulsion is necessary to get those most demotivated and demoralised back into the folds of citizenship, through the world of paid work (Mead, 1992, 1997; Deacon, 2004b, 2005).

Contractualist arguments form the third justification of conditionality, whereby welfare benefits and services can be justly utilised to enforce the obligations of claimants within a broader framework of contractual duties, which fall on both the state and individual citizens (Deacon, 2004b, 2005). Contractualists construct conditionality as a policy tool for ensuring that citizens meet their reciprocal duties, but these are framed within, and are themselves made conditional on, governments' own responsibilities. How embracive and egalitarian the duties of government are regarded varies according to the political persuasions of different academics within the contractualist tradition. Thus, the state's obligations under White's (2003) egalitarian form of contractualism are far more extensive than those advocated by the American democrat Ellwood (1988) or the more conservative Galston (2005).

Over the past 20 years, government ministers have, on occasions, employed all three justifications for increasing conditionality. However, both New Labour governments were, and the coalition government is, particularly keen on a contractual approach. New Labour subtitled its first 'social security' Green Paper, *A new contract for welfare* (DSS, 1998) and, more than 10 years later, the Conservative Party (2010) published its ideas for welfare reform measures under the tag line, *A new welfare contract*. While recent British governments' articulations of contractualism have focused policy attention on the responsibilities of individuals, there is also scope to employ contractualist ideas to consider the duties and obligations of the state.

Stuart White, the civic minimum and conditionality

Operating from within a contractualist perspective, White attempts to develop an egalitarian and social democratic defence of welfare conditionality by stressing the importance of linking duty to equality through a principle of reciprocity. His egalitarian form of contractualism is based on the premise that true justice requires an element of reciprocity, which can best be ensured through welfare conditionality (White, 2003; Deacon, 2007; White and Cooke, 2007). White develops the idea of a civic minimum to describe the conditions that must first be met for welfare conditionality to be fairly imposed as part of the government–citizen contract. He makes a distinction between justice as fair reciprocity in its ideal and non-ideal form, recognising that its ideal form might be unachievable in practice. Therefore, he bases his arguments on what would be necessary to obtain justice as fair reciprocity in a pragmatic and feasible 'non-ideal' form (White, 2003).

The preconditions for the realisation of justice as fair reciprocity encompass fair opportunity, fair reward, universality and diversity (White, 2003; Deacon, 2007; White and Cooke, 2007). The basic work obligation can only be justly enforced via conditionality if each individual has a fair chance of finding a job that pays a sufficient income to enable them to escape poverty. Further, for conditionality to be defensible it must be applicable to all (and not just recipients of public welfare) and recognise a diverse range of contributions (White and Cooke, 2007). As White (2003) acknowledges, these conditions are not easily obtainable and few advanced capitalist societies provide such a civic minimum. Where these conditions are not met, those unjustly disadvantaged as a result should have a proportionately reduced obligation to contribute (White, 2004). This principle of proportionality, when tied to the notion of justice as fair reciprocity, illustrates the demands that the contract places on both the state and its citizens (White, 2003, 2005; White and Cooke, 2007). White's work is important as it attempts to explore how and whether conditionality could be justly employed, with a particular focus on what would first be required from the state before demands could fairly be made of individual citizens. We will return to White's civic minimum in the concluding discussion in this chapter.

While it is relatively easy to find examples of government ministers employing various justifications for increasing welfare conditionality, it is far less easy to find analyses of the ways individuals employ such arguments in their attitudes to welfare conditionality. In analysing both disabled and non-disabled people's attitudes towards the appropriateness of applying welfare conditionality to disabled people, we have explored both the presence and absence of these justifications. Before looking at these findings, however, we briefly outline the methods employed in our study.

Methods

This chapter is based on the findings from a small-scale exploratory study into attitudes towards applying work-related welfare conditionality to disabled people. The qualitative research was conducted between 2007 and 2008, and coincided with a marked increase in the conditionality faced by many disabled people via New Labour's introduction of ESA. Three focus groups – two with disabled people (DSG1, DSG2) and one with non-disabled (NDG) people (15 participants in total) – were facilitated in Leeds. The groups were segmented according to whether or not participants were disabled because the aim of the study was to consider whether opinions and attitudes towards conditionality differed between disabled and non-disabled people.

For the three focus groups, a purposive sampling strategy was adopted with a reliance on snowballing to recruit appropriate participants. The groups followed a semi-structured format in order to keep the discussions focused and to enable effective comparison both within and, importantly, across groups (Morgan, 1997). Ethical concerns were paramount and at all times the researcher kept within the ethical guidelines of the British Sociological Association (BSA, 2002). Anonymity, confidentiality and informed consent were prioritised. In the following analysis, all names have been changed.

Data from the focus groups were analysed using detailed qualitative data protocols, involving immersion within the text, annotation of the text, the search for emergent themes, thematic coding and comparison between focus groups. In addition to the primary analysis of the data conducted by the researcher, and reported elsewhere (Patrick, 2011), this chapter discusses findings from a secondary analysis of the data undertaken by the joint authors. This secondary analysis was invaluable in providing fresh insight into the data, and a new reading of the data, which is particularly important given the time that has passed (both chronologically and in terms of the evolution in policy) since the study was undertaken.

Findings

Conditionality

The research found clear differences between the views of disabled and non-disabled participants regarding the appropriateness of applying work-related conditionality to disabled people. A key example of this was revealed in discussions around a fictional scenario where a depressed individual was compelled to work 16 hours a week after a medical examiner deemed him able to work. While all the non-disabled participants felt that this was the right course of action, none of the disabled participants agreed, considering this compulsion likely to further exacerbate the individual's impairment. Disabled participants such as Isobel (DSG2) were concerned that: "you're constructing circumstances where the depression is going to get a lot more serious". Dave (DSG2) agreed, arguing: "It's wrong because it's putting pressure on people, saying 'you must do this'. That can have further implications on the person's health so it's not right."

In criticising the application of conditionality in this scenario, some disabled participants stressed that an effective approach would focus on encouragement, rather than compulsion. Richard (DSG2) suggested the perversity of making a disabled person seek work, given the persistence of discrimination: "That person is going to have to go looking for jobs and the employers are just going to look on him negatively if he's got depression. That guy is going to go through interview after interview getting knocked back and he is just going to go down and down."

Outside of the specific scenario discussion, those non-disabled participants defending conditionality for disabled people employed both contractualist and paternalist justifications. John (NDG), for instance, took a contractualist approach, stressing disabled people's obligation to contribute where possible:

> 'If they [disabled people] just sort of sit back and give up, then yeah, their benefits should be reduced because they're not doing a great deal to try and improve things for themselves, to maybe get more integrated into a working life. At the end of the day, everybody else has to pay tax, and a certain amount of taxpayers' money is going to benefits and they should try their best to contribute as well.'

Similarly, another participant in favour of conditionality highlighted the contractualist argument that disabled people's obligations must be linked to the government's responsibility to provide appropriate support. Referring back to the fictional scenario of the depressed individual, Andy (NDG) said: "I think it's reasonable as long as he's given the right support and maybe monitored whilst he's working to make sure that it's not affecting his condition."

Paternalist arguments were employed to emphasise the value of work for disabled people alongside the need to motivate disabled people into work. Rochelle (NDG) described: "people going to work, having a routine, being with people, having to have a wash and get dressed and comb their hair and go out, it's all really important". This was echoed by Tom (NDG), who suggested that people on out-of-work benefits should be encouraged to work with charities to assist the voluntary sector and improve their own self-worth:

> 'There's a lot of charities out there who are struggling, and they need volunteers. And I think it would be a very good move for people who are out of work that are able to work to help with charities and things like hospices, this sort of thing.... I don't think there's many people who would object to that because they're giving some good to their community. Who wouldn't feel good about being able to contribute something to their community?'

Interestingly, some disabled participants also recognised the value of work, but felt that conditionality was a blunt and inappropriate device to apply to disabled people. Kathy (DSG1) explained: "I do personally think that work is a good thing, by and large, but I don't feel people should be forced into it when it's not appropriate." Some participants also recognised that conditionality could be conceptualised as a 'carrot and stick' approach:

> 'I don't like the idea of any government being able to use a carrot and stick approach to force people to behave in certain ways. People always have their own reasons for doing what they do. That's why I don't think it's always possible to use carrot and stick kind of, to use all these conditions.'
> (Dave, DSG2)

Welfare conditionality was seen as an effective policy mechanism by most of the non-disabled group, who seemed relaxed about using welfare instrumentally to encourage and prevent certain types of behaviour. By contrast, this was a concern for some of the disabled participants. Jane (DSG1), for example, felt that encouragement was more important than compulsion in enabling people to meet their responsibilities: "I generally agree that people should take some responsibility for themselves, and add some structure to their day. But it's about encouraging people to feel they can, not bending their arm up their back."

Demand-side barriers to work for disabled people and conditionality

Another central theme highlighted by the disabled participants was the suitability of the workplace and employment practices more generally. This, again, problematised the application of conditionality for disabled people. Disabled participants highlighted the barriers they and other disabled people faced regarding employment. Demand-side issues such as physical barriers, discrimination by employers, as well as stigma and stereotyping were all issues raised by participants that have consistently been highlighted as problematic in the employment of disabled people (for instance, Roulstone, 2004; Barnes and Roulstone, 2005).

With regard to gaining employment, the disabled participants were concerned that demand-side interventions were needed. Richard (DSG2) explained:

> 'The government is trying to get disabled people to go and find jobs, but the problem, no matter what government puts in place, it's the employer at the bottom. The last thing, if the employer doesn't want to know, they won't make reasonable adjustments, you just don't have a chance.'

However, the coalition government, like New Labour before it, has continued to focus policy attention on supply-side interventions (Yates and Roulstone, 2013). Support for employers was also mentioned by the NDG group. Rochelle suggested: "I think the only way they can do that is by investing in employers, when they employ somebody. Because I think realistically I don't think employers would employ someone who is disabled."

Rochelle's comment connects to another theme from the disabled participants' discussions concerning the idea that disabled people are not seen as being able to compete with non-disabled people for paid work:

'If you get a disabled person and a non-disabled person going for the same job ... I'm sure that employer, even though we've got the DDA [Disability Discrimination Act] and we've got ... reasonable adjustments, they would tend towards the non-disabled person because they could do everything and they don't have to go through the hassle of getting PAs [personal assistants]....' (Gail, DSG1)

Other disabled participants agreed with this view, and some spoke of their experience of discrimination in the workplace: "Obviously it depends on the size of the company, if you have a small organisation they're going to be very reluctant to employ a disabled person. I've had personal experience" (Richard, DSG2).

These kinds of statements indicate that, even with anti-discrimination legislation currently in place in Britain, paid work and its processes can be experienced as disabling. However, these concerns were largely the preserve of the disabled participants. By contrast, the non-disabled group were more focused on attitudes and perceptions – for example, a lack of confidence and motivation as reasons why disabled people do not work. As John (NDG) said: "It's about enticing them [disabled people] to do it.... It's a case of changing that mindset. Making them realise that although they're officially, medically classed as disabled, there is still a place in the workplace for them."

This kind of sentiment reflects an assumption that disabled people have 'given up' and, therefore, that some sort of incentive or condition is needed to get them into work. In brief, it is a paternalistic approach. Such an approach was one of New Labour's original justifications for ESA (DWP, 2008). Since 2008, however, changing economic conditions have arguably made finding employment even more difficult for disabled people, and yet, as we have seen, conditionality has been extended. Drawing on the work of White's (2003) notion of the civic minimum, this lack of recognition of the employment issues that disabled people face means that conditionality could be interpreted as entrenchment of injustice, because the starting point for disabled and non-disabled benefits claimants is unequal.

A welfare contract?

All the non-disabled participants thought that the contractual approach to conditionality was a good idea. John (NDG) was particularly enthusiastic:

'Sounds fantastic, yeah. It kind of lays down some ground rules. So if people are aware of what to expect from government, and if they want all those expectations to be met, then they have to provide certain things themselves … so if they're wanting support to be integrated into the workplace, then they need to help themselves by putting themselves out there and looking for employment.'

There was also some support for a contractualist approach among disabled participants. Dave (DSG2), for instance, saw it as having potential:

'I feel it could be a good thing to have a contract so that both sides understand precisely what is expected of each other, so you know what the government expects from you, and you also know precisely what kind of help you can expect from the government. Could be much more clear.'

The link between rights and contributions (responsibilities) was picked up across the focus groups. A number of participants – both disabled and non-disabled – suggested that disabled people should have a right to contribute and to have responsibilities in the same way as non-disabled people. As Isobel (DSG2) described:

'I would far rather pay into a social insurance scheme and get benefits from it than be seen to be some kind of hand-out victim or unwelcome employee … I need for my self-esteem and my self-worth, I need to be doing something purposeful and productive and positive, but I equally need the head space to know that I don't have to go tomorrow if I'm not physically able.'

This perspective was echoed by Andy (NDG): "[Disabled people should have] the right to have support to allow them to contribute to society and feel fulfilled." He felt that this right and responsibility to contribute could be linked to conditionality: "I think that if you want to be part of society then you've got to play by society's rules and contribute. If you don't you can't expect society to contribute to you" (Andy, NDG). Both Andy and Isobel's arguments showed elements of mutualist thinking, with Andy's in particular a fairly clear articulation of a mutualist defence of welfare conditionality.

Overall, it was clear that attitudes to welfare conditionality's applicability to disabled people differed considerably between the disabled and non-disabled participants in this research. While the non-disabled advocates of welfare conditionality employed mutualist, paternalist and contractual arguments, the disabled people were more likely to outline their concerns with the punitive and ineffective aspects of what one described as a 'carrot and stick' approach to welfare. Interestingly, though, several participants in all three groups saw potential in viewing the relationship between the state and citizen in contractual terms.

Discussion

This research into attitudes towards the appropriateness of applying work-related conditionality to disabled people found a clear difference in perspective between disabled and non-disabled participants. While the non-disabled people who participated in the study were enthusiastic about welfare conditionality being utilised in this way, all the disabled people in the study were opposed to it – arguing that it would be a blunt and punitive tool; ineffective in supporting disabled people into paid work. As Isobel (DSG2) explained: "I just think it's unfortunate that it's quite so punitive, in the way that it [conditionality] may affect us."

Disabled people's opposition towards conditionality in this research was for two linked reasons. First, such an approach was held to not understand the potential impacts of conditionality on disabled people. Mike (DSG2) suggested that governments needed "a much better understanding of what disability actually means to individuals before making policy decisions which ... affect millions of disabled people". Concerns were raised about the health impacts of increased conditionality, but respondents also pointed to other potential diswelfares of conditionality, such as increased stigmatisation of benefit claimants and an undermining of other forms of contribution, like volunteering and care work.

Second, there was recognition among disabled participants that the problem in terms of paid work was not disabled people being unwilling or unable to work, but that they were disabled by a lack of demand in labour markets, stigma and employer discrimination. Indeed, the policy prescription of welfare conditionality – carrots and sticks – to 'encourage' disabled people into paid work, clashes with a lived reality of endemic and persistent societal, disabling structures to their inclusion in the labour market. For example, some 92% of employers describe it as difficult or impossible to employ blind and partially sighted people, suggesting some rather deeply ingrained demand-side labour market barriers to their employment (Gentleman, 2011). Despite this, the Royal National Institute of Blind People anticipates that ESA's Work Capability Assessment (WCA) will find many blind and partially sighted people fit for work, who will then be placed on JSA and subject to comparatively tough conditions as part of their benefit entitlement (Gentleman, 2011).

These observations have important implications for the justifications that are used for the extension of conditionality. If disabled people are discriminated against in accessing paid work, they are going to struggle to fulfil their mutualist obligations. Furthermore, the lived experience of discrimination and disabling workplaces may be at odds with a paternalist reading of paid work as inherently rewarding and satisfying. Similarly, and most important for our purposes, they raise questions about the contractualist defence of conditionality.

We have seen that White (White, 2003; White and Cooke, 2007) employs the concept of a 'civic minimum' to focus on what first might be expected of the state before work-related conditionality can justly be imposed upon citizens. While White puts emphasis on work being available that allows employees to escape poverty, in Britain there remain real issues around in-work poverty and the continued growth in precarious and inflexible forms of employment. Furthermore, White (2003) argues that conditionality should apply to all citizens, and recognise forms of contribution beyond paid work (such as caring and volunteering), but Britain's conditionality regime is focused solely on paid work. It also remains primarily concerned with imposing conditionality on those reliant on social security benefits for all, or the majority, of their income. The deficit between White's civic minimum and what currently operates in Britain suggests that any imposition of work-related conditionality is inherently problematic.

Importantly, disabled people in Britain are particularly disadvantaged, being more likely to be in low-paid employment, and more likely to experience discrimination in their attempts to secure paid work (see Chapter One, this volume). For example, in 2012, the mean hourly wage rate of disabled people was £12.15, while that of non-disabled people was £13.25 (Office for Disability Issues, 2011). Disabled people in work are more likely than non-disabled people to say they would like to work more hours, suggesting that they are at greater risk of under-employment. Furthermore, figures suggest that disabled people are significantly more likely to experience problematic treatment at work than non-disabled people. In 2008, for example, 19% of disabled people experienced unfair treatment at work compared with 13% of non-disabled people (Office for Disability Issues, 2011).

Drawing on the principle of proportionality that informs the notion of fair reciprocity in White's work, it can be argued that it is particularly unjust to impose work-related conditionality on disabled people because paid work is something that they are disproportionately disadvantaged in accessing and keeping compared with non-disabled people. In this sense, advocates of social justice for disabled people (broadly conceived as fairness with a particular focus on equality of opportunity) might be wise to make use of White's notion of contractualism. Critically, it provides scope to scrutinise the responsibilities that the government ought to be fulfilling, and to identify the deficit between its contractual duties and actual practice – what we describe as the 'civic minimum deficit'. While this pragmatic approach could yield real results, it is also vital to interrogate whether extensive work-related conditionality can ever co-exist with social justice and equality of opportunity.

Conclusion

This chapter has discussed a small-scale study into attitudes towards the appropriateness of applying work-related conditionality to disabled people. Importantly, the research found a marked difference between the attitudes of the target group and those not likely to be directly affected, with disabled people being very critical of the imposition of work-related conditionality, which ESA in Britain entails.

The research reported here took place in 2008, just as ESA was being introduced. Reviewing the findings six years on, as the controversy and possible shortcomings with both ESA and its WCA receive continued attention (Citizens Advice Bureau, 2014; Spartacus Network, 2014), it is tempting to conclude that welfare conditionality and disabled people are indeed ill-suited companions. Certainly, the implementation of ESA thus far has been marked by high-profile examples of punitive sanctions and a common experience among disabled people of anxiety, worry and stress as they try to navigate the reformed benefit system (Garthwaite, 2013). Furthermore, there are overarching issues with a policy approach that places the corrective lens firmly on the steps disabled people need to take to enter work, given the endurance of demand-side issues to disabled people's equal opportunities in employment.

Importantly, though, politicians' rhetorical reliance on welfare contractualism, when considered in tandem with the work of contractualist theorist Stuart White (2003), means that there is perhaps scope to reconsider the relationship between the individual and the state in contractual terms by placing far more emphasis on the duty and obligations of the state itself. Currently, there is a large 'civic minimum deficit' between what White (2003) suggests are necessary preconditions for conditionality to be imposed justly, and what currently exists. There is a role for more research here, for example, the sketching out the component parts of a civic minimum for all, inclusive of the needs and rights of disabled people. There is also scope for contractualism to be utilised by campaigners from within the disabled people's movement who could invert the conditionality rhetoric by making further demands of the state.

However, in Britain, given the enduring barriers to disabled people's equal treatment in the workplace and society in general, there is little doubt that welfare conditionality is currently incompatible with social justice. With the government and the main political parties all committed to policy programmes that extend and entrench welfare conditionality, it is of critical import that researchers continue to listen to, and record, the perspectives of the real experts – those directly affected – on conditionality's impact and possible applicability.

References

Barnes, C. and Roulstone, A. (2005) '"Work" is a four-letter word: disability, work and welfare', in A. Roulstone and C. Barnes (eds) *Working futures? Disabled people, policy and social inclusion*, Bristol: Policy Press.

BSA (British Sociological Association) (2002) *Statement of ethical practice for the British Sociological Association*, updated May 2004, Durham: BSA www.britsoc.co.uk/equality/Statement+Ethical+Practice.htm

Burchardt, T. (1999) *The evolution of disability benefits in the UK: Re-weighting the basket*, CASE Paper, London: Centre for Analysis of Social Exclusion.

Citizens Advice Bureau (2014) *'Unfit for purpose': ESA is biggest problem for Citizens Advice clients*, London: Citizens Advice Bureau www.citizensadvice.org.uk/index/pressoffice/press_index/press_office-20140408.htm

Conservative Party (2010) *A new welfare contract*, London: Conservative Party, www.conservatives.com/~/media/Files/Downloadable%20Files/a_new_welfare_contract.ashx?dl=true

Deacon, A. (2002) *Perspectives on welfare: Ideas, ideologies, and policy debates*, Buckingham: Open University Press.

Deacon, A. (2004a) 'Justifying conditionality: the case of anti-social tenants', *Housing Studies*, 19(6), pp 911-26.

Deacon, A. (2004b) 'Can conditionality be justified?', in P. Collins and A. Rossiter (eds) *On condition*, London: The Social Market Foundation, pp 38-56.

Deacon, A. (2005) 'An ethic of mutual responsibility? Toward a fuller justification for conditionality in welfare', in C. Beem and L. Mead (eds) *Welfare reform and political theory*, New York, NY: Russell Sage Foundation, pp 127-50.

Deacon, A. (2007) 'Civic labour or doulia? Care, reciprocity and welfare', *Social Policy and Society*, 6(4), pp 481-90.

Deacon, A. and Patrick, R. (2011) 'A new welfare settlement? The coalition government and welfare-to-work', in H. Bochel (ed) *The Conservative Party and social policy*, Bristol: Policy Press, pp 161-79.

Dean, H. (2002) *Welfare rights and social policy*, Harlow: Prentice-Hall.

Driver, S. (2004) 'North Atlantic drift: welfare reform and the "Third Way" politics of New Labour and the new democrats', in S. Hale, W. Leggett and L. Martell (eds) *The Third Way and beyond: Criticisms, futures, alternatives*, Manchester: Manchester University Press, pp 31-47.

DSS (Department for Social Security) (1998) *New ambitions for our country: A new contract for welfare*, Green Paper, Cmnd 3805, London: The Stationery Office.

DWP (Department for Work and Pensions) (2008) *Raising expectations and increasing support: Reforming welfare for the future*, White Paper, Cm 7506, London: DWP.

DWP (2010) Speech: Welfare for the 21st century, 20 May, https://www.gov.uk/government/speeches/welfare-for-the-21st-century

DWP (2012) *Changes to sanctions for Employment and Support Allowance claimants from 3 December 2012*, http://webarchive.nationalarchives.gov.uk/20130627060116/http:/www.dwp.gov.uk/adviser/updates/esa-sanction-changes/

DWP (2014) *Employment and Support Allowance sanctions statistics*, https://www.gov.uk/government/collections/employment-and-support-allowance-sanctions

Dwyer, P. (2000) *Welfare rights and responsibilities: Contesting social citizenship*, Bristol: Policy Press

Dwyer, P. (2004) 'Creeping conditionality in the UK: from welfare rights to conditional entitlements?', *Canadian Journal of Sociology*, 29(2), pp 265-87.

Dwyer, P. (2008) 'The conditional welfare state', in M. Powell (ed) *Modernising the welfare state: The Blair legacy*, Bristol: Policy Press, pp 199-218.

Dwyer, P. and Wright, S. (2014) 'Universal Credit, ubiquitous conditionality and its implications for social citizenship', *Journal of Poverty and Social Justice*, 22(1), pp 27-35.

Ellwood, D.T. (1988) *Poor support: Poverty in the American family*, New York, NY: Basic Books.

Etzioni, A. (1997) *The new golden rule: Community and morality in a democratic society*, New York, NY: Basic Books.

Galston, W.A. (2005) 'Conditional citizenship', in L. Mead and C. Beem (eds) *Welfare reform and political theory*, New York, NY: Russell Sage Foundation, pp 110-26.

Garthwaite, K. (2013) 'Fear of the brown envelope: exploring welfare reform with long-term sickness benefits recipients', *Social Policy & Administration*, doi: 10.1111/spol.12049.

Gentleman, A. (2011) 'Blind people will lose £30 per week under new benefit regime, says RNIB', *The Guardian*, 16 February.

Giddens, A. (1998) *The Third Way: The renewal of social democracy*, Cambridge: Polity Press.

Gilbert, N. and Besharov, D. (2011) 'Welfare states amid economic turmoil: adjusting work-orientated policy', *Policy & Politics*, 39(3), pp 295-308.

Homeless Watch (2013) *A high cost to pay – the impact of benefit sanctions on homeless people*, London: Homeless Watch, http://homeless.org.uk/sites/default/files/site-downloads/A%20High%20Cost%20to%20Pay%20Sept13_0.pdf

Mead, L. (1992) *The new politics of poverty: The nonworking poor in America*, New York, NY: Basic Books.

Mead, L. (1997) 'Welfare employment', in L. Mead (ed) *The new paternalism: Supervisory approaches to poverty*, Washington, DC: Brookings Institute Press, pp 39-88.

Mead, L. (2011) 'Lawrence M. Mead replies to Ruth Patrick, "The wrong prescription: disabled people and welfare conditionality"', *Policy & Politics*, 39(2), pp 281-2.

Miscampbell, G. (2014) *Smarter sanctions: Sorting out the system*, London: Policy Exchange.

Morgan, D. (1997) *Focus groups as qualitative research*, London: Sage Publications.

Office for Disability Issues (2011) *Disability equality indicators*, London: Office for Disability Issues, http://odi.dwp.gov.uk/disability-statistics-and-research/disability-equality-indicators.php

Patrick, R. (2011) 'Disabling or enabling: the extension of work-related conditionality to disabled people', *Social Policy & Society*, 10(3), pp 309-20.

Patrick, R. (2012) 'All in it together? Disabled people, the coalition and welfare to work', *Journal of Poverty and Social Justice*, 20(3), pp 307-22.

Piggott, L. and Grover, C. (2009) 'Retrenching Incapacity Benefit: Employment Support Allowance and paid work', *Social Policy and Society*, 8(2), pp 159-70.

Roulstone, A. (2004) 'Disability, employment and the social model', in C. Barnes and G. Mercer (eds) *Disability policy and practice: Applying the social model*, Leeds: The Disability Press, pp 18-34.

Sacks, J. (2008) 'The age of greed is over: will the age of responsibility now begin?', BBC Radio 4, *Today*, 3 October, www.rabbisacks.org/thought-for-the-day-3rd-october-2008-the-age-of-greed-is-over-will-the-age-of-responsibility-now-begin/

Selznick, P. (2002) *The communitarian persuasion*, Washington, DC: Woodrow Wilson Center Press.

Spartacus Network (2014) *Beyond the barriers*, We are Spartacus, www.spartacusnetwork.org.uk/images/reports/BeyondTheBarriers.pdf

Stanley, K. and Lohde, L. (2004) 'Applying the framework', in K. Stanley, L. Lohde and S. White (eds) *Sanctions and sweeteners: Rights and responsibilities in the benefits system*, London: Institute for Public Policy Research, pp 25-82.

White, S. (2003) *The civic minimum*, Oxford: Oxford University Press.

White, S. (2004) 'Is conditionality unfair?', in P. Collins and A. Rossiter (eds) *On condition*, London: The Social Market Foundation, pp 16-35.

White, S. (2005) 'Is conditionality illiberal?', in C. Beem and L. Mead (eds) *Welfare reform and political theory*, New York, NY: Russell Sage Foundation, pp 82-109.

White, S. and Cooke, G. (2007) 'Taking responsibility: a fair welfare contract', in J. Bennett and G. Cooke (eds) *It's all about you: Citizen-centred welfare*, London: Institute for Public Policy Research, pp 26-44.

Wright, S. (2011) 'Steering with sticks, rowing for rewards: the new governance of activation in the UK', in R. Berkel, W. Graaf and T. Sirovatka (eds) *The governance of active welfare states in Europe*, Basingstoke: Palgrave Macmillan.

Yates, S. and Roulstone, A. (2013) 'Social policy and transitions to training and work for disabled young people in the United Kingdom: neo-liberalism for better and for worse?', *Disability & Society*, 28(4), pp 456-70.

THREE

Doing the 'hard yakka': implications of Australia's workfare policies for disabled people

Alan Morris, Shaun Wilson and Karen Soldatic

Introduction

In Australia, almost 19% of the population has a disability (ABS, 2009) and its prevalence will steadily rise with the increase in life-sustaining interventions and an ageing population (AIHW, 2008). The number of Australians receiving the Disability Support Pension (DSP)[1] has grown substantially. In 1990, there were around 316,000 DSP recipients (Yeend, 2011). By the beginning of 2014 there were about 825,000 (Maley, 2014). The proportion of the working-age population claiming the DSP grew from 4.3% to 5.5% between 1994 and 2012 (Maley, 2014). Increasingly, DSP recipients are women, at 43% in 2008, up from 26% in 1990 (ACOSS, 2011). The current cost of the DSP is around AU$15 billion per annum, representing about 21% of the welfare budget (Ireland, 2014).

In the name of promoting paid work and cutting costs, the main policy response to the rising DSP expenditure has focused on tightening the eligibility rules and assessment procedures and moving DSP recipients into work where possible or onto Newstart, Australia's stringent unemployment benefit. In April 2011, in a speech on the 'Dignity of Work', the-then Labor Prime Minister Julia Gillard concluded that 'there are many thousands of individuals on the Disability Support Pension (DSP) who may have some capacity to work' (Whiteford, 2011, npn). Later that year, the government made a series of changes to DSP policy, including tighter 'impairment tables' to reduce DSP eligibility and, for new clients under 35 years of age, a mix of initiatives were put in place to encourage employment. Partial pensions could be retained for people working up to 30 hours per week and new applicants who did not have a severe impairment had to participate in a 'programme of support' (typically focused on job search or employability) before becoming eligible for the DSP (Lunn, 2011; Australian Government, 2014a).

The result of these reforms, over time, is an anticipated wider use of Newstart as a benefit for disabled people. But a greater reliance on Newstart instead of the DSP will produce a severe loss of income for many disabled Australians. In January 2014, the Newstart benefit was just AU$250.50 (around £136) per week for single people, well below the AU$413.55 (around £225) available for single DSP clients. The single Newstart payment is well below the poverty line, which in September 2013 was estimated at AU$408.98 per week once housing is included (Melbourne Institute, 2013). Income poverty caused by Newstart has been criticised by commentators on the left and right (ACOSS, 2012; Denniss and Baker, 2012; Sloan, 2012; Morris and Wilson, 2014) and even by the Organisation for Economic Co-operation and Development (OECD) (Whiteford, 2010).

The conservative Coalition government that came to power in September 2013 is exploring 'merging' DSP into Newstart. An interim report released by the federal government in June 2014 recommends reserving the DSP for people with a permanent disability and no capacity to work. Disabled people 'who have current or future capacity to work could be assisted through the tiered working age payment to better reflect different work capacities' (Commonwealth of Australia, 2014, p 9). What a permanent disability means and how it will be established are not discussed. The 'tiered working age payment' is not defined, but the payment will probably be close to the much lower Newstart payment. The imposition of this recommendation could result in hundreds of thousands of people being forced off the DSP and onto a much lower payment. It would further underline the trend away from a framework of social protection for disabled people in favour of a workfare system whereby sanctions are used to force people to look for work when in receipt of a government benefit (see Peck, 2001).

Our objective in this chapter is to gain greater insight into the likely impacts of using Newstart as the primary income support programme for disabled people. The chapter has three main sections. The first outlines recent reforms in disability support. The second discusses the adequacy problems of the Newstart benefit and ongoing deficiencies in Australia's welfare-to-work model. The remainder of the chapter details the mixed-methods approach and results of a small research project conducted in inner-metropolitan Sydney in late 2012. The sample is not a cohort of disabled welfare recipients; rather, it includes disadvantaged Newstart clients whose disability status was not directly assessed. Still, the data serve a useful purpose. They highlight areas of hardship, 'hard yakka'[2], likely to be significant problems for a growing disabled cohort dependent on Newstart.

Reforms to income support for disabled Australians since the 1990s

Australia has a long history of social security measures for disabled people. Dating to 1908, disabled people who were defined as 'permanently incapacitated for work' had access to a centrally funded benefit (Kewley, 1980). Considerations of space mean that we cannot recount much of this history; rather, our task is to show that since the late 1980s, disability benefit payments have shifted towards a tougher work activation and benefit regime.

Australia's reformist Labor governments expanded Australia's social security spending substantially between 1983 and 1996 by around 6% of Gross Domestic Product (GDP). Labor legislated for a universal health insurance system (Medicare), more generous payments for poor families and universal superannuation (Wilson, 2013). But these social democratic trends were accompanied by a greater targeting of basic welfare benefits. In addition, by the late 1980s, there was growing consensus that obtaining benefits should be conditional on work-related undertakings, such as training, job-search and 'work-readiness' activities (Bessant, 2000). At first, the tougher, work-oriented approach was directed only at Australia's unemployed. In 1991, Newstart emerged as the new income support payment for unemployed people. The expectation was that it would only provide temporary support at a low level income while they made the transition to work. Consistent with Australian welfare design benefit has no time limit, although at the time of writing, the Coalition government had sought parliamentary support for an (effective) time limit for young unemployed people.

In 1991, the DSP was also introduced. It was to focus on the 'work capability' of disabled beneficiaries, not 'work incapacity' as was the case in the past (Cass et al, 1988). The disability assessment criteria were expanded and a dual-track assessment process was established. The dual-track assessment uses a medical determination to define impairment and a time-based work capacity assessment. Work–time capacity was defined as being able to work up to 30 hours per week. In practice, this resulted in many disabled people maintaining access to the new DSP while actively seeking work or receiving some payment when working part time.

The emphasis on employment and work activity was extended by the conservative Coalition government elected in 1996, led by Prime

Minister John Howard. In 1997, 'work for the dole' was introduced for young unemployed beneficiaries, obligating them to participate in community work programmes. Later, the government made participation compulsory for Newstart recipients under 50 years of age and tougher penalties were applied for 'breaches' of benefit conditions (Coad et al, 2006). The government's workfare approach also served to justify the late-1990s privatisation of the Commonwealth Employment Service. This led to a flourishing sector of non-governmental and private sector service organisations dependent on government funding (Soldatic and Pini, 2012).

The Howard government's disability support reforms emphasised greater conditionality, work activity and cost-cutting. The disability community/movement had long struggled for the right to work and access to employment (Clear and Gleeson, 2001; Morris, 2006). Indeed, the new generation of workfare policies under Prime Minister Howard can be seen as partially incorporating these claims. However, claims for access to employment were quickly subverted by the design of workfare, which was clearly motivated by hitching 'work participation' to the goal of reducing costs and welfare dependence (Soldatic and Chapman, 2010).

The new disability benefit funding model, developed in the late 1990s, was underpinned by a policy approach that social scientists have elsewhere called 'fast labour market attachment' (see Peck and Theodore, 2001). Accordingly, the funding of employment services became 'time limited' and 'outcome' focused, with payment of contracts directly tied to placing disabled people into 'any job' within 18 months (Australian Healthcare Associates, 2000). Employment services had clear financial incentives to engage in the practice of 'creaming' the 'most able of the disabled' into jobs (Kellie, 1998; Soldatic and Chapman, 2010; see also Chapters Four and Five, this volume). This practice contributed to the stratification of disabled clients into those judged too disabled to work and those 'able enough' to participate in what was usually the insecure end of the labour market (Grover and Soldatic, 2013). At the same time, the government agency administering social security, Centrelink, encouraged assessment staff to implement 'curbing' practices designed to discourage people from applying for the DSP and instead steer them onto Newstart (Australian Government, 2003, p 10). Many of the 'able enough' clients lost access to the DSP and were shifted onto Newstart even though their disability remained. Despite these reforms, the DSP was still viewed by policy elites as sheltering people from the government's mutual obligation requirements and from finding work (Newman, 1999).

The interaction between the DSP and Newstart benefit programmes that has emerged since the 1990s is important to our analysis. It serves as a reminder of overlapping definitional and categorisation processes involved with disability and unemployment. Actually, it suited policy makers in the 1990s to treat the DSP as an implicit policy tool for mitigating high levels of official unemployment (see Argyrous and Neal, 2003). However, as employment levels rose in the 2000s, the 'concealment' function served by the DSP became less necessary, and the level of benefit dependency was increasingly criticised. Echoing the views of policy makers, economists Cai and Gregory (2004) argued that the DSP had become a *de facto* unemployment programme, with higher entry rates onto the DSP during times of weak labour market conditions.

The Howard government attempted to further reduce access to the DSP in 2001 by reforming the time-based work assessment (the 30-hour work test). The proposed new qualification regime maintained the initial medical test to determine impairment, but sought to place any prospective DSP client onto Newstart if their work capacity was assessed at a much lower 15 hours per week (see Argyrous and Neale, 2003). Campaigns were mobilised across the country and the proposed change failed to gain parliamentary support on three occasions between 2001 and 2003 (Soldatic and Chapman, 2010). However, after the 2004 elections, the Howard government used its control of both the House of Representatives and Senate to finally introduce the unpopular 15-hour work test (the Job Capacity Assessment), and to shift all disability employment services out of the main welfare portfolio and into the Department of Employment and Workplace Relations (Soldatic, 2010). Work capacity assessment was outsourced to private companies. Many disabled people could no longer access disability benefits and were forced onto Newstart. As a result, their payments were substantially reduced and they no longer qualified for a range of concessions linked to the DSP (Soldatic, 2013). Disability employment services were given sanctioning powers and, as a condition of federal funding, were required to report clients who were judged to be flouting their benefit obligations (House of Representatives, 2005, p 7). Consequently, more clients were 'breached' (sanctioned), losing up to eight weeks' benefit (Commonwealth Ombudsman, 2007).

Hopes and disappointments: Labor reforms after 2007

Before discussing the income support and work reforms under Labor, it is necessary to give a more complete overview of Labor's disability reform agenda between 2007 and 2013. Clearly, our emphasis in this chapter is on the trend towards stricter eligibility, reduced payments and greater conditionality for Newstart and the DSP. This focus is not intended, however, to ignore the powerful reform energies that emerged during Labor's term in office and from within the disability community.[3] Labor's far-reaching plan for a National Disability Insurance Scheme (NDIS) gained bipartisan parliamentary support during Julia Gillard's tenure as Prime Minister (2010-13). The scheme provides a new funding base for financing disability services, with an expected annual cost of AU$14 billion (Buckmaster, 2013). However, the return of a Coalition government has seriously slowed the roll-out of the NDIS and its level of funding, approach and scope are now uncertain. However, its genesis is a reminder that mobilisation from the disability movement with the support from political progressives can still influence welfare reform paths dominated by neoliberal and paternalistic ideas.

Disappointingly, Labor's return to office in 2007 did not produce the same reformist spirit when it came to the DSP. The 15-hour per week work-test criteria and mutual obligation requirements were kept in place, and there was a further tightening of the Job Capacity Assessment (see Table 3.1). Indeed, in the financial year 2007-08, 35% of DSP applications were rejected (ACOSS, 2012). Despite the tightening of eligibility, by 2009 the DSP accounted for 37% of total working-age income support recipients (ACOSS, 2011, p 9), making it a target for further efforts to curb its growth. In 2011, the Labor government further tightened eligibility for the DSP and imposed even stricter work tests. Part of this involved another comprehensive review of the DSP medical impairment test (Grover and Soldatic, 2013).

A further key shift took place in 2011. Disabled people under 35 years of age with a capacity to work for eight hours or more per week now had to wait for 36 months before they could access the DSP (only people with assessed 'severe impairment' in this age group immediately qualify for the DSP). During the waiting period, clients are placed on Newstart (PWDA, 2011). In July 2012, Labor legislated that all DSP claimants under the age of 35 must undergo activity tests (Grover and Soldatic, 2013). Compulsory 'participation plans' and ongoing interviews are embedded throughout the new requirements (see Table 3.1). Access to the DSP for disabled people under the age of 35 became conditional on successive failures to find work over a two-year period. The National Welfare Rights Network concluded at the time that as many as four in 10 people with work incapacity would not qualify as disabled under the new assessment regime

(NWRN, 2011). It remains unclear how many DSP applicants have been directly affected. However, with the change in government in September 2013, these reforms will now be extended to all present DSP recipients under the age of 35.

Table 3.1: Welfare streams for disabled people according to assessed work capacity in Australia

Assessment	Less than 15 hours	15-30 hours	30+ hours
Entry programme	DSP	Newstart	Newstart
Payment	AU$413.55 per week (single person)*	AU$250.50 per week (single person)*	AU$250.50 per week (single person)*
Conditions	No activity testing required. DSP reduced by 50c for each dollar earned above $152 per fortnight.	Required to search for jobs and undergo activity testing. Newstart reduced by 50c for each dollar earned above $62 and up to $250 per fortnight and by 60c in the dollar for earnings above $250 per fortnight.	Required to search for jobs and undergo activity testing. Newstart reduced by 50c for each dollar earned above $62 and up to $250 per fortnight and by 60c in the dollar for earnings above $250 per fortnight.
Special assistance measures	Access to a range of pension benefits, such as highly subsidised pharmaceuticals, rental assistance, educational supplement and subsidised transport. The DSP is one of the key eligibility criteria for state/territory-funded disability support services, such as in-home support, disability counselling, aids and equipment, subsidised taxis and companion cards.	Access to a range of pension benefits, such as highly subsidised pharmaceuticals, rental assistance and educational supplement. Do not qualify for state/territory-funded disability support schemes that require DSP receipt for eligibility.	Access to the Health Care Card, which has lower-level subsidises than those available on the DSP. No access to state/territory-funded disability support schemes.

Note: * Payment rate in January 2014

Source: Australian Government (2014b, 2014c, 2014d)

Given that only around 10% of DSP clients earn a labour market income, the Labor government's 2011 reforms made concessions designed to facilitate work participation by liberalising the benefit cut-off rules. Those assessed capable of no more than 15 hours of work per week no longer had their benefits cut off if they worked longer hours (Yeend, 2011). This change provides greater support to people whose hours of work vary with their ability to manage their disability and recognises that the majority of these workers access employment within casual and contingent labour markets. Labor also committed to additional subsidies for employers hiring disabled people (a subsidy of AU$3,000 per DSP recipient for providing 26 weeks' employment at 15 hours per week) and proposed compensation for productivity losses incurred by employing disabled people (Australian Labor Party, 2011).

We would not expect the benefit modifications and subsidies to employers announced during Labor's term in office to have made a major difference to the employment and income security of disabled welfare recipients, especially as labour markets have weakened further.[4] It was unclear at the time of writing whether the Coalition government will retain these incentives. More needs to be done, and more needs to be done of a different kind, to achieve higher and sustained employment levels of disabled people. The NWRN (2011, npn), for example, has called for 'further guaranteed investment to support people into jobs and commitments from large public and private sector employers to employ more people with disabilities'.

Newstart and job assistance: impact on disabled people

Obstacles to returning to work are accentuated by weak labour markets (see, for example, Peck, 2001). According to a 2009 Australian Bureau of Statistics survey, disabled respondents most frequently cited 'their own ill health and disability' (35%) and then 'lack of skills or education' (13%) as barriers to working (ABS, 2012, p 11). Labour force participation rates for disabled people in Australia are low. In 2009, only 54.3% of disabled people were in the labour force compared with 83% without a disability (ABS, 2009) and Australia ranked 21 out of 27 OECD countries for labour force participation of disabled people (OECD, 2009).

Welfare-to-work reforms are altering the Newstart cohort in fundamental ways. Almost 20% of Newstart clients are now assessed as having 'partial capacity to work' as a result of tightened access to the DSP (Australian Government, 2012, p 65). Moreover, the duration of income support dependence among the Newstart cohort reveals that for many, the period of benefit receipt is not brief. Often, clients receive different payments over time. Government data show that, in June 2012, some 62% of Newstart recipients were on (some form of) income support for a year or more; and 46% of the Newstart population were classified as 'very long-term' recipients (that is, they had received income support for two years or more) (Australian Government, 2012, p 63). These proportions have changed little since 2002. The average duration of income support for Newstart clients is around 180 weeks (Australian Government, 2012, p 63), but this figure rises to a disturbing five years for Newstart clients assessed with a partial capacity to work (Australian Government, 2012, p 81).

Lengthy periods of dependence on Newstart raise particular problems for recipients, especially given the low level of the Newstart benefit and the correspondingly high levels of poverty among recipients (Morris and Wilson, 2014). Elsewhere, we have discussed the potential for 'scarring' – the reduction of human capabilities brought about by lengthy periods of unemployment (Morris and Wilson, 2014). Newstart clients with a disability are particularly prone to scarring because of their lengthy periods of dependence on Newstart and their likely further loss of capability during that experience (see, for example, the joint submission of federal government departments to the federal Senate Inquiry into the adequacy of Newstart: Australian Government, 2012, p 69). The effects of long-term unemployment on physical and mental health are well known (Morris, 2002; Rosenthal et al, 2012), so it is not surprising that the data indicate that many long-term income support clients are likely to eventually move from Newstart to the DSP.

The data indicate that moving from Newstart to employment is not typically easy or rapid. Just 21% of new Newstart recipients are in full-time work three months later, with a total of 48% getting a job (of any kind) in the same period. Indeed, the majority (52%) remain unemployed or leave the labour market altogether (Australian Government, 2012, p 71). Ongoing questions about the performance of job assistance programmes, now privatised, in assisting long-term unemployed people have been raised elsewhere (see Davidson, 2011; Morris and Wilson, 2014). Poor performance in placing long-term unemployed clients is particularly critical to prospects for a larger disabled clientele on Newstart; job placement for Newstart clients with a partial capacity to work is extremely poor. The joint department submission to the Senate Inquiry on the adequacy of Newstart found that: 'Only three per cent of the job placements achieved for Newstart Allowance job seekers since the start of JSA [Job Services Australia] have been achieved for job seekers with a partial work capacity' (Australian Government, 2012, p 72).

An empirical study of doing the hard yakka

Given these developments in, and problems of, the Newstart programme, we now consider issues that they raise for people assessed with a partial capacity to work. A mixed-methods study involving Newstart recipients (not assessed for disability status) in inner-metropolitan Sydney was undertaken by two of the authors (Morris and Wilson) in the second half of 2012. The study was assisted by approximately 40 students in a senior undergraduate research course at the University of New South Wales and had university ethics approval. The study was conducted with clients of the Inner West Skills Centre (IWSC) – an employment services provider – at three sites in Sydney.

The two elements of the research were semi-structured interviews with Newstart clientele ($n = 20$) and self-completion questionnaires ($n = 54$). The study focused on the impact of living on Newstart.[5] Topics included in the research included:

- coping on the income from Newstart;
- dealings with Centrelink (the government's 'shopfront' welfare centres) and job assistance agencies;
- social networks and social isolation;
- job prospects;
- public perceptions of Newstart.

Interviewees were recruited through self-selection, with our study advertised via a poster and a sheet to record names of people interested in participating. Informed consent was obtained at the time of the interview.

Without access to clients' telephone numbers, and a poor response to mail contact, we abandoned a randomised sampling strategy in favour of availability sampling. This involved depositing a number of questionnaires for clients to complete at the three sites, with a display providing information about the study. A larger number of responses was obtained, but the non-random sampling strategy limits our ability to draw statistically based inferences from the data. Still, the survey data add to the small repository of available quantitative data about the experience of Newstart recipients and maintain descriptive value.

A life of hard yakka: living on the Newstart benefit

Four primary interrelated themes emerged from the data analysis with particular importance to the growing cohort of disabled welfare recipients who are now Newstart recipients, but assessed as having a partial capacity to work. These themes are:

- the inadequacy of the Newstart benefit and experiences of deprivation;
- poor housing and health;
- limited social networks, exclusion and isolation;
- difficulties in finding and keeping work.

These are discussed in turn. Taken together, they reveal how recipients dependent on the Newstart benefit engage in what we see as hard physical and emotional work. Managing on low incomes and searching out work in tough, precarious labour markets are constant stresses on self-respect and wellbeing.

Benefit inadequacy and the experience of deprivation

Almost all the interviewees commented on the severe financial difficulties encountered living on Newstart, confirming the now widely accepted inadequacy of the benefit (Saunders, 2011; Whiteford, 2011; Denniss and Baker, 2012; OECD, 2012). In our sample, 66% of respondents disagreed with the proposition that 'Newstart is enough to live on'. Just 20% agreed with this statement. Survey data suggested a trend towards greater disagreement with this statement among long-term unemployed people in the sample. Indeed, long-term unemployed interviewees talked at length about the severe hardships from increasingly diminishing resources. Housing costs are also likely to drive client perceptions of inadequacy, a subject discussed in more detail below.

Newstart recipients found it exceptionally hard to live on the Newstart benefit and were aggrieved that it was so much less than other benefits. Eric,[6] for example, told us: "It is hard because you tend to live from pay to pay and that is not really a good way to live because the amount provided is basically a minimum. When you compare it to other allowance like the [age] pension, they are paid double compared to us." The struggle to manage money over the fortnightly Newstart payment period can be a real skill. This was apparent in Leanne's experience:

'Well if you've got to pay your rent, put credit for your phone, there isn't a lot left.… You have to worry about, okay, what am I going to do and how am I going to do this, you know, because you have to get your basics – rent, food, phone credit 'cause you need your phone. So once you've done those three things there's not a ton left.… So there are times when you are left with not a lot of money or maybe no money for maybe a day or two until you get your next pay.'

Leanne's description was echoed in the responses of others. Sam, an older client, also spoke of the stress of running out of money: "I go without, you know, or you borrow off mates." He also spoke of only eating once a day and having to scavenge for tobacco: "Couple of places around where I live, we help each other out. So, they wanna smoke, they come and ask. You need a dollar, if they got it they will give it to ya. If not, you go walking around the streets picking up cigarette butts."

Recently, quantitative measures of benefit inadequacy have been established with the use of deprivation indicators. These measures first establish what the community considers essential items (to avoid poverty) so that the deprivation of these items is an effective measure of poverty or benefit inadequacy (see Saunders and Wong, 2011). These indicators also offer further insight into the specific types of deprivation that affect different sub-populations, including those dependent on social security payments.

Our survey included questions attempting to gauge deprivation. Figure 3.1 presents responses to the question: 'Do you have enough money for….?'. The figure shows the 'no' results in percentages (that is, the percentage of people who could not afford each item) in the dark grey bars of the bar chart. 'Not applicable' responses are represented by the light grey bars.[7] The data displayed indicate a high incidence of deprivation (above 50%) for several items considered essential, including:

- dental care;[8]
- household appliances;
- electricity and gas;
- rent/mortgage payments;
- good-quality food;
- clothes.

Despite Australia's subsidised pharmaceutical scheme, 42% of our survey sample said that they could not afford to buy the medication they needed.

Figure 3.1: Deprivation incidence of essential items among Newstart client sample, 2012 (%)

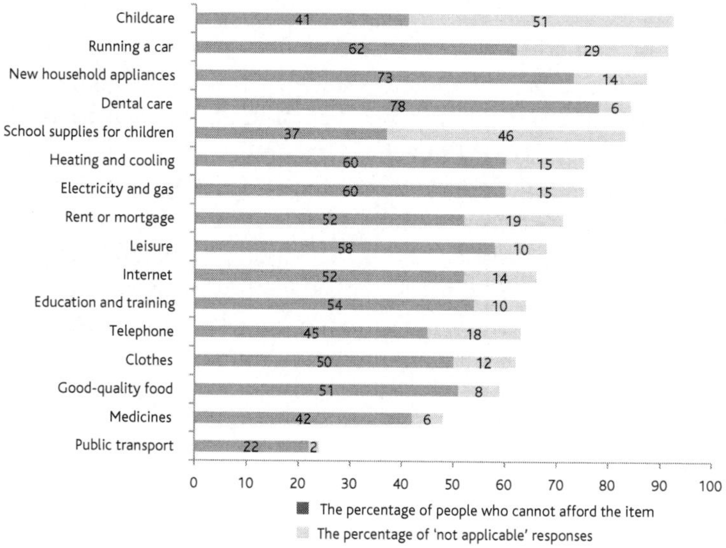

Housing and health

Housing costs are at the epicentre of Australia's poverty problem (Morris, 2010; ACOSS, 2012), so it is hardly surprising that our participants experienced severe housing stress. The interviewees who were renting in the private rental sector had to use a considerable proportion or all of their income for basic accommodation. Jason, for example, observed that Newstart "is clearly not enough. I'm in a very, very basic grotty place ... I've had to dig into my savings quite a lot and but no I could not live off the $550 or something a fortnight I receive".

Another interviewee (Jim) was living in a backpackers' hostel: "I am very lucky because I'm staying at a backpackers' hostel, which is the cheapest I can get.... You need an overseas passport to be able to be at a backpackers' hostel. Because I am able to speak Chinese ... they think I am a tourist." Sub-standard living conditions were by no means exceptional, as Greg told us:

'From the outside it looks like quite a healthy building but the inside, I have no electricity. I have no fridge. I have no hot water to shower. I have a unit the size of this room, 35 square metres, that after the roof collapsed because of water pouring in from above still has not been repaired after four and a half years ... but I can't afford to move out ... so I am stuck there.'

Poor living conditions were matched by poor physical and/or mental health among some respondents. Studies continue to confirm that unemployment contributes to poor physical and mental health (see Rosenthal et al, 2012). Minimal incomes meant that recipients often found it difficult to look after themselves adequately. Ben elaborated: "They [people on Newstart] can't afford the rent. It's not a healthy, productive system.... In fact I'd say it's ... destructive in many cases. That's my experience." Coping with the stress of managing money and poor-quality (often shared) housing is likely to present particular difficulties for the large number of clients with mental health problems who are now on Newstart. Sally, for example, captured how her situation accentuated her vulnerabilities:

'I've had, unfortunately, suffered from depression for several years and because of that, you keep losing.... So, there [are] many, many barriers people are confronted with. It's not a lack of, [I] don't consider myself stupid or incapable. I have all the capabilities there but how do I get there? It's very, very frustrating.... It's difficult. I can only do so much 'cause I'm running out of steam. Does that make sense?'

Social networks, exclusion and isolation

Previous studies confirm that people who are unemployed for lengthy periods tend to have poorer social networks or 'social capital', which, in turn, further hampers their return to work (Lin, 1999; Korpi, 2001). This 'vicious cycle' was evident in comments by interviewees who described having to avoid going out with friends (due to a lack of money) or not asking for a loan so as not to 'overstretch' friendships. Jeff, for example, commented: "You sort of, you can't really do anything that much because you can't go out ... with friends and family ... you don't have the financial resources." And Phil described how his social circle had contracted: "With any paid sort of work I can keep up with my mates and, as it stands, I can't participate in any nights out, or events they go to, or dinners or anything like that.... It impacts on your social life, dramatically. I mean, I'm talking about everything."

Still, family and friends remained important sources of financial support: 59% of respondents asked for help from family and 49% asked for help from friends. The impact of longer-term unemployment on coping and social networks appears particularly significant, suggesting greater reliance on external (and more risky) sources of support, such as charities, pay-day lenders and even begging. In our survey sample, those who were unemployed for longer than a year reported a higher incidence of asking for money from people on the street (25% versus 4% of those who were unemployed for less than a year), from pay-day lenders (25% versus 13%) and from charities (61% versus 38%).

Many of the interviewees told of how limited finances affected their social connections. Sally could not afford to go out: "You ... don't really have a life. I stay at home, or I come here [the job centre].... You can't go out.... Your main focus is meant to be looking for work but you can't look for work 24/7. It drives you nuts." Not surprisingly, unemployment generates social stigma. As Tim said: "When it comes to meeting friends ... once people find out that you are unemployed and for this long basically they just don't want to know you." The difficulty of establishing and keeping long-term intimate relationships was also noted by some interviewees. The survey data confirmed this. Four fifths of our sample were single (including those who were divorced or separated).

Finding and keeping work

As we have seen, Newstart recipients with a partial capacity to work have particularly poor job placement outcomes, leading to people remaining on the Newstart programme for long periods (an average of five years according to the Australian Government, 2012, p 81). A growing body of research and commentary indicates that the design of Newstart *contributes* to the problem of long and difficult transitions, something hinted at by the federal government's own departmental reporting (Australian Government, 2012). Meanwhile, free-market economist Judith Sloan (2012, npn) has observed: 'Patently inadequate support may have some unintended consequences that actually work against the aim of the policy to encourage people into suitable work', while Davidson (2011; see also Clark et al, 2001; Young, 2012) notes that long-term unemployed people become harder to employ because of the 'scarring' effects of unemployment and that most Newstart programmes offer limited assistance in reversing poor job prospects.

The potential for scarring, it seems, is more likely to impact on *already* disadvantaged jobseekers. Interviewees spoke of feeling demoralised after continual rejections. Ralph commented: "I can see why people get demoralised.... They feel like second-rate citizens, particularly those, those people who have been on it [Newstart] for an extended period.... They can lose hope and ... they can almost not feel a part of society." Jim spoke of how hard the job market was and that the job-search office had not helped him find his way back into employment:

'They didn't help me much.... They try, but they are overrun. There is not enough staff. You know they are overrun and coming here since for like the last four months ... and ... nothing has happened you know.... You ring up about a job and it is gone two minutes after it is in the paper.'

After a spate of disappointments, some interviewees had abandoned their job search altogether. The more skilled clients felt that the work activation programmes did not work for them. Sally commented: "There is no provision for mature-aged, educated people. It targets low-skilled labourers only, and everyone is forced into it. It's pretty much, if you can't make it on your own, tough."

Conclusions

Disabled people face greater barriers to finding and staying in work than most unemployed people (Morris, 2006; Sayce, 2011). When they *do* find work, the evidence indicates that they are also more likely to be concentrated in less-skilled work and casual jobs, with minimal autonomy (Barnes and Mercer, 2005). It is encouraging that, as a result of the disability movement's advocacy, policy makers in Australia are recognising the employment needs of this group. Recent reforms to benefits and the redesign of employment assistance programmes appear to be acknowledging the patterns of work capacity that disabled Australians are able to manage even if policies continue to make unrealistic assumptions about their employment opportunities. Indeed, a more critical reading of recent reform trends cannot avoid the conclusion that the disability movement's progressive claims for decent work have been subverted by a neoliberal policy framework mainly interested in 'jobs' and a 'partial ability to work' as mechanisms to reduce benefit levels and availability. An indication of this is that in 2012 over 80% of the non-profit disability labour market services were re-contracted out to for-profit provider employment agencies, with questionable commitment to disabled people's right to decent and equitable work (DEN, 2012).

The concluding point is this: a critical sociology of welfare reform in this area must draw a distinction between policies that encourage employment and income security *as a right* and policies that do little more than push disabled people into deregulated labour markets as a way of *unburdening* state budgets. Policy *rhetoric* emphasises the right to work and participation, but policy *detail* reveals increasing bureaucratic imperatives and mechanisms designed to pressure disabled people into Newstart where financial support is minimal and employment support is often patchy and ineffective.

This study has focused on disadvantaged jobseekers on the Newstart programme in inner-metropolitan Sydney. As stated, we did not collect specific data from this cohort about the incidence or level of disability. This research highlights the intense pressures for survival and self-justification felt by people on Newstart. These pressures include severe financial difficulties; unstable, inadequate and unaffordable housing; higher risks of social isolation, exclusion and 'scarring' as the period of unemployment drags on; and, for many, serious difficulties in re-entering the workforce.

Taking these experiences as a guide, we are able to identify evidence of the specific risks attached to the Newstart programme and their potential to accentuate difficulties for disabled people already coping with physical and/or mental health problems. We would expect these difficulties to be compounded by the longer than average periods on Newstart recorded by disabled claimants. While economists talk of the *scarring* impact of long-term unemployment, disability researchers talk of the *disabling* impacts of ill-equipped government programmes. Newstart risks generating a state of despair and 'inbetweenness' for its clients assessed with disabilities, offering neither adequate income support nor the prospect of stable, decent and suitable work.

Notes

[1] The DSP is a government benefit paid to people who have a physical, intellectual or psychiatric condition that prevents them from working for more than 15 hours per week. In order to qualify, applicants have to have a medical assessment and a 'job capacity assessment'.

[2] 'Hard yakka' is Australian rural slang for hard work. In Australia, this term is used to describe the hard physical labour of blue collar employment. We co-opt this term to contest the notion that life on welfare is easy and encourages laziness. Our empirical

findings suggest otherwise – welfare recipients undertake a form of 'hard work' in managing the daily grind of poverty and often marginalised social status.

[3] Labor's Parliamentary Secretary for Disability and Children's Services, Bill Shorten, for example, was critical in the government in pushing for major disability insurance reforms.

[4] In October 2013, the unemployment rate was 5.7%. In April 2007, it was 4.5%.

[5] A small number of responses ($n = 7$) were from respondents aged under 22, the current age of eligibility for Newstart. We have assumed that these respondents were in receipt of Youth Allowance, effectively an equivalent to Newstart for younger Australians with different eligibility and payment rates. Their responses have been preserved in the sample.

[6] All names of participants used are pseudonyms.

[7] Although the 'not applicable' response includes instances where the respondent did not have that expense due to life circumstances (for example, the respondent did not have children), this type of response often carried further clues about deprivation in situations where the respondent was excluded from a spending category altogether. For example, the costs of running a car are avoided by not owning one.

[8] In 2012, the Gillard Labor government put in place low-cost or free basic dental care for low-income Australians (people in receipt of welfare payments and children in low-income families).

Acknowledgements

This chapter is dedicated to Patricia Frost from the Inner West Skills Centre who passed away in April 2014. Patricia was a tireless fighter for people on Newstart. Patricia and Lisa Fowkes provided invaluable advice and assistance. We would also like to thank workers within the disability civil society employment providers who provided information about the Labor government's privatisation strategies within the sector. Particular thanks go to the students of the 2012 SLSP 3002 Newstart project class at the University of New South Wales who ably contributed at all stages to the survey and interview research reported in this chapter.

References

ABS (Australian Bureau of Statistics) (2009) *Survey of disability, ageing and carers*, Canberra, ACT: ABS.

ABS (2012) *Australian Social Trends, 2012*, cat. no. 4102.0, March – disability and work, Canberra, ACT: ABS.

ACOSS (Australian Council of Social Services) (2011) *Beyond stereotypes: Myths and facts about people of working age who receive social security*, ACOSS paper 175, Strawberry Hills, NSW: ACOSS, http://acoss.org.au/images/uploads/beyond_stereotypes.pdf

ACOSS (2012) *OECD joins growing call for increase in Newstart allowance*, www.acoss.org.au/media/release/oecd_joins_growing_call_for_increase_in_newstart_allowance

AIHW (Australian Institute of Health and Welfare) (2008) *Disability in Australia: Trends in prevalence, education, employment and community living*, AIHW bulletin no. 61, June, Canberra, ACT: Australian Government, www.aihw.gov.au/publications/index.cfm/title/10751

Argyrous, G. and Neale, M. (2003) 'The "disabled" labour market: the disability support program and unemployment', *Journal of Australian Political Economy*, 51, pp 5-25.

Australian Government (2003) *Budget paper no. 2*, Canberra, ACT: Commonwealth of Australia.

Australian Government (2012) *Submission to the Senate Inquiry on the adequacy of the allowance payment system for job seekers and others*, joint agency submission, no. 38, Canberra, ACT, https://senate.aph.gov.au/submissions/comittees/viewdocument.aspx?id=6ecdecea-2f8d-42a8-b422-a7b3499ffd7b

Australian Government (2014a) *Guide to social security law* (version 1.203), http://guidesacts.fahcsia.gov.au/guides_acts/ssg/ssguide-1/ssguide-1.1/ssguide-1.1.a/ssguide-1.1.a.30.html

Australian Government (2014b) *Disability support pension payments*, Canberra, ACT: Department of Human Services, www.humanservices.gov.au/customer/services/centrelink/disability-support-pension

Australian Government (2014c) *Newstart Allowance*, Canberra, ACT: Department of Human Services, http://www.humanservices.gov.au/customer/services/centrelink/newstart-allowance).

Australian Government (2014d) *Waiting Periods,* Canberra: Department of Human Services (Canberra, www.humanservices.gov.au/customer/enablers/waiting-periods

Australian Healthcare Associates (2000) *Interim report on the case based funding trial*, Canberra, ACT: Commonwealth of Australia.

Australian Labor Party (2011) *Supporting Australians with disability into work*, 10 May 10, www.alp.org.au/6020/federal-government/news/supporting-australians-with-disability-into-work/

Barnes, C. and Mercer, G. (2005) 'Disability, work and welfare: challenging the social exclusion of disabled people', *Work, Employment & Society*, 19, pp 527-45.

Bessant, J. (2000) 'Regulating the unemployed: Australia's work-for-the-dole scheme', *Journal of Australian Studies*, 24, pp 75-84.

Buckmaster, L. (2013) *National Disability Insurance Scheme*, Canberra, ACT: Australian Government, www.aph.gov.au/About_Parliament/Parliamentary_Departments/Parliamentary_Library/pubs/rp/BudgetReview201213/NDIS

Cai, L. and Gregory, B. (2004) 'Labour market conditions, applications and grants of disability support pension (DSP) in Australia', *Australian Journal of Labour Economics*, 7(3), pp 375-94.

Cass, B., Gibson, F. and Tito, F. (1988) *Towards enabling policies: Income support for people with disabilities*, Canberra, ACT: Commonwealth of Australia.

Clark, A.E., Georgellis, Y. and Sanfey, P. (2001) 'Scarring: the psychological impact of past unemployment', *Economica*, 68(270), pp 221-41.

Clear, M. and Gleeson, B. (2001) 'Disability and materialist embodiment', *Journal of Australian Political Economy*, 49(1), pp 34-55.

Coad, M., Finlay, J., Raper, M. and Thomas, G. (2006) *Welfare to work or unworkable welfare?*, Sydney, NSW: National Welfare Rights Network, www.vcoss.org.au/documents/VCOSS_docs/Welfare/NACLC_welfarework.pdf

Commonwealth of Australia (2014) *A new system for better employment and social outcomes: Interim report of the Reference Group on Welfare Reform to the minister for social services*, Canberra, ACT: Department of Social Services.

Commonwealth Ombudsman (2007) *Application of penalties under Welfare to Work (report no 16)*, Canberra, ACT: Commonwealth of Australia.

Davidson, P. (2011) 'Did "work first" work? The role of employment assistance programs in reducing long-term unemployment in Australia (1990–2008)', *Australian Bulletin of Labour*, 37(1), pp 51-96.

DEN (Disability Employment Network) (2012) *Operations bulletin*, 5 December, Melbourne: DEN.

Denniss, R. and Baker, D. (2012) 'Are unemployment benefits adequate in Australia?', *Policy Brief no. 39*, Canberra, ACT: The Australia Institute, https://www.tai.org.au/index.php?q=node%2F19&pubid=991&act=display

Grover, C. and Soldatic, K. (2013) 'Neoliberalism and disability social (in)security in Australia and Britain', *Scandinavian Journal of Disability Studies*, 15(30), pp 216-32.

House of Representatives (2005) *Official Hansard*, 9 November, Canberra, ACT: Commonwealth of Australia.

Ireland, J. (2014) 'Disabled not rorting the disability pension, disability discrimination Commissioner Graeme Innes hits back', *Sydney Morning Herald*, 12 March.

Kellie, D. (1998) 'Unemployed? Board the enterprise for a brave new world and a "real" job: a critique of the new strategy for reducing unemployment', *Australian Journal of Social Issues*, 33, pp 285-302.

Kewley, T. (1980) *Australian social security today: Major developments from 1900 to 1978*, Sydney: University of Sydney Press.

Korpi, T. (2001) 'Good friends in bad times? Social networks and job search among the unemployed in Sweden', *Acta Sociogica*, 44, pp 157-70.

Lin, N. (1999) 'Social networks and status attainment', *Annual Review of Sociology*, 25, pp 467-87.

Lunn, S. (2011) 'Gillard tightens disability pension', *The Australian*, 30 July.

Maley, J. (2014) 'The disabled will need to fight for themselves', *The Canberra Times*, 17 May.

Melbourne Institute (2013) *Poverty lines Australia*, Melbourne: University of Melbourne, http://melbourneinstitute.com/downloads/publications/Poverty%20Lines/Poverty-lines-Australia-Sept-2013.pdf

Morris, A. (2002) 'The social costs of unemployment', *The Economic and Labour Relations Review*, 13(2), pp 207-25.

Morris, A. (2006) 'Pain and mythology: disability support pension recipients and work', *Australian Review of Public Affairs*, 7(1), pp 49-59.

Morris, A. (2010) 'Policies relating to homelessness and affordable housing in Australia', in A. Nevile (ed) *Human rights and social policy: A comparative analysis of values and citizenship in OECD countries*, Cheltenham: Edward Elgar, pp 154-73.

Morris, A. and Wilson, S. (2014) 'Struggling on the Newstart unemployment benefit in Australia: the experience of a neoliberal form of employment assistance', *Economic Labour Relations Review*, 25(2), pp 202-21.

Newman, J. (1999) 'The future of welfare in the 21st century', paper presented at the National Press Club, Canberra, 29 September, www.facs.gov.au/newman.nsf/v1/sdiscusswelfare.htm

NWRN (National Welfare Rights Network) (2011) 'Disability support pension changes untested, unfair and unacceptable', 14 April, https://www.welfarerights.org.au/news/2011/4/14/disability-support-pension-changes-untested-unfair-and-unacceptable

OECD (Organisation for Economic Co-operation and Development) (2009) *Sickness, disability and work: Keeping on track in the economic downturn*, London: OECD Directorate for Employment, Labour and Social Affairs.

OECD (2012) *Activating jobseekers: How Australia does it*, Paris: OECD.

Peck, J. (2001) *Workfare states*, New York, NY: Guilford Press.

Peck, J. and Theodore, N. (2001) 'Exporting workfare/importing welfare-to-work: exploring the politics of Third Way policy transfer', *Political Geography*, 20, pp 427-60.

PWDA (People with Disability Australia) (2011) *PWD e-bulletin*, no. 71, Strawberry Hills, NSW: PWDA.

Rosenthal, L., Carroll-Scott, A., Earnshaw, V., Santilli, A. and Ickovics, J. (2012) 'The importance of full-time work for urban adults' mental and physical health', *Social Science and Medicine*, 75, pp 1692-6.

Saunders, P. (2011) *Down and out: Poverty and exclusion in Australia*, Bristol: Policy Press.

Saunders, P. and Wong, M. (2011) 'Using deprivation indicators to assess the adequacy of Australian social security payments', *Journal of Poverty and Social Justice*, 19(2), pp 91-101.

Sayce, L. (2011) *Getting in, staying in and getting on: Disability employment support fit for the future*, London: The Stationery Office.

Sloan, J. (2012) 'Newstart needs a boost', *The Drum*, 31 October, www.abc.net.au/unleashed/3609716.html

Soldatic, K. (2010) 'Disability and the Australian neoliberal workfare state', PhD dissertation, University of Western Australia, Perth, Australia.

Soldatic, K. (2013) 'Appointment Time: Disability and Neoliberal Workfare Temporalities', *Critical Sociology*, vol 39, no 3, pp 405-19, http://dx.doi.org/10.1177/0896920511430168

Soldatic, K. and Chapman, A. (2010) 'Surviving the assault? The Australian disability movement and the neoliberal workfare state', *Social Movement Studies*, 9(2), pp 139-54.

Soldatic, K. and Pini, B. (2012) 'Continuity or change: disability policy and the Rudd government', *Social Policy & Society*, 11(2), pp 183-96.

Whiteford, P. (2010) 'Why unemployment benefits need to be increased', *Inside Story*, 7 December, http://inside.org.au/why-unemployment-benefits-need-to-be-increased/

Whiteford, P. (2011) 'Will the government slow the growth of disability support pension numbers?', *Inside Story*, 12 May, http://inside.org.au/growth-of-disability-support-pension-numbers/

Wilson, S. (2013) 'The limits of low tax social democracy? Welfare, tax, and fiscal dilemmas for Labor in government', *Australian Journal of Political Science*, 48(3), pp 286-306.

Yeend, P. (2011) 'Budget 2011–12: disability support pension reforms', *Budget Review 2011–12*, Canberra, ACT: Parliament of Australia, www.aph.gov.au/About_Parliament/Parliamentary_Departments/Parliamentary_Library/pubs/rp/BudgetReview201112/Disability

Young, C. (2012) 'Losing a job: the nonpecuniary cost of unemployment in the United States', *Social Forces*, 91(2), pp 609-34.

Part Two
Social policy, work and
disabled people

Why are the policies and organisations seeking to help disabled people access work failing?

Bruce Stafford

Introduction

Social security governance and policies are not immune to wider political and economic ideas. Specifically, in Britain, employment policies aimed at disabled people have been subject to marketisation and performance management regimes that reflect neoliberalism and the New Public Management turn in public administration (Hughes, 2003; Carmel and Papadopoulos, 2009; Flynn, 2012), as well as being a means to achieve 'efficiency savings' in Whitehall (see, for instance, Gershon, 2004, p 38). In recent years, successive governments, through the responsible department, the Department for Work and Pensions (DWP), have implemented programmes that involve private and third sector organisations competitively tendering to deliver programmes targeted at working-age people, including disabled people (see, for example, DWP, 2006, 2007b, 2008, 2010, 2011, 2012, 2013a, 2013c; Freud, 2007; Finn, 2009a; Damm, 2012). This shift in service provision has also happened in other countries, and is controversial (Davies, 2008; Finn, 2009b; Grover, 2009; Work and Pensions Committee, 2013).

These market-based programmes seek to assist disabled people in receipt of incapacity-related benefits[1] to move into, or towards, 'sustained' paid work via a variety of (mainstream) employment programmes. Typically, however, these initiatives have only relatively small impacts on employment. This is not to deny that employment programmes have successfully placed some disabled people in employment (see Bambra et al, 2005), rather to argue that the people most in need of support are the least well served by these programmes. This occurs because the contracts have an incentive structure that rewards contractors for working with, and placing in employment, participants who are more job ready. Providers are then more likely to meet performance targets and, importantly for their finances, generate revenue income. Two examples of these programmes – the New Deal for Disabled People (NDDP) and Pathways to Work (PtW) – are presented in this chapter to illustrate the argument that the marketisation of such provision can disadvantage many disabled people in the labour market. The DWP commissioned evaluations of both programmes (see Stafford et al, 2007; Dorsett, 2008; Knight et al, 2013), and this chapter draws on the author's involvement in the evaluation of the NDDP and published work on PtW. These evaluations used quantitative and qualitative methodologies to examine how the programmes worked and were implemented, and their impact on participants, notably their exits from benefits and moves into employment. The evaluations were commissioned as part of New Labour's commitment to evidenced-based policy making and sought to influence the development not only of policy, but also of practice.

The chapter begins by providing an overview of the two programmes and their funding regimes. It then considers the outcomes and impacts of the two programmes, as a prelude to discussing why those furthest from the labour market might be poorly served by contracted-out provision. The characteristics of participants who were less likely to find employment under both programmes are then outlined before some concluding comments are presented.

The policies and delivery organisations

Before outlining the two programmes, it is important to emphasise the heterogeneous nature of the target population. Not only do recipients of incapacity-related benefits vary by demographic characteristics such as gender, age and health, some are also closer to the labour market than others (see, for example, Dorsett, 2008; DWP, 2013b). Those closer to the labour market share characteristics associated with being job ready, such as having higher educational attainment, possessing a driving license and being a homeowner. However, some disabled people face multiple barriers to finding employment. In addition to their disability, for instance, they may lack basic skills, have a fluctuating work history and/or are members of the black and minority ethnic community and so on (Hayllar and Wood, 2011; Coleman et al, 2013). In brief, even if they were not disabled by society, some recipients would encounter difficulties in the labour market due, for example, to low skill levels and/or age.

The introduction of NDDP was announced in 1997 and more details were given in two 1998 consultation papers on welfare reform (DSS,

1998a, 1998b). It was piloted in 1998 and a revised programme was rolled out nationally in 2001. NDDP was initially delivered by 64 job brokers, who were public, private or third sector organisations, for example, local authorities, disability charities, recruitment agencies and training providers (McDonald et al, 2004). Some of these organisations had a wealth of experience of working with disabled people, but for others this was a new client group. There was some variation in the services provided by job brokers, but they often included assessment of basic skills, vocational advice, job-search support, training and work placements. Some contractors also provided participants with a financial incentive if they entered employment.

PtW was proposed in a 2002 Green Paper (DWP, 2002), piloted in several locations in Britain, judged to be 'very successful' (DWP, 2007a) and then rolled out to other areas. Initially, the British public employment service, Jobcentre Plus, which is part of the DWP, delivered the programme. However, provision was contracted out in two waves, in December 2007 (phase 1) and April 2008 (phase 2), to areas not previously covered by the programme (NAO, 2010; Knight et al, 2013). The completion of phase 2 meant that the whole of Britain was covered by PtW. Eleven organisations, the overwhelming majority of which were private sector organisations, with the remainder from the third sector, were awarded 34 area-based contracts (NAO, 2010; Knight et al, 2013). Under this so-called 'provider-led' model, the contractor led provision covered 60% of Britain (NAO, 2010). Elsewhere, Jobcentre Plus delivered the programme, but used external contractors and the National Health Service to support provision.

For a time, NDDP and PtW ran alongside one another. NDDP continued in those areas where Jobcentre Plus delivered PtW. However, NDDP provision was replaced by PtW in provider-led areas, although the contractors were required to provide an equivalent service to NDDP. PtW ended in Jobcentre Plus and contracted-out areas in March/April 2011. As a non-specialist disability programme, it was replaced by the coalition government's Work Programme (Sayce, 2011).

PtW was designed to provide an earlier and more intensive intervention than that offered by NDDP (NAO, 2010). PtW also offered a financial incentive for those who had returned to work (£40 per week for the first 12 months of employment) and a Condition Management Programme designed to help benefit recipients to manage their condition so that they might gain employment.

NDDP was a *voluntary* programme. It had a take-up rate of around 3% of the eligible population (Stafford, 2012). However, for most *new* incapacity-related benefit claimants, participation in PtW was *mandatory*, and they had to attend, and engage with, six work-focused interviews with an adviser while they remained on benefit. Jobcentre Plus staff conducted the first interview in all areas, but in provider-led areas the contractors undertook any remaining interviews. Those failing to attend an interview without 'good cause' risked a 20% benefit sanction being imposed, with a further 20% reduction for each subsequent failure to attend (Mitchell and Woodfield, 2008; see also Dorsett, 2008). Existing claimants and those new claimants not obliged to take part could volunteer to join PtW.

While there were programmatic differences between NDDP and PtW, they shared a number of commonalities. Both were designed to help reduce the number of people claiming incapacity-related benefits by one million over a 10-year period (DWP, 2006), and to provide more tailored, individualised work-focused support to participants in order to help them enter paid work. The programmes also included post-employment support to participants. Importantly, the provision of both programmes was subject to competitive tendering by the DWP. External providers tendered to deliver the relevant programme for a specific geographical area or areas. Some areas were covered by more than one contractor – so users had some degree of choice. Often contractors outsourced aspects of their service to local public, private and/or third sector bodies, creating a 'supply chain'. These arrangements could range from formal sub-contracts through service-level agreements to more informal arrangements (see Stafford et al, 2004; Hudson et al, 2010). The DWP did not always know with whom its prime contractors had sub-contracted or worked with informally (McDonald et al, 2004; Hudson et al, 2010; NAO, 2010).

The DWP, which wished to encourage innovation in service delivery under both programmes, did not specify the services that contractors were required to provide, although there were some minimum requirements, for example the formulation of participants' Action Plans under NDDP and the provision of the Condition Management Programme under PtW. However, there is little evidence that the contractors in either programme delivered new interventions to serve disabled people (Corden et al, 2003; Hudson et al, 2010). Providers in both programmes delivered 'tried-and-tested' interventions.

These were not the only two policies for disabled people. For example, a new incapacity benefit (Employment and Support Allowance) was introduced in 2008, changes to anti-discrimination legislation were made and there were complementary Jobcentre Plus specialist disability programmes[2] such as Access to Work and the (then) Work Preparation programme, the Job Introduction Scheme and the

WORKSTEP employment programme (NAO, 2005; Sayce, 2011).[3] Nonetheless, the main employment programmes for disabled people between 2001 and 2010 were NDDP and subsequently PtW.

Performance and funding regimes

The DWP monitored providers' performance against contracted job outcome targets and by conducting regular reviews of performance. The targets were designed to ensure that policy goals were met and that the providers did not exceed the programmes' budgets.

The programmes shared a funding model – 'outcome-related funding' or 'payment by results'. While the details of their funding regimes varied and changed over time, providers in both programmes received the majority of their income through placing participants in (sustained) employment. In both cases, providers received a fee (a small lump sum under NDDP and a monthly payment for PtW), a payment for a job entry and a further payment if the employment was sustained (that is, the employment lasted for 26 weeks[4]) (Stafford et al, 2007; Hudson et al, 2010). So, for instance, 70% of the PtW contract value was paid on performance in terms of job entries (50%) and job sustainability (20%) (McDonald et al, 2007). A difference between the programmes was that the payment per job outcome made to job brokers under NDDP varied between providers (depending on what they had bid) (Stafford, 2012), but was the same for all PtW providers (Hudson et al, 2010).

In practice, contractors in both programmes could underperform relative to the target number of jobs (Corden et al, 2003; Lewis et al, 2005; CPA, 2010; NAO, 2010; Stafford, 2012). Overbidding by contractors and for PtW the 2008 financial crisis and related recession (Hudson et al, 2010) meant their revenue income was less than expected. Not only did this mean that contractors could face cash-flow problems or have insufficient working capital if they did not meet their targets, but also that they had a strong financial incentive to find employment for participants closer to the labour market because they were easier to help and timelier in generating revenue income.

The DWP formally and informally amended contracts to help contractors' cash-flow (Corden et al, 2003; Lewis et al, 2005; Hudson et al, 2010; NAO, 2010). For example, the DWP could 're-profile' underperforming job brokers' monthly targets by reducing their target number of registrations and job entries (in some cases by as much as 50%) (Davis et al, 2006). Nonetheless, some contractors and partner organisations made financial losses (Corden et al, 2003; Lewis et al, 2005; McDonald et al, 2007; CPA, 2010; Hudson et al, 2010). So, for instance, a survey by the National Audit Office (NAO, 2010) showed that one third of the prime contractors and two thirds of subcontractors expected to make a financial loss from their involvement in PtW. Consequently, some had to subsidise the programmes from other schemes, some reduced resources allocated to the programmes and some terminated their contracts or did not seek to renew them (Corden et al, 2003; Stafford et al, 2004; Greenberg and Davis, 2007; Stafford et al, 2007; Grover, 2009; Hudson et al, 2010; NAO, 2010). Any reduction in resources led to a fall in the service 'offer' to participants, for example, limiting or withdrawing access to training courses.

Outcomes achieved and impacts

The DWP commissioned evaluations of the impacts of the two programmes on benefit receipt and employment (see Orr et al, 2007; Knight et al, 2013), and the National Audit Office also investigated the impact of the PtW programme (NAO, 2010). The impact studies report 'average' outcomes for participants, and acknowledge that in addition to the programmes there are other factors (such as the attitudes of employers) that influence whether a disabled person successfully gains paid work. In general, the employers participating in the programmes were the 'usual suspects', that is, employers with a good track record of employing and retaining disabled people.

The rate at which recipients exited incapacity benefits was higher for NDDP participants compared with non-participants. So, for instance, the exit rate for participants was 13 to 16 percentage points higher than for non-participants after 24 months (Orr et al, 2007). For PtW the situation was more complex. The Jobcentre Plus-led pilot PtW did not significantly increase the flow of participants off incapacity benefits (Dorsett, 2008). However, the later Knight et al (2013) analysis, which measured the impact of the phase 1 contractors on all benefits, shows that the providers significantly reduced the proportion of recipients by 1.8 percentage points. The National Audit Office study (NAO, 2010) found that some new claimants flowed off benefit earlier than had there been no PtW programme. However, this was mainly attributed to the associated moving of the timing of the medical assessment for incapacity benefit from six months to three months and not to the programme. Early exits from benefit were also due to recipients wishing to avoid the 'prospect' of the mandatory work-focused interviews (NAO, 2010).

NDDP did help some disabled people move into employment. Between July 2001 and November 2006, there were 260,330 programme registrations, of which 110,950 (or 43%) resulted in jobs by

November 2006 (Stafford et al, 2007). Indeed, the proportion finding employment increased over time (Orr et al, 2007). For example, 32% of those registering between July 2001 and June 2002 found work within 12 months, and this increased to 44% for those registering between December 2004 and November 2005. The NDDP also had some success at securing sustainable employment for participants. For instance, of those participants gaining employment during the period up to August 2006, most (57%) had been in continuous employment of least 13 weeks. Interestingly, the employment rate was higher for NDDP participants residing in PtW areas (39%) compared with those living in areas not yet covered by PtW (29%) (Legge et al, 2006). The reason for this was unclear, but it might be because participants in PtW areas were eligible for a short-term financial incentive for entering work.

By the end of March 2009, approximately 15% of PtW participants had found paid work (NAO, 2010). Early evaluation findings suggested that over a period of time (18 months), the Jobcentre Plus-led pilot PtW were successful in gradually increasing the employment rate of people who initially enquired about the service (Dorsett, 2008), but this increase mainly occurred among those who were *not* in receipt of benefits (at around 18 months) (Dorsett, 2008). The National Audit Office subsequently found that the programme had a relatively low, or no, impact on employment rates (NAO, 2010).

Critically, for the argument presented here, the private and third sector contractors performed no better than Jobcentre Plus in achieving participants' moves into employment (Knight et al, 2013). Indeed, Jobcentre Plus performed better than the providers in getting participants who were *mandated* to take part in the programme into jobs over the period December 2007 to July 2009 (11% compared with 9%) (NAO, 2010). It also follows that the contractors had a higher proportion of voluntary participants in employment (40% compared with 9%). This inequity in job outcomes for participant types reflects the incentive structures of the programme. Because voluntary participants were more motivated to find paid work they were easier to place in employment than the mandated ones (Hudson et al, 2010; NAO, 2010).

For those participants obtaining employment, the jobs could be low paid and not always sustainable (see NAO, 2010; Hayllar and Wood, 2011). In the NDDP the jobs tended to pay above the National Minimum Wage (Legge et al, 2006), and most participants (around a quarter) entered routine, unskilled occupations (Kazimirski et al, 2005; Legge et al, 2006); for example, driving, domestic work, retail and security work (Corden et al, 2003). In the provider-led PtW, a half of the jobs were in low-skilled (semi-routine or routine) occupations (Hayllar and Wood, 2011). The relatively low-paid and low-skilled work that the participants from both programmes tended to obtain could be because the contractors focused on job outcome targets. They found it easier to place people in this type of employment than in higher-quality jobs (NAO, 2005).

Why is market provision problematic?

As the above discussion shows, there were some positive outcomes for some disabled people. However, not all participants were equally well served. The programmes' neoliberal design – prioritising the contracting-out of provision and using financial incentives to influence individual and organisational behaviour – worked against certain disabled people (those furthest away from the job market). Those furthest away from being job ready were disadvantaged, because of adverse selection and moral hazard, which are inherent in these sorts of schemes.

Adverse selection

There is evidence of information asymmetry in the procurement process (that is, of adverse selection). Some of the external providers for both NDDP (Corden et al, 2003) and PtW (NAO, 2010) underestimated the difficulties and complexity of the client group they were seeking to place in employment. As a consequence, they lacked the resources (notably staff), employment measures and time to address the full range of needs of the population they were meant to serve. It also meant that they 'overbid' when submitting their tenders. In other words, some organisations intentionally or unintentionally (due to, say, a lack of understanding of the needs of the client group) proposed unrealistic performance targets. Consequently, they secured contracts at the expense of those submitting less ambitious, but more feasible bids (see Davis et al, 2006; CPA, 2010). Similarly, the DWP appears, in accepting the targets in contractors' tenders, to have lacked information on the providers' ability to deliver. Indeed, the National Audit Office is critical of the DWP's failure to adequately review the PtW bids (NAO, 2010).

Moral hazard

When provision is contracted out, there is a risk of 'moral hazard', namely that the contractor undertakes behaviour that was not intended by the principal (in this case the DWP). There are risks of:

- 'cream-skimming' or 'cherry picking' when providers have the opportunity to select who participates in their provision;
- 'creaming' when contractors provide more intensive support to those participants who are more job ready; and/or
- 'parking' when providers offer limited (the minimum), or no, support to those deemed further from the labour market.

All three behaviours arise so that providers can meet set job outcome targets and generate sufficient cash-flow. They also help frontline staff manage their caseloads (Lewis et al, 2005).

NDDP was a voluntary programme and there is some evidence of cream-skimming by job brokers. Participants requiring a lot of support might not be registered by job brokers for the programme, or could be referred back to Jobcentre Plus for more specialist help (Corden et al, 2003; Lewis et al, 2005; Davis et al, 2006). However, there is also evidence that not all job brokers engaged in 'cream skimming' as some reported operating 'open' registration policies and practices and sought to make their services widely available (Corden et al, 2003; Lewis et al, 2005).

Creaming and parking occurred in both programmes. There is qualitative evidence that job brokers tended to prioritise participants who were more job ready (Corden et al, 2003; Lewis et al, 2005). The criteria used to assess job readiness varied between job brokers, but could include the amount of time and resources needed to secure a job entry and the extent of the participants' engagement with the service (Corden et al, 2003; Davis et al, 2006). Other factors could also affect prioritisation of participants, such as the relative buoyancy of the local labour market (Corden et al, 2003). Some job brokers had formal systems for prioritising or banding participants according to their job readiness.

Judgements about job readiness and concerns about funding could also affect the type of NDDP services provided to people. Harder-to-reach participants could have less frequent, and fewer, contacts with job brokers and/or were referred to other services (Corden et al, 2003; Lewis et al, 2005). Conversely, participants entering or sustaining work for 13 weeks could receive a financial incentive paid by some job brokers (Lewis et al, 2005). The payments were typically grants to cover the cost of, for example, clothing and equipment, and were for relatively modest sums (around £100).

The view that NDDP was for people who were close to the labour market was shared by Jobcentre Plus advisers (Dickens et al, 2004). Indeed, the view that only job-ready recipients were suitable for the NDDP led some Jobcentre Plus advisers to refer only these claimants to job brokers (Corden et al, 2003).

Qualitative and quantitative research also provides evidence of creaming and parking in PtW. Four case studies by Hudson et al (2010) show that providers used 'traffic light systems' and numerical categories to classify the job readiness of participants. The classification systems influenced the amount of time and the type of support given to participants. Those judged most job ready were 'creamed', while those seen as furthest from the labour market were 'parked', receiving the minimum standard of service (Hudson et al, 2010; see also Tennant et al, 2010). Job readiness also influenced referrals to partner organisations. Prime providers creamed their caseload to the extent that they 'served those customers who were considered more likely to enter work, while partner agencies attended to the not directly work-related needs of customers who were not immediately ready for employment' (Hudson et al, 2010, p 3). That is, participants facing greater barriers to work were passed down the supply chain (Hudson et al, 2010). This in turn could adversely affect the partner organisations' cash-flow.

Tennant et al (2010), in a qualitative study of the phase 2 provider-led PtW, report that participants were aware of creaming and parking practices by contractors. Those further away from the labour market:

> ... perceived that advisers spent less time with them during their [work-focused interviews] once it was apparent that they were not ready to enter the labour market in the near future... Other customers also perceived that advisers tailored the level of support for preparing them for paid employment (e.g. access to or funding for courses) according to their perceptions of how close the customer was to moving into work. (Tennant et al, 2010, p 71)

Hayllar and Wood (2011) report on a telephone and internet survey of new and repeat incapacity benefits recipients in phase 1 provider-led PtW areas, and conclude that it is difficult to assess whether parking and creaming of participants occurred. However, they find that 77% of respondents received some form of work-related activity (such as help with applying for a job or with writing a curriculum vitae) to support them into employment (Hayllar and Wood, 2011). This means that nearly a quarter of participants received no such assistance from their provider. While these participants may not have wished to enter employment for a number of reasons (such as their assessment of their health condition), it does mean that, contrary to the policy intent, they were effectively 'parked' by the contractors. Although the PtW contractors achieved a relatively high level of attendance by participants at multiple work-focused interviews, this could mask '"parking" by providers of groups of customers who are harder to help. This could occur where customers continue to be asked to attend meetings, but these are cursory and do not lead to significant assistance' (Hayllar and Wood, 2011, p 32). As Hayllar and Wood (2011, p 62) poignantly observe: 'Although being "parked" might have been the most appropriate approach for these customers in their own view, it might be argued that these were precisely the groups who should be challenged and actively offered assistance.' Hudson et al (2010, p 4) succinctly conclude that provider-led 'Pathways outcome-based contracts do not reflect an expectation that providers will work with the harder to help'.

Policy makers have sought to address moral hazard in the design of programmes (Finn, 2009a), for instance, by differential pricing, whereby contractors receive a higher payment for the hardest to help (Finn, 2012). This, however, does not eliminate the financial incentives to cream and park (Simmonds, 2011; Work and Pensions Committee, 2011; Rees et al, 2013; Work and Pensions Committee, 2013). The coalition government's contracted-out Work Programme replaced the provision provided by NDDP and PtW and utilises differential pricing in an attempt to minimise moral hazard for disabled people. However, emerging evidence is that employment outcomes for disabled people are poorer than for non-disabled people (which may reflect creaming and parking by providers) (Rees et al, 2013; Work and Pensions Committee, 2013). Hence, moral hazard is difficult to eliminate in a market-based, outcome-driven system (see Mulheirn and Menne, 2008; Finn, 2009a).

Who might be adversely affected?

The evaluations of both programmes identify a number of factors that were statistically associated with moves into employment. Some of these factors help to provide a 'picture' of sub-groups who were less well served by contracted provision. The sub-groups identified as least likely to enter employment vary by analysis, but *include* participants:

- whose self-assessed health status had continued to be 'poor' or who had not improved while on the programme;
- who had a mental health condition;
- who lived alone;
- who rented from a social landlord;
- who had no qualifications or poor basic skills (and did not have a driving licence);
- who had a fluctuating work history;
- who had low motivation and/or lacked confidence;
- who were members of a black and minority ethnic group;
- who were male (Kazimirski et al, 2005; Legge et al, 2006; Hayllar and Wood, 2011).

Taken together, these characteristics suggest that those participants who might traditionally be viewed as furthest from the labour market were the least likely to enter employment under either programme.

In the multivariable statistical models used to identify these factors, the key variables were gender, health status and educational attainment, although the studies did not always include the same variables. Having a mental health condition was identified in all three analyses, but was only significant at the 5% level. This possibly underestimates the link between mental health and employment outcomes because survey respondents' mental health status will be based on their primary condition, whereas many of those coded as having a physical or learning disability will have depression, anxiety and stress as secondary conditions.

Conclusion

The argument here is *not* that the two programmes did not help some people into employment (clearly the NDDP did), nor that participants were not overall satisfied with the service, as they were (see, for example, Hayllar and Wood, 2011), rather that the marketisation of the programmes meant that some people were better served than others. Moreover, those least well served were not a random sample of the programmes' participants but tended to be those in most need of support. It is in this sense that the policies and organisations designed to help disabled people find work are failing.

A related consequence is that providers are overly concerned with job outcomes, rather than with some individuals' significant, albeit possibly tentative, steps towards the labour market. Improvements in 'soft' outcomes, such as an improvement in self-confidence, are undervalued.

To paraphrase Bill Clinton: 'It's the market stupid.' Policies inspired by neoliberalism and the logic of the market create an incentive structure in which those in most need of the help and support of providers, because they are those with the most complex needs and greatest barriers to employment, are the least likely to generate revenue and so are the least likely to be served. A far more effective policy response might be to tackle the structural factors, such as employer discrimination, that disabled people face in the labour market, to adopt a more 'holistic' approach that prioritises 'soft' outcomes in employment programmes and, for those further from the labour market, to introduce individual budgets so that people and not providers have funding to purchase specialist support (Sayce, 2011).

Notes

[1] The benefits include Incapacity Benefit, Income Support claimed on the grounds of disability, Severe Disablement Allowance and their replacement (in October 2008) Employment and Support Allowance.

[2] Contractors referred participants back to Jobcentre Plus to access these specialist employment programmes.

[3] *Access to Work* was a grant paid to those about to start paid employment, self-employment or a work trial and it helped to cover the extra costs that someone with a disability might incur, such as the need for work adaptations, specialist equipment, a support worker, certain travel costs and so on. *Work Preparation* aimed to improve a disabled person's employment options, self-confidence and work-related skills through short-term work placements. The *Job Introduction Scheme* was a weekly grant payable to employers for up to six weeks (and exceptionally 13 weeks) to assist towards the extra costs of employing a disabled person. *WORKSTEP* was designed to provide a tailored package of support for disabled people with significant and complex barriers to finding and retaining work. Provision in the open labour market and in businesses designed to employ disabled people was contracted out to local authorities, and third and private sector organisations, and also delivered by REMPLOY (an executive non-departmental public body of the DWP). Following the recommendation of the government-commissioned Sayce review (2011) of disability employment and training, the government announced in 2012 that subsidies paid to REMPLOY would end and its factories sold or closed. Work Preparation and WORKSTEP were replaced by Work Choice in October 2010. *Work Choice* is a voluntary programme that offers help with moving into work and in-work support, and its provision is contracted out. Provision includes advice, training, work trials and job search assistance. Emerging

evaluation findings suggest that many of the issues discussed in this chapter also apply to Work Choice (see Purvis et al, 2013).

[4] In 2003, the DWP reduced this to 13 weeks to help job brokers with their cash flow.

References

Bambra, C., Whitehead, M. and Hamilton, V. (2005) 'Does "welfare-to-work" work? A systematic review of the effectiveness of the UK's welfare-to-work programmes for people with a disability or chronic illness', *Social Science & Medicine*, 60(9), pp 1905-18.

Carmel, E. and Papadopoulos, T. (2009) 'Governing social security: from protection to markets', in J. Millar (ed) *Understanding social security: Issues for policy and practice* (2nd edn), Bristol: Policy Press, pp 93-109.

Coleman, N., Sykes, W. and Groom, C. (2013) *Barriers to employment and unfair treatment at work: A quantitative analysis of disabled people's experiences*, Research Report no. 88, Manchester: Equality and Human Rights Commission.

Corden, A., Harries, T., Hill, K., Kellard, K., Lewis, J., Sainsbury, R. and Thornton, P. (2003) *New Deal for Disabled People national extension: Findings from the first wave of qualitative research with clients, job brokers and Jobcentre Plus staff*, DWP Research Report W169, Sheffield: Department for Work and Pensions.

CPA (Committee of Public Accounts) (2010) *Support to incapacity benefits claimants through Pathways to Work*, HC 404, London: The Stationery Office.

Damm, C. (2012) *The third sector delivering employment services: An evidence review*, TSRC Working Paper no. 70, Birmingham: Third Sector Research Centre, University of Birmingham.

Davies, S. (2008) 'Contracting out employment services to the third and private sectors: a critique', *Critical Social Policy*, 28 (2), pp 136-64.

Davis, A., Pound, E. and Stafford, B. (2006) *New Deal for Disabled People extensions: Examining the role and operation of new job brokers*, DWP Research Report no. 384, Leeds: Corporate Document Services.

Dickens, S., Mowlam, A. and Woodfield, K. (2004) *Incapacity Benefit reforms — the personal adviser role and practices*, DWP Research Report no. W212, Sheffield: Department for Work and Pensions, http://web.policystudiesinstitute.org.uk/pdf/2004/report212

Dorsett, R. (2008) *Pathways to Work for new and repeat Incapacity Benefits claimants: Evaluation synthesis report*, Research Report no. 525, Leeds: Corporate Document Services.

DSS (Department of Social Security) (1998a) *New ambitions for our country: A new contract for welfare*, Cm 3805, London: The Stationery Office.

DSS (1998b) *A new contract for welfare: Support for disabled people*, Cm 4103, London: The Stationery Office.

DWP (Department for Work and Pensions) (2002) *Pathways to Work: Helping people into employment*, Cm 5690, London: The Stationery Office.

DWP (2006) *A new deal for welfare: Empowering people to work*, Cm 6730, London: The Stationery Office.

DWP (2007a) *In work, better off: Next steps to full employment*, Cm 7130, London: The Stationery Office.

DWP (2007b) *Ready for work: Full employment in our generation*, Cm 7290, London: The Stationery Office.

DWP (2008) *DWP commissioning strategy*, Cm 7330, London: The Stationery Office.

DWP (2010) *Building bridges to work: New approaches to tackling long-term worklessness*, Cm 7817, London: The Stationery Office.

DWP (2011) *Disability employment support: Fulfilling potential government's response to the consultation on the recommendations in Liz Sayce's independent review Getting in, staying in and getting on*, Cm 8312, London: The Stationery Office.

DWP (2012) *The Work Programme*, London: DWP.

DWP (2013a) *DWP commissioning strategy 2013 consultation*, London: DWP.

DWP (2013b) *Fulfilling potential: Building a deeper understanding of disability in the UK today*, London: DWP.

DWP (2013c) *The disability and health employment strategy: The discussion so far*, Cm 8763, London: The Stationery Office.

Finn, D. (2009a) *Differential pricing in contracted out employment programmes: Review of international evidence*, DWP Research Report no. 564, London: Department for Work and Pensions.

Finn, D. (2009b) 'The "welfare market": private sector delivery of benefits and employment services', in J. Millar (ed) *Understanding social security: Issues for policy and practice* (2nd edn), Bristol: Policy Press, pp 275-93.

Finn, D. (2012) *Sub-contracting in public employment services: The design and delivery of 'outcome based' and 'black box' contracts: Analytical paper*, Brussels: European Commission, DG Employment, Social Affairs and Inclusion.

Flynn, N. (2012) *Public sector management* (6th edn), London: Sage Publications.

Freud, D. (2007) *Reducing dependency, increasing opportunity: Options for the future of welfare to work: An independent report to the Department for Work and Pensions*, Leeds: Corporate Document Services.

Gershon, P. (2004) *Releasing resources to the front line: Independent review of public sector efficiency*, Norwich: HMSO.

Greenberg, D. and Davis, A. (2007) *Evaluation of the New Deal for Disabled People: The cost and cost-benefit analyses*, DWP Research Report no. 431, London: Department for Work and Pensions.

Grover, C. (2009) 'Privatizing employment services in Britain', *Critical Social Policy*, 29(3), pp 487–509.

Hayllar, O. and Wood, M. (2011) *Provider-led Pathways to Work: The experiences of new and repeat customers in phase one areas*, DWP Research Report no. 723, London: DWP.

Hudson, M., Phillips, J., Ray, K., Vegeris, S. and Davidson, R. (2010) *The influence of outcome-based contracting on provider-led Pathways to Work*, DWP Research Report no. 638, London: Department for Work and Pensions.

Hughes, O. (2003) *Public management and administration: An introduction* (3rd edn), Basingstoke: Palgrave Macmillan.

Kazimirski, A., Adelman, L., Arch, J., Keenan, L., Legge, K., Shaw, A., Stafford, B., Taylor, R. and Tipping, S. (2005) *New Deal for Disabled People evaluation: Registrants' survey – merged cohorts (cohorts one and two, waves one and two)*, DWP Research Report no. 260, Leeds: Corporate Document Services.

Knight, G., Salis, S., Francavilla, F., Radu, D., Hevenstone, D., Mocca E. and Tousley, B. (2013) *Provider-led Pathways to Work: Net impacts on employment and benefits*, Working Paper no. 113, London: Department for Work and Pensions.

Legge, K., Magadi, M., Phung, V.-H., Stafford, B., Hales, J., Hayllar, O., Nevill, C. and Wood, M. (2006) *New Deal for Disabled People: Survey of registrants – report of cohort 3*, DWP Research Report no. 369, Leeds: Corporate Document Services.

Lewis, J., Corden, A., Dillon, L., Hill, K., Kellard, K., Sainsbury, R. and Thornton, P. (2005) *New Deal for Disabled People: An in-depth study of job broker service delivery*, DWP Research Report no. 246, Leeds: Corporate Document Services.

McDonald, M., Shaw, M. and Ayliffe, R. (2007) *Independent inquiry into DWP Pathways to Work contracting*, London: ACEVO.

McDonald, S., Davis, A. and Stafford, B. (2004) *Report of the Survey of Job Brokers*, DWP Research Report no. WAE197, Sheffield: Department for Work and Pensions.

Mitchell, M. and Woodfield, K. (2008) *Qualitative research exploring the Pathways to Work sanctions regime*, DWP Research Report no. 475, Leeds: Corporate Document Services.

Mulheirn, I. and Menne, V. (2008) *The Flexible New Deal: Making it work*, London: Social Market Foundation.

NAO (National Audit Office) (2005) *Gaining and retaining a job: The Department for Work and Pensions' support for disabled people*, HC 455, London: The Stationery Office.

NAO (2010) *Support to incapacity benefits claimants through Pathways to Work*, HC 21, London: The Stationery Office.

Orr, L., Bell, S. and Lam, K. (2007) *Long-term impacts of the New Deal for Disabled People: Final report*, DWP Research Report no. 432, Leeds: Corporate Document Services.

Purvis, A., Foster, S., Lane, P., Aston, J. and Davies, M. (2013) *Evaluation of the Work Choice Specialist Disability Employment Programme: Findings from the 2011 early implementation and 2012 steady state waves of the research*, Research Report no. 846, London: Department for Work and Pensions.

Rees, J., Whitworth, A. and Carter, E. (2013) *Support for all in the UK Work Programme? Differential payments, same old problem ...*, TSRC Working Paper no. 115, Birmingham: Third Sector Research Centre, University of Birmingham.

Sayce, L. (2011) *Getting in, staying in and getting on: Disability employment support fit for the future*, Cm 8081, London: The Stationery Office.

Simmonds, D. (2011) *Work Programme results: Perform or bust*, Working Brief no. 7, London: Centre for Social and Economic Inclusion.

Stafford, B. (2012) 'Supporting moves into work: New Deal for Disabled People findings', *Scandinavian Journal of Disability Research*, 14(2), pp 165-76.

Stafford, B., with Ashworth, K., Davis, A., Hartfree, Y., Hill, K., Kellard, K., Legge, K., McDonald, S., Reyes De-Beaman, S., Aston, J., Atkinson, J., Davis, S., Evans, C., Lewis, J., O'Regan, J., Harries, T., Kazimirski, A., Pires, C., Shaw, A. and Woodward, C. (2004) *New Deal for Disabled People (NDDP): First synthesis report*, DWP Research Report no. W199, Sheffield: Department for Work and Pensions.

Stafford, B. with others (2007) *New Deal for Disabled People: Third synthesis report – key findings from the evaluation*, DWP Research Report no. 430, Leeds: Corporate Document Services.

Tennant, R., Kotecha, M. and Rahim, N. (2010) *Provider-led Pathways: Experiences and views of implementation in phase 2 districts*, DWP Research Report no. 643, London: Department for Work and Pensions.

Work and Pensions Committee (2011) *Work Programme: Providers and contracting arrangements: Volume I: Report, together with formal minutes, oral and written evidence*, HC 718, London: The Stationery Office.

Work and Pensions Committee (2013) *Can the Work Programme work for all user groups? Volume 1: Report, together with formal minutes, oral and written evidence*, HC 162, London: The Stationery Office.

FIVE

Disabled people, welfare reform and the balance of rights and responsibilities

Dan Heap

Introduction

The increased conditionality that has been the hallmark of recent reform of benefits for disabled people in Britain has been justified, often explicitly, on the grounds that those disabled people required to seek work will be given appropriate support. Through a series of qualitative interviews with policy makers and a review of relevant literature and qualitative data, this chapter seeks to examine the extent to which increased conditionality has been accompanied by increased support for disabled people to access paid work. The chapter argues that what began in the mid-2000s as a genuine attempt to extend employment support to disabled people marginalised from the paid labour market has faded in recent years. This appears to be as a result of changed labour market policy priorities as a result of the economic crisis that began in 2008 and the failure of the Pathways to Work programme (PtW). The Work Programme (WP) that was, at least in part, a replacement for PtW, however, makes limited formal recognition of the additional labour market barriers that disabled people face and does little to stop disabled people from being excluded by service providers.

Concurrently, welfare reform has continued apace, with 900,000 people with disabilities or health conditions experiencing some additional conditionality (Beatty and Fothergill, 2011). Unlike, for example, in Scandinavian countries, where benefits reform has been bound up closely with and accepted by social partners in exchange for improved support, disabled people claiming working-age benefits in Britain have few formal rights to employment services or to redress if excluded from them. Looked at this way – as an (im)balance between permanent changes in the value and conditions of benefits with services of highly variable availability and quality – reform of working-age disability benefits emerges as even more punitive than has hitherto been appreciated.

The rest of this chapter is divided into five sections. The first section explores the nature of the welfare settlement between the state and disabled working-age benefit claimants that emerged in the 2000s – one supposedly underpinned by the state and the claimants' mutual rights and responsibilities. The second section examines the subsequent shift from small-scale specialist employment support to more mainstream employment support for a much larger group of disabled claimants. Marshalling relevant evidence, the third section judges the adequacy of this type of support in the WP according to three offered criteria:

- access;
- quality and availability;
- performance in getting disabled people into work.

The fourth section briefly highlights the ways in which the experiences of welfare-to-work schemes involving disabled people in Britain have parallels with those elsewhere in Europe. The final section sets out the conclusions to the chapter.

'Balancing rights and responsibilities' and the emergent welfare settlement for disabled people

The publication of the Freud Report in 2007 appeared to signal a major shift in Britain's welfare-to-work strategy. Freud's starting point was the assumption that unemployment as usually understood had fallen 'probably to near the frictional level' (Freud, 2007, p 51). Consequently, he advocated a refocusing of welfare-to-work policy away from the frictionally unemployed to, instead, three groups – older people, Incapacity Benefit (IB) claimants and lone parents – 'facing multiple disadvantage and long term benefit dependency' (Freud, 2007, p 51). Greater levels of employment for these groups, Freud argued, was necessary if the government was to reach its then recently adopted 80% employment target, for they represented 95% of those people who had been claiming benefits for more than a year. Despite representing two thirds of the workless population, these groups tended to have relatively poor access to work-focused support – just 14% of the welfare-to-work budget was spent on them – and what support was available was offered on what Freud (2007) referred to as a 'client group' basis that related to problems perceived to be common to all those people receiving a particular benefit, rather than on a genuinely individual basis. That IB claimants had hitherto been 'written off' – provided with no or minimal back-to-work support and left, instead, on benefits with little chance of experiencing paid employment – was a strong theme of welfare reform from the mid-2000s onwards and one in which the Freud Report was anchored.

Freud recommended that the Department for Work and Pensions (DWP) should free up Britain's state-provided employment service, Jobcentre Plus, to focus on short-term unemployed people, while building a network of contracted provision to help support long-term workless people, principally members of the three groups outlined above, and IB claimants in particular, into paid employment. He saw this as a necessary step in justifying the extension of conditionality to the benefits of all working-age benefits claimants other than parents with very young children and people with seriously incapacitating illnesses or disabilities. He noted (Freud, 2007, p 1), for example, 'with the least advantaged in receipt of more individualised support, the rights and responsibilities of all benefit recipients should be brought more closely into line'. Such ideas framed the then Labour government's White Paper, *Raising expectations and increasing support: Reforming welfare for the future* (DWP, 2008), the following year. It promised more intensive and extensive support on the understanding that most IB claimants would be required to access it once transferred to Employment and Support Allowance (ESA). This is a crucial point. Much of the recent extensive reform to IB and related benefits in Britain has been justified on the grounds that more and better employment support would be provided to match the increased demands made on claimants.

Thus, how the nature of the welfare-to-work settlement between the state and disabled people is viewed depends to a significant extent on how the demands on claimants are balanced by the employment-related support that is offered. In the absence of any existing frameworks to judge the balance of rights and responsibilities for disabled jobseekers, three criteria derived from the government's own pledges and from the literature on specialist disability employment services are used in this chapter to judge this balance.

First, given that recent governments in Britain have sought to apply conditions to a much broader range of claimants than previously, governments needs to show that they are providing support to this full range of claimants, from those closest to employment to those with multiple and complex barriers to paid work. Limited support has long been available through the New Deal for Disabled People (NDDP) and predecessor programmes, and through general Jobcentre Plus services, but providing support to the range of claimants that governments have been seeking to activate will require a radical step-change in the design, delivery and assessment of employment support for disabled people. The evidence from elsewhere in Europe is that governments find it more difficult to develop services and successfully engage people in them the further those people are away from the labour market (OECD, 2010).

Second, the right type and mix of services needs to be provided. Specialist services have been provided through NDDP and the WORKSTEP employment programme, but on a relatively small scale and with mainly voluntary claimants, usually considered the easiest to help. Mental health support in particular is not well developed, with mental health conditions being the primary or secondary reason for claiming for 50% of the IB population at the time of the *Raising expectations* White Paper (DWP, 2008). Ensuring that there is the capacity in such support in the quantity that is needed is a significant challenge.

Third, an equitable settlement would require any measure or programme in which disabled people are required to participate to have a reasonable rate of success. In his study of how the rights of claimants are framed in active social policy legislation in Finland, Denmark and Sweden, van Aerschot (2013, p 9), for example, establishes the 'principle of proportionality', which suggests that there should be 'a suitable balance between the probable results of activation measures and the effects of these measures on the basic rights of the recipient'. Arguably, compelling claimants to access support that is unlikely to help them find work is no more significantly progressive than not providing support. While there is certainly value in support that moves claimants towards employment without necessarily achieving an employment outcome – the 'distance travelled' model – such a model has not underpinned recent governments' approaches in Britain, which focus almost exclusively on job outcomes.

From specialist to mainstreamed employment support: Pathways to Work to the Work Programme

PtW was the culmination of much of the thinking that New Labour governments had done in the early and mid-2000s around the best way to 'help' IB claimants to access paid work. It was in some ways a step-change because it was the first disability employment programme in Britain to contain some element of compulsion. New IB claimants and ESA claimants assessed as being capable of moving towards work[1] were required to attend work-focused interviews or face a benefit sanction of up to 25%. The Condition Management Programme component of PtW – delivered by the National Health Service in the Jobcentre Plus-led version of the scheme and by contractors in the provider-led version and offering advice on managing health conditions and disabilities within an employment context – was also noticeable for being the first national, large-scale health and disability-related employment service (see Chapter Four, this volume). Most importantly, it dwarfed NDDP and previous schemes in terms of the number of people served (1.8 million entries for 1.25 million individuals; DWP, 2011) and cost, which had reached approximately £1 billion when the decision was made to end the programme (NAO, 2010).

The subsequent realisation that PtW had little impact in increasing job outcomes (NAO, 2010), particularly given the positive results of initial evaluations (made on the basis of erroneous data), appeared to cause a crisis of confidence in extant approaches to the activation of sick and disabled claimants. This led to discussions of the possibility of supporting sick and disabled claimants within a more general employment programme. As one of the DWP officials involved in the operation of Pathways noted in one of a series of interviews with the author in 2011 and 2012;[2] "Some providers were struggling to achieve targets and this led to discussion about whether having a separate specialist disability programme is the right way forward or whether disabled people could be helped just as well if not better through a flexible mainstream programme."

The first economic crisis of the 21st century, coming at around the same time that PtW was being evaluated, was the second main factor in the movement away from a specialist programme towards a unified one for all claimants. According to a senior DWP adviser involved in the PtW strategy, interviewed in the year after it was cancelled, the need to be seen to be dealing with the increase in the number of unemployed people as a consequence of the economic crisis drew focus away from the disadvantaged groups identified by Freud:

> 'From the middle of 2008 the ministerial focus shifted a lot towards jobseekers and people who had been on benefit six to twelve months, so much focus went on to how to boost support for people who had been unemployed for a while but aren't yet long-term unemployed. The civil service are very responsive to what the ministers are focused on. If ministers aren't cracking the whip on an issue then it can drift and I think IB/ESA support for people with health

conditions and disabilities did get a bit lost there from mid '08 onwards.'

The launch of new initiatives for newly unemployed people appeared to have diverted funds from expanding support for sick and disabled claimants, as a DWP strategist involved in developing policy at the time argued:

'Nobody has actually said "this comes out at the expense of scrapping schemes for disabled people" but you have to think that if we hadn't been spending all that money introducing new initiatives on helping the short-term, and particularly youth, unemployed, then there might have been more space.'

The specific desire to assist sick and disabled claimants into work looks to have been subsumed into a general strategy of lowering unemployment in which any job entry is seen as a positive outcome. This change was observed by a senior DWP ministerial adviser:

'DWP were incredibly enthusiastic about [PtW] for a very long time until they completed all their evaluations and found that unfortunately it didn't appear to have any impact. Which then I think to some extent with the onset of the recession was an important factor in them saying "let's just package all this up in a single programme; let's actually worry less about people on IB and let the market sort it out" and assume that any job entry is a bonus rather than what had really happened in the last 10 years or so, up until two years ago [2009], *which was a real effort to improve the support for people on IB.*' (Emphasis added)

However, such an approach – what can be described as the 'single gateway' approach – is problematic. There is, for instance, the issue of resource allocation between competing groups of non-employed claimants. Mabbett (2003, p 23) notes that: 'Mainstreaming can also have a flip side, whereby special recognition through separate institutions and arrangements is lost. At the level of provision, losses may be connected with intensified competition for resources from other disadvantaged groups, and the withdrawal of special services for disabled people.' The issue here is how national authorities ensure that resources are apportioned fairly in programmes between participants who have different employment support needs, so that those with the least barriers to work do not get the most help and those with more complicated labour market needs get less support; the well-known problem of 'creaming' and 'parking' in employment programmes (Bredgaard and Larsen, 2008; Shutes, 2011; Chapter Four, this volume). In addition, single gateway programmes may also mean that those claimants who have distinct needs may become lost through a single, centrally defined regime that is not particularly appropriate and which is imposed on them.

The Work Programme: access, service provision and performance for disabled jobseekers

These concerns appear to be borne out by the experience of the first two-and-half years of the WP. While claimants of IB and ESA were supposed to be a major focus of the WP, their participation has run significantly below what was expected. Innovation and the provision of specialist support service appears to be limited and the fears of 'parking' of claimants with the most complex needs are being realised.

Accessing the Work Programme

The first year of the WP saw referrals of IB and ESA claimants running far below what was originally expected. The Centre for Social and Economic Inclusion (Coleman, 2011) predicted that by 2014, 78% of the WP caseload would have some current or previous connection to ESA or IB and around 25% of total referrals were expected to be from the ESA/IB caseload (ERSA, 2011). Instead, the first year saw less than half this figure. Forecasts for the participation of ESA claimants have been revised down, even though the overall forecast for flows into the programmes has been increased by 32% since tendering. The result, in the words of a DWP official involved in its design, is that the WP is becoming "largely a JSA [Jobseeker's Allowance] programme". One of the principal explanations for this is the relatively high work-readiness requirement that frames it. Original plans to refer all ESA claimants assessed as being capable of work-related activity into the programme were shelved in favour of only those claimants considered ready for work within three months (Bivand, 2011). This was a fundamental change in the nature of the programme because the WP was supposed to assist claimants adjudged furthest from employment. However, the consequent very low inflow of claimants was a source of considerable embarrassment for the DWP and subsequent revisions to six and then

12 months had the desired effect of increasing the flow of ESA/IB claimants into the programme. However, it remains below the original expected levels (Riley et al, 2014). While the increased enrolment is to be welcomed, it is the case that much of the increase is accounted for by new ESA claimants. Claimants with longer claim histories – and arguably, therefore, the most in need of support – are still not accessing the scheme in the volumes originally expected (see Figure 5.1). This appears to bear out concerns that the WP would not serve the full range of disabled claimants, from the least to the most disadvantaged.

Figure 5.1: Work Programme referral volumes by payment group, June 2011 to December 2013

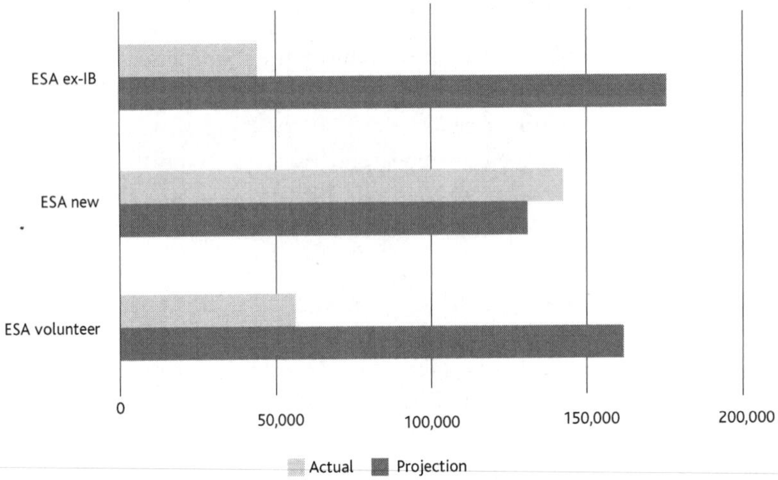

Source: DWP Work Programme Tabulation Tool

The relatively low referral rates are concerning. This is because it is the scheme in which the majority of welfare-to-work effort is invested and, therefore, there is relatively limited support outside of it. Even for those who do enrol, the relatively low referral rates are likely to mean that providers cannot achieve the required economies of scale to adequately invest in specialist support services and, therefore, provide support to sick and disabled claimants (Riley et al, 2014).

Quality and availability of specialist support

The WP is a significant departure from previous programmes in that it does not closely specify what services are to be offered. It operates on a 'black box' basis, which means, in contrast to providers delivering a prespecified set of services, as was the case with previous programmes, they are free to design their own intervention regimes and are responsible to government only on their performance in getting claimants into employment. It was the DWP's expectation that the payment-by-results model would drive innovation in the development of specialist support and, thus, mandating a specific set of interventions – as PtW was criticised for doing (NAO, 2010) – was not necessary.

WP providers, however, appear to be converging around a relatively standardised and familiar set of measures – for example, job coaching and assistance with job search, Curriculum Vitae (CV) writing and interview skills (Work and Pensions Select Committee, 2013) – applied to most claimants. Evidence of specialisation and innovation is relatively rare. Providers report that they focus on such standardised support because it can be provided in-house or sourced cost free. More specialist support for claimants with specific needs is sometimes available through specialist sub-contractors, but is not widely used due to cost constraints and doubts surrounding whether such support would lead to an employment outcome (Newton et al, 2012). This helps to explain why the involvement of such providers has not been at the level originally expected, with a significant number leaving the programme due to too few referrals (Rees et al, 2013).

A further common theme is what has become known as 'inappropriate referrals'. Providers have complained that they are receiving too many claimants with very severe barriers to work – particularly surrounding mental health conditions – that cannot be realistically addressed given the structure of the WP payment systems (Newton et al, 2012). The operation of the ESA's Work Capability Assessment (WCA) is almost certainly to blame for this. A large number of claimants have been reassessed, after receiving IB for often lengthy periods of time, and are now considered ready for work or work-related activity, and thus eligible for WP intervention. However, the accuracy of the WCA has been widely questioned (Gulland, 2011), with even claimants suffering from terminal illness being assessed as being capable of work (Citizens Advice Bureau, 2010). This has resulted in the ESA/IB caseload being much more diverse than the WP was originally designed for and more diverse than providers had planned for. Once again, this questions the wisdom of merging most existing support into the programme.

The limited provision of specialist support for disabled claimants on the WP appears to have two major causes. First, the level of funding that was expected to be available did not ultimately materialise:

Prime contractors went into [the WP] with the intention that they would have their key subcontractors, who would deliver across the board, but that where more specialist help was needed they would have a pool, if you like, of money to refer people to. I think the further we have gone down the process, the more prime contractors found that there just simply is not the money in it for that ... there is *very, very little money for any interventions that do not have a clear job outcome.* (Caroline Taunt, Prince's Trust,[3] in Work and Pensions Select Committee, 2011, question 93, emphasis added)

The low referral rate appears to be part of the reason behind this limited funding. On the initial caseload projections, spending for each ESA claimant would have been £1,169, but on current referral rates it is around half this, at £690 (Riley et al, 2014). It is predicted to have fallen further from 2014 as attachment fees – the amount paid to the provider to take the claimant on – are phased out. Across the five-year programme as a whole, this equates to a total spend of £350 million on sick and disabled people, as opposed to the initial expectation of £730 million, figures that are both substantially below the cost of the previous PtW. Riley et al's (2014) projection that this would only pay for relatively limited support – an initial interview, a 30-minute intervention every two months, one in 20 claimants getting additional support to manage their disability, a 1:370 adviser:claimant ratio and an average additional spend on such support of £30 per participant over their two-year participation – appears to be accurate in the light of participant surveys, which report the majority of ESA/IB claimants getting limited or no support (Crowther and Sayce, 2013; Newton et al, 2012).

The design of the WP contracts – focused largely on job outcomes – appears to militate against sick or disabled claimants for whom the journey to employment is likely to be longer and for whom a positive outcome may not be realistic in the short term. The majority of the payments made to providers are awarded once the claimant enters work and stays employed, with only a small attachment fee of £400 to £600 made when the claimant is taken on by the provider. Given that most job outcomes come within the first six months, there is little incentive for providers to offer intensive support in the later stages of the two-year period: the 'prospect of continued support is bleak especially in the second year' (Simmonds, 2011, p 5). This is likely to worsen as an issue as attachment fees are removed. Welfare-to-work providers asked to give evidence to the House of Commons' Work and Pensions Select Committee's investigation into the early implementation of the WP confirmed this concern that the strict work focus of the programme would encourage providers to ignore those participants for whom quick entry into the workplace would not be a realistic possibility:

> We focus, for example, on disabled young people, lone parents or young people in or leaving care, and I think there is a real risk with the Work Programme that those groups might be ignored. When you are solely looking at the customer journey from not being in work to being in work, *you can omit those that need more complex support.* (Caroline Taunt, Prince's Trust, in Work and Pensions Committee, 2011, question 63, emphasis added)

There now seems to be an acceptance by both the DWP and providers that as currently constituted the WP is likely to fail those claimants whose needs cannot easily and quickly be met. As a further former DWP official interview told me:

> 'So the differential pricing in the Work Programme contains a break against creaming and parking but the reality is there will still be creaming and parking within payment groups and often the differences between payment groups arguably *are not large enough to drive provider behaviour,* something the providers themselves say.... I think that they understand that they haven't got this right and there will be creaming and parking. I think you're looking at 10-20% of participants that will effectively be written off. Providers are looking to get about 40% of their caseload into work and to my mind they can't afford to provide a bells and whistles service to everybody.... What worries us is that they will appear two years later with two years more of not being in the labour market, even more disadvantaged and you end up spending even more money.' (Emphasis added)

Even though the parking of vulnerable claimants appears to be widespread and obvious, the DWP can do relatively little to manage provider behaviour to ensure that sick and disabled claimants get more appropriate support. This is because there is an absence of central standards and only a minority of prime providers have their own minimum standards that mention such claimants. A Treasury official involved in the setting up of the programme expressed concerns in this regard:

> 'I think a critical point is that there are no centralised minimum standards attached to the Work Programme so it entirely depends on what the providers offer. They have to set their own minimum standards and those vary quite widely. It's entirely conceivable that somebody could go through two years of the Work Programme and not really receive the meaningful intervention that addresses their barriers to work. Providers will say with justification that they can't afford to do that, they have to get results or they'll go bust. In employment programmes *there are no rights: just responsibilities.*' (Emphasis added)

Pathway to what? Work Programme outcomes for ESA/IB claimants

Given the apparent limited specialist support available and incentives to provide such support, it should be unsurprising that the WP has not been particularly successful for claimants of ESA or IB. Against an initial target of 13% of the monthly intake achieving a job outcome within one year, the latest figures show the programme achieving only 5% overall (see Figure 5.2). Figure 5.2 demonstrates two main issues. First, that ESA/IB claimants have the worst prospects of any of the main groups referred to the WP in terms of job outcomes. In particular, ex-IB claimants who have been transferred to ESA are particularly poorly served – that is, those with the longest period out of work and thus most in need of successful support – with less than 2% successfully being placed in paid work. While the proportion for new ESA claimants is better (at about 5%), it is still poor compared with participants in receipt of JSA. Second, the year-on-year trends for ESA/IB participants are very different from those for JSA participants. For the former the proportion securing paid work has been consistently poor, whereas for the latter, significant improvement is visible, particularly in the first year.

Figure 5.2: Percentage of monthly intakes of referrals to the Work Programme achieving a job outcome within 12 months following referral, June 2011 to December 2012

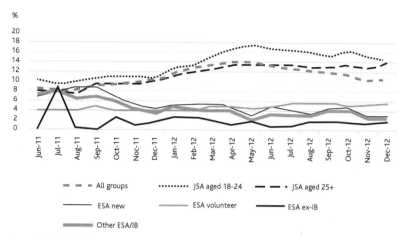

Source: DWP Work Programme Tabulation Tool

Experiences from abroad

The experience of other countries that have sought to get sick and disabled claimants into work is remarkably similar to that of Britain, despite differences in welfare and governance contexts. For example, Social Code II, introduced as part of Germany's Hartz reforms, forced more claimants into its work-first activation schemes by requiring anyone deemed to be considered 'employable' (defined as being able to work three hours per week) to access them. The effect has been similar to that of the WCA in Britain, leading to a large number of claimants with support needs related to their disability moving into the most conditional, most strongly work-first grouping. Rauch and Dornette (2010) found that as a result, local employment offices in Germany were inundated with claimants for whom there was little capacity to help. They note, for example, that: 'Even people with severe disabilities are classed as "employable". Consequently, possible rehabilitation needs are often neglected if not requested directly by the person concerned' (Rauch and Dornette, 2010, p 64). As in Britain, the sheer number of people they were charged with supporting (caseloads more than doubled from a caseworker ratio of 1:75 to 1:171), combined with new management procedures that required staff to pursue the quickest and least expensive path for getting people back to work, meant that people with more than basic support needs were essentially parked on out-of-work benefits.

In Denmark too, while the most work-ready disabled claimants can access highly regarded, supported and subsidised employment schemes (see Chapter Eight, this volume), recent efforts to assist those with more complex barriers to work have faced difficulty with limited local capacity to provide specialist support, and the inability of central government to incentivise service providers to support the full range of claimants (Heap, 2013).

Conclusion

Disabled people have long moved in and out of British governments' target population when it comes to increasing employment and reducing the cost of social welfare support (Stone, 1984), but disabled people's experience of welfare reform in the past 10 years is distinct from previous decades in that disabled people have experienced a slew of highly regressive changes to their benefits. On a number of occasions these have been explicitly justified on the assurance that more and better support would be made available to help support sick and disabled claimants into paid work. However, while demands on claimants and changes to their benefits in Britain have been permanent, the support such claimants are offered for securing employment wax and wane in terms of both quality and quantity.

The new system of employment support appears not to be able to meet disabled claimants' individual needs. Given the focus on rapid entry into employment and the emerging system's failure to appreciate the gradual and often long-term nature of their return-to-work trajectories, disabled people are, at best, at risk of being pushed to the periphery of the government's welfare-to-work support strategy, and, at worst, being denied access altogether. Those who do tend to access it are poorly served by it, with, for example, ESA/IB claimants having the lowest success rate of all groups of the programme, and far below what was expected. Britain, therefore, appears to fail on the three criteria – employment support accessible to all disabled claimants of conditional benefits, the provision of high-quality and specialist services, and offering claimants good prospects of finding employment – used in this chapter to judge whether it is adequately balancing the increased demands made on claimants by increasing employment-focused support.

All this appears to be compounded by the fact that the pressure to make employment support more inclusive dissipated very rapidly after the onset of the economic crisis that started in 2008 and the failure of previous programmes. What looked at one point to be a genuine desire to improve support for the most disadvantaged claimants has been subsumed into a more general attempt to get workless people into employment and to reduce the cost of paying benefits, with disabled people no longer being a specific focus of welfare-to-work policy.

Given these observations, the current situation in Britain is similar to that observed of the New Deals employment programmes by Evans (2001) at the turn of the 21st century:

> The policy history of social security has no background of helping the hard to serve beyond cash payment and the ES's [Employment Service] history has been based on servicing a pre-selected group who were also not hard to serve. There is thus a worry that structural-organisational change will not see service-rich provision for welfare to work as a priority other than for the under-25s. It is difficult to see how the distribution of resources, so prominently skewed to the easiest to serve at present, can be reallocated other than by a 'wait and see' policy (this means that, as unemployment levels fall, the harder to serve will eventually get nearer to the front of the queue, but presumably still some way behind the continued demands of the frictionally unemployed). While this approach may make sense in economic terms as an efficient rationing of current resources, *it cannot also carry the label of equal opportunity.* (Evans, 2001, p 59, emphasis added)

Since 2001, Britain has had nearly 15 years of experience of attempting to support what governments have considered 'hard-to-help' claimants, particularly those in receipt of disability benefits, access paid work. However, they have not seemingly been able to ensure such equality of opportunity in access to adequate employment services. A truly progressive and transformative project would need to be underpinned by a more informed understanding of the nature of disabled people's transitions from worklessness to employment, by a broader vision of how sick and disabled people might contribute to society than has hitherto guided welfare-to-work policy, and by an enforceable right to support services that enables them to do so.

Notes

[1] Those people claiming ESA or who are in the process of moving from IB to ESA undergo the Work Capability Assessment (WCA) to determine their eligibility. Claimants considered capable of work immediately are moved to Jobseeker's Allowance.

Applicants assessed as not being capable of work immediately or engaging in activities to quicken their entry to work are placed in the ESA's Support Group (SG). Applicants considered not to be capable of work immediately, but capable of engaging with such activities are placed in ESA's Work Related Activity Group (WRAG). There is no conditionality for people in the SG, but those applicants in the WRAG face mandated activities.

[2] The findings in this chapter come from a wider three-year (2010–13) project funded by the Economic and Social Research Council, examining the development of active labour market policy for sick and disabled benefit claimants of working age in Europe over the past 10 years. Denmark and Britain were the focus of the research. Thirty interviews were conducted in 2011 and 2012 with a number of current and former government officials, and representatives from disabled persons' organisations and other relevant bodies.

[3] The Prince's Trust is a young person's charity established by the Princes of Wales. It offers training programmes, provides mentoring support and offers financial grants to build the confidence and motivation of disadvantaged young people. WP participants can access services offered by the Trust.

References

Beatty, C. and Fothergill, S. (2011) *Incapacity Benefit reform: The local, regional and national impact*, Sheffield: Centre for Regional Economic and Social Research.

Bivand, P. (2011) 'Can The Work Programme succeed?', *Working Brief*, February, London: Centre for Economic and Social Inclusion.

Bredgaard, T. and Larsen, F. (2008) 'Quasi-markets in employment policy: do they deliver on promises?', *Social Policy and Society*, 7, pp 341-52.

Citizens Advice Bureau (2010) *Work Capability Assessment independent review – call for evidence: Submission from Citizens Advice*, London: Citizens Advice Bureau, www.citizensadvice.org.uk/citizens_advice_response_to_esa_review_sept_2010__2_.pdf

Coleman, N. (2011) *Opening up employment for all: The role of assessment in the Work Programme*, London: Centre for Economic and Social Inclusion, www.cesi.org.uk/publications/opening-employment-all-role-assessment-work-programme

Crowther, N. and Sayce, E. (2013) *Taking control of employment support*, Working Paper, London: Disability Rights UK, www.disabilityrightsuk.org/sites/default/files/pdf/takingcontrolofemploymentsupportexecsummary.pdf

DWP (Department for Work and Pensions) (2008) *Raising expectations and increasing support: Reforming welfare for the future*, Cm 7506, London: The Stationery Office.

DWP (2011) *Provider-led Pathways to Work: Official statistics: October 2011*, London: DWP, https://www.gov.uk/government/uploads/system/uploads/attachment_data/file/200533/pl_pathways1011.pdf

DWP Work Programme Tabulation Tool, http://tabulation-tool.dwp.gov.uk/WorkProg/tabtool.html

ERSA (Employment Related Services Association) (2011) *Press comment: Work Programme providers call for urgent action on Employment Support Allowance referrals*, London: ERSA

Evans, M. (2001) *Welfare to work and the organisation of opportunity: Lessons from abroad*, CASE Report 15, London: Centre for Analysis of Social Exclusion, http://eprints.lse.ac.uk/28306/1/CASEreport15.pdf

Freud, D. (2007) *Reducing dependency, increasing opportunity: Options for the future of welfare to work*, London: Department for Work and Pensions.

Gulland, J. (2011) 'Ticking boxes: decision-making in Employment and Support Allowance', *Journal of Social Security Law*, 18(2), pp 69-86.

Heap, D. (2013) 'Reforming welfare for sick and disabled people in the UK and Denmark', Panel on Shame, Stigma and Austerity (with B. Baumberg and R. Walker), Social Policy Association (SPA) Annual Conference, 'Social Policy in Changing Times', University of Sheffield, UK, 8-10 July.

Mabbett, D. (2003) 'Why have disability categories in social security?', *Benefits*, 38(11), pp 163-8.

NAO (National Audit Office) (2010) *Support to incapacity benefits claimants through Pathways to Work*, London: HMSO.

Newton, B., Meager, N., Bertram, C., Corden, A., George, A., Lalani, M., Metcalf, H., Rolfe, H., Sainsbury, R. and Weston, K (2012) *Work Programme evaluation: Findings from the first phase of qualitative research on programme delivery*, London: Department for Work and Pensions.

OECD (Organisation for Economic Co-operation and Development) (2010) *Sickness, disability and work: Breaking the barriers: A synthesis of findings across OECD countries*, Paris: OECD.

Rauch, A. and Dornette, J. (2010) 'Equal rights and equal duties? Activating labour market policy and the participation of long-term unemployed people with disabilities after the reform of the German welfare state', *Journal of Social Policy*, 39(1), pp 53-70.

Rees, J., Taylor, R. and Damm, C. (2014) *Does sector matter? Understanding the experiences of providers in the Work Programme*, TSRC Working Paper 92, Birmingham: Third Sector Research Centre, University of Birmingham.

Riley, T., Bivand, P. and Wilson, T. (2013) *Making the Work Programme work for ESA claimants: Analysis of minimum performance levels and payment models*, London: Centre for Economic and Social Inclusion.

Shutes, I. (2011) 'Welfare-to-work and the responsiveness of employment providers to the needs of refugees', *Journal of Social Policy*, 40(4), pp 1-18.

Simmonds, D. (2011) 'The Work Programme: perform or bust', *Working Brief*, May, London: Centre for Economic and Social Inclusion.

Stone, D.A. (1984) *The disabled state*, Philadelphia, PA: Temple University Press.

van Aerschot, P. (2013) *Activation policies and the protection of individual rights: A critical assessment of the situation in Denmark, Finland and Sweden*, Farnham: Ashgate.

Work and Pensions Select Committee (2011) *Oral evidence on the Work Programme: Providers and contracting arrangements – Wednesday 12 January*, www.publications.parliament.uk/pa/cm201011/cmselect/cmworpen/uc718-i/uc71801.htm

Work and Pensions Select Committee (2013) *Can the Work Programme work for all user groups? First report of session 2013–14: Report, together with formal minutes, oral and written evidence*, www.publications.parliament.uk/pa/cm201314/cmselect/cmworpen/162/162.pdf

SIX

Disabled people and employment in Poland

Monika Struck-Peregończyk

Introduction

The Republic of Poland is a Central European country with a population of 38.5 million people. It is estimated that between 12.2% and 21.5% of the Polish population can be considered as disabled. The lower figure comes from the last National Census carried out in 2011 (CSO, 2013a, p 24), which defines a disabled person as 'a person who has an appropriate disability certificate or a person who does not have such a certificate but has a limited ability to perform basic activities for their age (play, learning, work, activities of daily living)'. The higher figure is derived from the 2009 European Health Interview Survey. It defines disability as 'limitations in activities people usually do because of health problems for at least the past six months' (CSO, 2011, p 70). It is estimated that almost half of those people who might be defined as disabled in Poland are of working age.

In this chapter, the employment position of disabled people in Poland is discussed. The prevailing view in Poland is that it is desirable for disabled people to work. However, as we shall see, it is the case that disabled people there are more likely to not be working than they are to be working. This chapter examines policies in Poland that are supposed to help disabled people access paid employment and critically engages with them. The chapter is divided into three main sections. The first section focuses on the legal status of disabled people in Poland, in particular the way a right to work for disabled people has been construed in Poland. This section examines employment policies before and after the collapse of Communism in 1989 in Poland and discusses the effectiveness of the Polish quota-levy system. It also examines supply-side policies used to address the low level of employment among disabled people. The second section examines the social security system for disabled people in Poland. The third section examines employment opportunities in the open and sheltered labour markets and discusses disabled people's experiences of paid work.

Disability and paid work

While Poland does not have comprehensive disability rights law, the rights of disabled people are protected by various international and domestic Acts. There was an attempt to create a universal Act that would concern most of the areas of disabled people's lives (it was to be entitled the Act on Equal Opportunities of Persons with Disabilities). However, the Bill was shelved[1] and the attention of the Polish government was devoted to the ratification of the United Nations' (UN) 2006 *Convention on the rights of persons with disabilities* (UN, 2006). This happened in 2012, but there are still regulations and practices that need changing in order to achieve full compliance with the Convention (Błaszczak, 2012).

Disability is defined in Polish law as a 'permanent or temporary inability to fulfil social roles due to permanent or long-lasting impairment, in particular resulting in inability to work' (Act on Vocational and Social Rehabilitation and Employment of Persons with Disabilities 1997).[2] To be acknowledged as disabled, a person has to obtain an appropriate legal certificate, either on the level of disability they have and/or on their incapacity to do paid work. The first type of certificate is issued by 296 Disability Assessment Boards (DABs) in Poland. DABs comprise a medical doctor and other specialists, such as a psychologist, a school counsellor, a career development professional and/or a social worker. The range of professionals sitting on a board is determined by the nature of the certificate being sought.

DABs determine the level of disability that an individual can be considered to have through a medical examination and an interview with the specialists noted above. DABs can determine three levels of disability: mild, moderate and significant. The certificate of disability includes recommendations concerning:

- employment;[3]
- training;
- the provision of orthopaedic equipment and other types of disability equipment;
- social and care services;
- the necessity for permanent or long-term care or assistance from another person.

The certificate is a basis for obtaining various benefits and services. However, it does not grant access to Poland's disability pension.

In contrast, disability pension is granted on the basis of the second type of disability certificate, which is issued by a practitioner at the Social Insurance Institution[4] (SII) and concerns work incapacity. The assessment for this certificate is based on a medical examination, any other relevant medical documentation and a questionnaire on the place and character of the last employment the individual had. The certificate may state that a person has:

- a partial incapacity to work;
- a total incapacity to work; or
- a total incapacity to work and an inability to lead an independent life.

A person is regarded as incapable of work if they are judged to have lost the capacity to do paid work due to an impairment of the body and have little chance to regain the capacity to work after retraining. Total incapacity to work suggests that a person has lost capability to do any work while partial incapacity to work suggests that they have lost, to a considerable degree, the capability to do work corresponding to their level of qualifications. Inability to lead an independent life means that the person needs permanent and long-term care and support to meet their essential daily needs. In 2012, the SII issued 764,600 certificates. The majority (81.8% or 625,500) acknowledged the disability of the applicant, finding them incapable of working (SII, 2013).

As can be seen, definitions of degrees of disability and incapacity to work are based on the medical model of disability (see Kaplan, 2000, p 354), concentrating on inability and ignoring the importance of barriers to employment and other aspects of disabled people's lives. Ideas such as 'incapable of work' lead to a frequent belief on the part of employers that disabled people are not able to work at all. Moreover, some disabled people are convinced that work is forbidden for them (Kutyło et al, 2009, pp 106-7; Kryńska and Pater, 2013, p 126). The need for change in the assessment system has only been discussed in the last few years. The system is criticised as being complicated, concentrating on inability to work, rather than ability to work, and not taking into consideration the actual needs of a particular disabled person.[5] Both the Government Plenipotentiary for Disabled People[6] and the Supreme Audit Office[7] have suggested that the system of assessment should be unified, or that SII should take over all the issues connected to the assessment of capability to work.[8] This may lead to the loss of the employment support for some disabled people as it will be in the interests of SII, which is at the same time a benefit provider, to limit the numbers of certified disabled people.

The *Charter of rights of persons with disabilities* (Resolution of the Sejm of 1 August 1997, M.P. no. 50, item 475) embodies the right of disabled people 'to work in the open labour market in accordance with their qualifications, education and abilities, to receive career counselling, and when the disability and state of health so require – the right to work in conditions adapted to needs of people with disabilities'. By ratifying the UN *Convention on the rights of persons with disabilities*, Poland confirmed Article 27 (that is, it recognised the right of disabled people to work on an equal basis with others). However, although the employment rate of disabled people has grown over the last few years, it is still very low at 22.4% of disabled people of working age. This figure is over three times lower than the figure for non-disabled people (69.7%). At the same time, the unemployment rate[9] of disabled people is 17.9%, compared with 10.3% for non-disabled people (Labour Force Survey, 2013). Employment policies for disabled people have been developed, but often remain ineffective. The reasons for this, as we shall see, are complex.

The employment of disabled people during Communism

Before 1989, in the time of Communism and the planned economy in Poland, it was believed that the best way to provide jobs for disabled people was to create special 'cooperatives of invalids'.[10] These were a type of sheltered enterprise whose aim was not only employment for disabled people, but also social and medical rehabilitation. The percentage of disabled people employed in cooperatives was to be at least 70% at a regional level (Majewski, 1995, p 132). The cooperatives enjoyed some privileges, such as, for example, the monopoly of manufacturing certain goods (for instance, schoolbags, curtain hooks and elements of protective clothing) and providing some services (for instance, cloakroom attendance). In 1988, there were 422 cooperatives employing 203,000 disabled people,[11] part of them in the 'outwork system'[12] (Hulek, 1998, pp 23-4). However, disabled people were also employed in establishments outside of the cooperatives. From 1967, establishments employing more than 500 workers were obliged to organise and adjust workplaces to the needs of disabled people. It is estimated that in the late 1980s about 600,000 disabled people were employed in the open labour market in this way (Thornton, 1998). However, employers preferred to hire those who were perceived as the most efficient, which, together with prevailing lack of access and attitudinal barriers, led to the exclusion of more severely disabled people from employment in the open labour market. The prevailing idea, therefore, was that the problems faced by disabled people would be solved inside the cooperatives (Thornton, 1998).

Following the collapse of Communism in 1989 and the development of a market economy, the emergence of mass unemployment meant that many disabled workers lost their jobs. The cooperatives lost their privileges and were unable to compete with new private companies. The number of disabled people employed in the cooperatives fell drastically to 80,000 in 1991 (Jaworski, 2009, p 58). There was a need for a new system of employment support for disabled people, which led to the passing of the Act on Employment and Vocational Rehabilitation of Persons with Disabilities 1991. The aim of the Act was to create mechanisms that would enable disabled people to work in the new economic climate, not only in sheltered enterprises, but also in the open labour market. The regulations introduced a quota-levy system modelled on the French system that at the time was popular in the countries of Central and Eastern Europe. As Thornton (1998, npn) notes, at that time a quota-levy approach was 'a central plank of newly created policies to promote mainstream employment of disabled persons in the new market economies'. The 1991 Act was then revised and replaced with the Act on Vocational and Social Rehabilitation and Employment of Persons with Disabilities 1997, which, apart from being lengthier and more detailed, also concerned social rehabilitation.

Employment policies and the quota-levy system

The quota-levy system that Poland adopted means that employers of 25 or more workers have a duty to ensure that at least 6% of their employees are disabled people. If the quota is not met, the employer is obliged to pay into the State Fund for Rehabilitation of Disabled Persons (SFRDP). This fund is used to help support the employment of disabled people and to help fund their social and vocational rehabilitation. However, the system applies only to the public sector and larger private companies,[13] and in both public and private sectors more than a half (55% in April 2014) of employers do not meet the quota.[14]

There are also financial incentives aimed at encouraging employers to employ disabled people. Those that meet the quota (or that are not obliged to do so, but who nevertheless employ disabled people) are entitled to a monthly subsidy from the SFRDP. This means employers who do not fulfil their legal obligations to employ disabled people contribute to employing them elsewhere. The aim of the subsidy is to partially fund the salaries of disabled workers and its level depends on the worker's degree of disability. In 2014, the subsidy amounted to PLN 1,800 per month (approximately £350) in the case of people with significant disabilities, PLN 1,125 (approximately £220) in the case of people with moderate disabilities and PLN 450 (approximately £88) in case of people with mild disabilities.[15] These sums may be raised by PLN 600 (approximately £118) in the case of people with 'special conditions' (for example, mental health issues, learning disability, pervasive developmental disorder, epilepsy or visual impairment). The aim of the differences in the amount of subsidy available was to create a financial incentive for employers to employ more people with significant degrees of disability and 'special conditions'. In practice, employers often seek workers with moderate or significant degrees of disability who, at the same time, would be as productive as non–disabled workers (Giermanowska, 2007; Kryńska and Pater, 2013).

The subsidy system should encourage employers to hire disabled people as it allows them not only to avoid paying the levy, but also to receive the subsidies. However, gaining and accounting for this type of financial support is quite complicated, which discourages many employers (Barczyński and Radecki, 2008; Bartkowski et al, 2009). This problem is exacerbated by the frequent changes in law. For example, the Act on Vocational and Social Rehabilitation and Employment of Persons with Disabilities 1997 has been changed more than 60 times since its introduction.[16]

There are also other financial incentives for employers, such as grants to cover all or some of the costs of equipping the workplace or employing workers supporting a disabled person at work. The first type of grant can cover the costs up to 15 times the amount of the average wage, on the condition that the employer ensures that a disabled person will be employed for at least 36 months. In 2012, grants were made for equipment at 1,783 workplaces at a cost of nearly PLN 70 million (approximately £14 million). The second type of grant can cover the costs of employing sign language interpreters and workers supporting disabled people at work. In 2012, these grants covered the employment of 223 people who supported 543 disabled employees. Employers may also apply for the reimbursement of the costs of training of their disabled employees. However, in 2012, only two employers did (*Informacja rządu RP...*, 2013, pp 59–60).

Although such financial inducements may encourage the recruitment of disabled people, they may also signal to employers that disabled people are less capable and have less to offer compared with other potential employees. It may also lead to the treatment of disabled people as a potential form of cheap labour. There are employers who employ disabled people merely because of the subsidies (Smoczyńska and Sijko, 2007; Kryńska and Pater, 2013). For a majority (72%) of employers the possibility of gaining the subsidies is the decisive factor in employing disabled workers (Bartkowski et al, 2009, p 33). The result in the case of many disabled people is low-paid, low-skill and low-status employment (Thornton and Lunt, 1995; Kryńska and Pater, 2013). This is because the level of the subsidies does not depend on the wages paid to disabled workers, which encourages employers to create low-cost jobs.[17]

Jaworski (2009, p 131) argues that the Polish quota-levy system did not achieve its main goals (increasing employment opportunities for disabled people and reducing differences between the employment situation of disabled and non-disabled people). The ineffectiveness of the quota-levy system may, for instance, be demonstrated by the fact that the employment rate of disabled people in the civil service remained at the level of 2.8% in 2011. None of the government ministries has met the quota. Some have been obliged to incur considerable expenses because of that. Ironically, the SII had to pay as much as PLN 24,304,000 (approximately £4,960,800) to the SFRDP in 2012 (*Informacja rządu RP...*, 2013, p 78). To increase the number of disabled workers in the civil service, new regulations were introduced in November 2011. Since then, central and local government departments where the employment rate of disabled people is below the quota have been required to give priority in employment to disabled people.[18] As yet, there are no data to indicate that this mechanism has helped to increase the employment rate of disabled people in the civil service. One of the problems is that disabled people rarely meet the job requirements because, as is the case in many countries (see Chapter Nine, this volume), disabled people face discrimination in education in Poland. Therefore, they tend to have lower levels of education and fewer necessary skills. It is, therefore, difficult for them to be among the five best candidates, the number of people in a group of candidates that would give the disabled person priority in employment (*Informacja rządu RP...*, 2013, p 79).

There is still much to do as far as supply-side policies are concerned to address the low employment rates of disabled people. However, there are policies, such as those in relation to training courses, job placements, career counselling and start-up business grants, aimed at increasing the employability of disabled people in Poland. One of the most popular is the policy on job placements. In 2012, over 8,000 disabled people took part in such placements, with 42% of participants securing employment following their placement. In the same year, 5,230 disabled people also completed training courses and over 18,000 received career counselling. A disabled person wishing to set up an enterprise may receive a start-up grant of up to 15 times the amount of the average wage. In 2012, more than 1,200 disabled people received such grants (*Informacja rządu RP ...*, 2013, pp 57, 61). These services and programmes are run by labour offices[19] (*urzędy pracy*) and are available to those disabled people who are registered as either *unemployed* or *jobseekers not in employment*.[20] There is no pressure on disabled people to make use of these programmes. On the contrary, insufficient financial resources limit the number of potential beneficiaries. A further problem is the fact that labour offices often fail to recognise the needs of disabled people and do not support them effectively (Wolski, 2010; Kryńska and Pater, 2013).

Supported employment (for example, with the support and assistance of a job coach in finding and maintaining employment) has gained recognition in Poland, but it is still not widely used. The first attempts to introduce supported employment were made by non-governmental organisations (NGOs)[21] at the beginning of 21st century and encompassed mainly learning disabled people and people living with mental health problems. Then the SFRDP ran a programme between 2007 and 2010 entitled Job Coach – Supported Employment for Disabled People. It then introduced a second programme to run between 2013 and 2014 entitled Job Coaching as a Way of Increasing Employment of Disabled People.[22] Supported employment is also used in various projects funded by the European Union (EU). Due to the variety of sources of financing, the number of people taking part in supported employment is difficult to determine.

According to a study by Zub et al (2008), the vocational integration system of disabled people in Poland is still poorly developed. Its main weaknesses include:

- inadequate legislative solutions;[23]
- poor cooperation between the main actors of the system;[24]
- barriers and limitations on the part of the institutions (Zub et al, 2008).

Moreover, supply-side policies in Poland often lack cohesion and comprehensiveness and their implementation depends largely on the financial resources available at the level of central and local institutions. The programmes offered by labour offices often lack flexibility and because of this they do not address needs arising from a particular disability and do not take the actual capabilities of a specific disabled person into consideration. This lack of individual support often means that it does not reach those who would really need it (Arczewska et al, 2014, p 103). It is possible that a more personalised system would be helpful, but it would have to be implemented with deliberation in order to avoid a 'cherry-picking' approach where only disabled people who are closest to the labour market get support (see Yates and Roulstone, 2013; also Chapters Four and Five, this volume).

Welfare and work

In Poland, a disabled person may not work and receive financial support in the form of disability pension. There are two main types of disability pensions: an 'inability to work pension' and a 'social pension'. The former is a contributory benefit available to those who have worked for a certain period of time; the latter is a non-contributory and non-means-tested[25] benefit available to those who do not have work experience and became disabled in their youth.[26] In March 2014, over one million Poles were entitled to an inability to work pension and 267,000 were entitled to a social pension (SII, 2014). All disabled people can also qualify for benefits from the social welfare system. These are non-contributory, but means tested. The income threshold is set at a very low level (for example, PLN 542 per month (approximately £106) in case of a person living alone and PLN 456 per month (approximately £89) for a person living with their family).[27] However, financially the possibility of not working can hardly be enjoyed. The average amount of social pension is PLN 705.41 per month (approximately £138), which is much less than the minimum wage (PLN 1,680 per month, approximately £329) but too much to be entitled to benefits from the social welfare system. An inability to work pension is higher at an average of PLN 1,541.40 per month (approximately £302) (71.5% of pensions are below PLN 1,600, approximately £314), but it is still below the level of the minimum wage.[28]

The disability benefits noted above are arguably disadvantageous to those disabled people who would like to exercise their right to work. Both types of pensions are, in fact, 'incapability' pensions and are, therefore, only available to people deemed incapable of working. The regulations concerning this matter are not clear and often contradictory. According to Article 12 of the Act on Old-Age and Disability Pensions from the Social Insurance Fund 1998, a person deemed totally incapable of work is unable to do any work. However, the same legal Act suggests that they might work in sheltered living conditions or adapted workplaces (Article 13). Theoretically, it is possible to combine a disability pension with income from work. The pension is reduced when a person earns more than 70% of the average monthly wage and suspended when the earned income exceeds 130% of the average wage. In practice, the SII often uses these contradictions to treat all working disabled people as capable of work,[29] thus depriving them of benefits, which acts as a disincentive to taking up employment (Waszkielewicz, 2012).

The current system does not take into account the extra costs of having a disability. It focuses only on the (in)ability to work. Thus, a disabled person who is in paid employment risks losing their disability benefits. If they do, they are treated as any non-disabled person, despite having to cover all the extra costs related to their disability. If they happen to lose their job, they often find it very difficult to regain the right to disability pensions (Waszkielewicz, 2012). This disincentive effect contributes to the findings about the so-called 'benefit trap' – that 40% of disabled people are afraid of losing their benefits if they take up work (Klyszcz, 2011). However, as we have noted, it is not the case that disability benefits deliver high incomes to disabled people. As is the case in many countries, disabled people are more likely to live in poverty in Poland compared with non-disabled people. So, for example, families with a disabled member face a 21.9% risk of poverty, compared with a 14.6% risk across households without disabled members (CSO, 2013b). This is linked to the low levels of both benefits and wages for disabled people. In 2013, for instance, the inability to work pension was the main source of income for 57.9% of disabled people of working age; only 23% relied mainly on their earned income.[30] In addition, there are disabled people in Poland who are incapable of working, but are not eligible for either the inability to work pension or the social pension (Waszkielewicz, 2012). Those disabled people have to rely on social welfare benefits that, as we have seen, provide only a subsistence income, or on the support of their family.[31]

Disabled people's experiences of paid work in Poland

We have seen that a small proportion (22.4%) of disabled people of working age are in paid employment in Poland. It is estimated that more than 40% of them are employed in the open labour market.[32] The majority of subsidised workplaces (66%) are in the sheltered labour market. There are two types of sheltered workplaces in Poland: sheltered enterprises (*zakłady pracy chronionej*) and vocational activity enterprises (*zakłady aktywności zawodowej*). An employer who employs 25 or more workers may apply for the status of a sheltered enterprise if at least 50% of its employees have a disability (including at least 20% with a significant or moderate degree of disability). In December 2013, there were 1,416 sheltered enterprises in Poland employing over 177,000 disabled people.[33] The primary role of the sheltered enterprises is to create workplaces for people with a significant degree of disability, and who would, therefore, have problems securing employment in the open labour market. However, this role is not being fulfilled. For example, figures from 2013 suggest that open labour market enterprises employ a higher percentage of people with a significant degree of disability (8.4%) compared to the sheltered enterprises (6.2%).[34]

This observation is perhaps not surprising because the role of sheltered enterprises has slowly been decreasing and there is a visible tendency to limit the state's support for them. So, for example, in April 2014, the amount of the subsidies for sheltered enterprises decreased and were made comparable to the level of subsidies available for open market enterprises. This change evoked negative reactions from the sheltered employers, which warned that these changes may lead to a drop in the employment rate of disabled people.[35]

Vocational activity enterprises offer employment to people judged to have a significant degree of disability and, in some cases, also to those judged to have a moderate degree of disability. Their purpose is to prepare disabled people for work in the open labour market through social and vocational rehabilitation and support. They have an important, but still quite a minor, role as they are so few in number. There were only 69 such enterprises, employing 2,655 disabled people, in 2013. The main reasons for such a limited number of these enterprises include:

- problems with financing;[36]
- unfavourable legislation;
- a lack of motivation for the organisers;[37]
- difficulties associated with the application process (PORC, 2009, p 61).

It can be seen that the open market is still not inclusive enough, especially for people with more severe disabilities. In recent years, therefore, there has been an increasing interest in the social enterprise sector as a promising source of employment opportunities for disabled people. In 2004, a new form of cooperative – the social cooperative – was introduced. It is a form of social enterprise aimed at the social and professional (re)integration of its members. A social cooperative can be set up by the people 'in danger of social exclusion' due, among other things, to disability, unemployment, homelessness and/or addiction. In April 2014, there were 1,059 social cooperatives in Poland. There are, however, no data concerning the number of disabled people who are employed by them.

Discrimination and job satisfaction

There are laws protecting disabled people against discrimination in employment – non-discrimination provisions are embodied in the Labour Code and the Act on Employment Promotion and Labour Market Institutions 2004. However, the notion of *reasonable accommodation* was incorporated into the Polish legal system only in 2010. It took 10 years for Poland to adopt EU Council Directive 2000/78/EC (of 27 November 2000), establishing a general framework for equal treatment in employment and occupation.

Employers are often reluctant to employ disabled workers due to misconceptions and stereotypes. They fear that disabled workers will be less productive, more dependent and require costly accommodations (Bartkowski et al, 2009; Kryńska and Pater, 2013). The common stereotypical image of a disabled person as a wheelchair user leads to widespread belief that architectural barriers make it impossible to employ disabled people, regardless of the nature of their disability. However, the group who are felt to be the least employable by employers are blind people, people with mental health problems and learning disabled people (Sobczak, 2007; Bartkowski et al, 2009). It is evident that employers are afraid of employing disabled people as their level of knowledge about disability is very low. It seems, therefore, that there is a need for initiatives aimed at changing employers' attitudes. However, disability awareness training is still quite a new concept in Poland. Although there are training courses for employers, they usually concern the legal regulations governing the employment of disabled people and the possibility of profiting from employing disabled people by drawing on wage subsidies from the SFRDP. Similarly, employers' knowledge about the concept of 'disability management' in the workplace is very low. Less than a third (28%) have heard about it (Bartkowski et al, 2009, p 30).

Research shows that disabled people in Poland still face discrimination when applying for work and during their time in employment (Bartkowski, 2007). Poliwczak (2007), for instance, in her research with 395 disabled people, found that almost 30% had experienced discrimination when applying for a job (for example, not being accepted for a job once disability had been revealed) and almost

17% were discriminated against at work (for example, by receiving lower wages, by experiencing harassment, by encountering prejudice regarding their productivity or by their employer's refusal to respect the additional entitlements of disabled workers[38]). Nevertheless, those disabled people who are in employment almost universally (98%) find it to be an important factor in their lives and are quite satisfied with their work.[39] The level of job satisfaction, however, depends on the degree of disability (the higher the degree of disability, the greater the proportion of people satisfied with their work) and the aspect of work being considered. Disabled workers in Poland are most satisfied with their working conditions and relationships with colleagues and direct superiors, and are least satisfied with their salary, job security and opportunities for promotion and career development (Jajor and Zadrożna, 2010).

Conclusion

As it is known that the situation in the labour market in Poland is difficult and the opportunities for disabled people are not equal to those of non-disabled people, the view that disabled individuals are responsible for their own worklessness is not common. As far as supply-side policies are concerned, the nature of the attempts to raise the employment level of disabled people has been more 'encouraging' than 'pressurising'. However, this situation may soon change as it will be difficult for Poland to achieve the Europe 2020[40] employment rate target without raising disabled people's employment rate. As the demand-side solutions are regarded as expensive and ineffective,[41] the government is likely to concentrate on supply-side solutions, perhaps similar to those implemented in Britain and other countries. This would lead to greater welfare conditionality, which, if experiences in other countries (see, for example, Chapters Two and Three, in this volume) are anything to go by, could have detrimental effects on the situation of those disabled people deemed as 'capable' of working, but who still face substantial barriers to employment. In the current situation, such solutions might leave many disabled people in Poland with even lower incomes and little chance of employment.

Notes

[1] The first draft of the Bill was created by disabled people's organisations in 2008. The government attempted to create its version of the Bill based on this draft. However, there were so many critical comments in the consultation stage that in 2010 it was

decided that a new Bill would be created. There is little to suggest that this has been done (http://orka2.sejm.gov.pl/IZ6.nsf/main/61035664).

[2] However, there are also other definitions of disability. For example, the *Charter of rights of persons with disabilities* defines disabled people as those 'whose physical, mental or intellectual ability either permanently or temporarily impairs, restricts or prevents daily life, education, work and performing social roles, in accordance with the legal and customary standards' (Resolution of the Sejm of 1 August 1997, *Charter of rights of persons with disabilities*, M.P. no 50, item 475).

[3] As far as employment recommendations are concerned, people who are assessed as having significant and moderate degrees of disability are those who are unable to work or able to work only in sheltered working conditions, while those assessed as having a mild degree of disability are those whose ability to work has been significantly reduced by an impairment. However, assessment of a significant or moderate degree of disability does not exclude the possibility of a disabled person being employed by an employer who does not provide sheltered working conditions if they adapt the workplace to the needs of that person or employ the person as a teleworker.

[4] The assessment is also carried out by the Ministry of National Defence and the Ministry of the Interior in the case of uniformed services and their families, and the Agricultural Social Insurance Fund (KRUS) in the case of farmers and their families.

[5] Although the certificates of disability issued by DABs should include various recommendations, they are usually laconic and very general.

[6] The Government Plenipotentiary for Disabled People is the Secretary of State in the Ministry of Labour and Social Policy who supervises the execution of tasks specified by the Act on Vocational and Social Rehabilitation and Employment of Persons with Disabilities 1997 – see www.niepelnosprawni.gov.pl/english-version-/the-government-plenipotentiary-/.

[7] The Supreme Audit Office is the top independent state audit body whose mission is to safeguard public spending – see www.nik.gov.pl/en/about-us/.

[8] www.nik.gov.pl/najnowsze-informacje-o-wynikach-kontroli/nik-o-orzecznictwie-zus.html; http://praca.gazetaprawna.pl/artykuly/683570,powiatowy_system_orzekania_o_niepelnosprawnosci_czeka_reforma.html. Now the SII decides about the right to disability pensions, but the basis for the employment support for disabled people is still the certificates issued by DABs.

[9] In accordance with EUROSTAT recommendations, the unemployment rate relates to the people aged 15 to 74 who are not employed, are actively looking for work and are available to take up work. Only those who have a valid disability certificate are regarded as disabled for the statistics.

[10] The term 'invalids' was widely used until the 1990s when the term 'disabled people' gained popularity and started to appear in legislation and everyday use.

[11] In 1988, there were 3.2 million with a disability certificate, according to the 1988 National Census.

[12] Whereby work was carried out in off-site facilities, usually the homes of workers.

[13] Ninety-six per cent of Polish enterprises are 'micro enterprises' (that is, they employ 10 or fewer employees).

[14] According to the information obtained from the SFRDP, in April 2014, 22,820 employers met the quota while 27,883 employers did not meet the quota and were obliged to contribute to the SFRDP.

[15] In comparison, the minimum wage in Poland in 2014 was PLN 1,680 per month (approximately £329).

[16] These frequent changes may serve as an example of a 'vicious circle of bureaucracy' (Gąciarz and Giermanowska, 2009, p 10).

[17] However, the amount of the monthly subsidy may not exceed 90% of the actual wage costs incurred.

[18] A person with a disability has priority in employment when in a group of no more than five best candidates.

[19] Labour offices are state run. There is no system of private sector employment agencies targeted at disabled people in Poland.

[20] A disabled person may register in the labour offices as unemployed if they are able and willing to accept at least half-time work and they are not entitled to any disability benefits. If a disabled person has the right to a disability pension, they can be registered as a jobseeker not in employment and, thus, may use some services and labour market programmes.

[21] NGOs are defined in Poland as non-profit organisations that are not a part of the public sector. The term encompasses associations and foundations, as well as trades unions, self-regulating organisations and professional associations. It is estimated that there are approximately 80,000 NGOs in Poland. About 10% of these declare that one of the fields of their activities is supporting disabled people (data from http://bazy.ngo.pl).

[22] The aim of this programme is to develop, test and implement uniform procedures for the recruitment, training, monitoring and management of the work of a job coach.

[23] Issues related to the work and social security of disabled people are regulated by various Acts. This hinders their coordination and harmonisation. Moreover, legal regulations are complicated and unstable (as, for example, those related to the rights and duties of employers).

[24] These are at the central level (Ministry of Labour and Social Policy, Government Plenipotentiary for Disabled People and the SFRDP), the regional level (province governors and marshals' offices and their units, including regional labour offices) and at the local level (local governments and their units, including labour offices).

[25] Although there are certain restrictions regarding combining the pension with some other types of benefits or ownership of an agricultural property.

[26] Until they turned 18 or, in the case of students, 25.

[27] In 2013, over 400,000 people claimed social welfare benefits or services because of disability.

[28] All the data are from March 2014.

[29] Kaplan (2000, p 361) notes a similar contradiction in the American law as being 'a catch-22 situation: if the individual has held a job, then this is proof that the individual is not disabled and therefore cannot use the ADA [Americans with Disabilities Act 1994] to seek a remedy for employment discrimination'.

[30] Data from www.niepelnosprawni.gov.pl/niepelnosprawnosc-w-liczbach-/warunki-zycia/

[31] In 2011, for 2.2% of certified disabled people the main source of income was social welfare benefits; for 9.7% it was the support of their family (CSO, 2013a).

[32] www.niepelnosprawni.gov.pl/niepelnosprawnosc-w-liczbach-/rynek-pracy/archiwum-danych-dotyczacch-rynku

[33] www.niepelnosprawni.gov.pl/niepelnosprawnosc-w-liczbach-/dane-od-wojewodow-o-zpch/

[34] The data apply to the employers that received subsidy from the SFRDP – available at www.niepelnosprawni.gov.pl/niepelnosprawnosc-w-liczbach-/sod-pfron/

[35] See the appeal of the Polish Organisation of the Employers of Disabled People – available at www.popon.pl/images/stories/AKTUALNOSCI/pliki_2013/Apel_POPON.pdf

[36] Vocational activity enterprises (VAEs) are financed mainly by the SFRDP and by the local government. Their limited financial resources make it impossible to create more such enterprises. The SFRDP allocated PLN 58 million (approximately £11.8 million) for VAEs in 2013 (SFRPD, 2014).

[37] Vocational activity enterprises may be set up by *municipalities* or *poviats* (both are units of administrative division in Poland), as well as by NGOs.

[38] Workers with moderate or significant degree of disability are entitled to an additional 10 days' leave, to an additional 15 minutes' break per day at work and, in most cases, to shorter working hours (35 instead of 40 hours a week).

[39] Jajor and Zadrożna (2010), for example, found an average score of 7.41 on a 10-point scale, where a score of 1 was very dissatisfied and a score of 10 was very satisfied.

[40] http://ec.europa.eu/europe2020/pdf/themes/18_employment_target.pdf

[41] In 2013 alone, for example, the SFRDP spent PLN 3.2 billion (approximately £65 million) on employment subsidies, which were granted to 24,590 employers (SFRDP, 2014).

References

Arczewska, M., Giermanowska, E. and Racław, M. (2014) 'Pracodawcy i nowy model polityki społecznej wobec aktywności zawodowej osób niepełnosprawnych' [Employers and a new model of social policy towards labour market activity of disabled people], in E. Giermanowska (ed) *Zatrudniając niepełnosprawnych: Dobre praktyki pracodawców w Polsce i innych krajach Europy* [Employing the disabled: Best practices of employers from Poland and other European countries], Cracow: AGH.

Barczyński, A. and Radecki, P. (2008) *Identyfikacja przyczyn niskiej aktywności zawodowej osób niepełnosprawnych* [Identification of the reasons for the low vocational activity of disabled people], www.pfron.org.pl/ftp/dokumenty/EQUAL/Kluczowa_rola_gminy/identyfikacja__przyczyn_niskiej_akt_mozliwosci_przel_barier_zatrudniania.pdf).

Bartkowski, J. (2007) 'Młodzi niepełnosprawni a instytucje i struktury wsparcia' [Young disabled people vs institutions and structures of support], in E. Giermanowska (ed) *Młodzi niepełnosprawni o sobie: Rodzina, edukacja, praca* [Young disabled people about themselves: Family, education, work], Warsaw: ISP.

Bartkowski, J., Gąciarz, B., Giermanowska, E., Kudlik, A. and Sobiesiak, P. (2009) *Pracodawcy o zatrudnianiu osób niepełnosprawnych: Jak jest? Co można zmienić?* [Employers about the employment of disabled people: What is it like? What can be changed?], Warsaw: ISP.

Błaszczak, A. (ed) (2012) 'Najważniejsze wyzwania po ratyfikacji przez Polskę Konwencji ONZ o Prawach Osób Niepełnosprawnych' [The most important challenges for Poland after the ratification of UN Convention on the Rights of Persons with Disabilities], *Biuletyn RPO*, no. 10, Warsaw.

CSO (Central Statistical Office) (2011) *Stan zdrowia ludności Polski w 2009 r.* [State of health of the Polish population in 2009], Warsaw: CSO.

CSO (2013a) *Ludność i gospodarstwa domowe: Stan i struktura społeczno-ekonomiczna: Część I: Ludność* [Population and households: State and socio-economic structure: Part I: Population], Warsaw: CSO.

CSO (2013b) *Household Budget Survey in 2012*, Warsaw: CSO.

Gąciarz, B. and Giermanowska, E. (2009) 'Uwarunkowania skutecznej realizacji polityki integracyjnej wobec osób niepełnosprawnych' [Determinants of effective implementation of integration policies for disabled people], *Analyses and Opinions*, no. 100, The Institute of Public Affairs, www.isp.org.pl/files/11261748260723827001257850019.pdf

Giermanowska, E. (2007) 'Nietypowe formy zatrudnienia – proces instytucjonalizacji zatrudnienia młodych osób niepełnosprawnych na otwartym rynku pracy' [Atypical forms of employment – the process of institutionalization of employment of young disabled people in the open labour market], in E. Giermanowska (ed) *Młodzi niepełnosprawni – aktywizacja zawodowa i nietypowe formy zatrudnienia* [Young disabled people – vocational activation and atypical forms of employment], Warsaw: ISP.

Hulek, A. (1998) *Z dziejów polskiej rehabilitacji inwalidów i innych osób niepełnosprawnych jako służby społecznej* [From the history of rehabilitation of invalids and other disabled people seen as social service], Warsaw-Rzeszów: Polskie Towarzystwo Walki z Kalectwem.

Informacja rządu RP o działaniach podejmowanych w 2012 r. na rzecz realizacji postanowień uchwały Sejmu RP z dnia 1 sierpnia 1997 r. Karta Praw Osób Niepełnosprawnych [Information of the government of the Republic of Poland on the activities undertaken in 2012 in order to implement the Charter of Rights of Persons with Disabilities], Warsaw, 2013.

Jajor, A. and Zadrożna, A. (2010) *Zadowolenie osób niepełnosprawnych z pracy. Raport TNS OBOP dla Państwowego Funduszu Rehabilitacji Osób Niepełnosprawnych* [Job satisfaction of disabled people: The report of PORC for the State Fund for Rehabilitation of Disabled Persons], Warsaw: TNS OBOP.

Jaworski, J. (2009) *Praca dla osób niepełnosprawnych w zwalczaniu ich wykluczenia społecznego: Ocena polskiego systemu wspierania zatrudnienia osób niepełnosprawnych* [Work for disabled people as a way of combating social exclusion: Evaluation of the Polish system of supporting disabled people's employment], Warsaw: IPiSS.

Kaplan, D. (2000) 'The definition of disability. perspective of the disability community', *Journal of Health Care Law and Policy*, 3(2), pp 352-64.

Klyszcz, L. (2011) *Pułapka świadczeniowa a aktywność zawodowa i społeczna osób niepełnosprawnych* [Benefit trap and vocational and social activity of disabled people], Cracow: Fundacja Instytut Rozwoju Regionalnego.

Kryńska, E. and Pater, K. (2013) *Zatrudnienie osób niepełnosprawnych – perspektywy wzrostu* [Employment of disabled people – prospects for growth], Warsaw: IPiSS, https://www.ipiss.com.pl/?projekt-badawczy=publikacje-8

Kutyło, Ł., Stronkowski, P., Wolińska, I. and Zub, M. (2009) *Bariery i możliwości integracji zawodowej osób niepełnosprawnych w województwie podkarpackim: Raport z badań* [Barriers and chances of labour market integration of disabled people in the Podkarpacie region: Research report], Warsaw: WYG International.

Labour Force Survey, data from 1993 to IV quarter of 2013, www. niepelnosprawni.gov.pl/niepelnosprawnosc-w-liczbach-/bael/

Majewski, T. (1995) *Rehabilitacja zawodowa osób niepełnosprawnych* [Vocational rehabilitation of disabled people], Warsaw: CBRON.

Poliwczak, I. (2007) *Wyrównywanie szans osób niepełnosprawnych na rynku pracy* [Giving equal employment opportunities for disabled people], Warsaw: KIG-R.

PORC (*Public Opinion* Research Centre) (2009) *Zakłady Aktywności Zawodowej: Raport z badania TNS OBOP dla Państwowego Funduszu Rehabilitacji Osób Niepełnosprawnych* [Vocational activity enterprises: Research report by PORC for the State Fund for Rehabilitation of Disabled Persons], Warsaw: PORC.

SFRPD (State Fund for Rehabilitation of Disabled Persons) (2014) *Sprawozdanie z realizacji planu rzeczowo-finansowego z działalności Państwowego Funduszu Rehabilitacji Osób Niepełnosprawnych w 2013 roku* [A report on the implementing of the material and financial plan by SFRDP in 2013], Warsaw: SFRPD.

SII (Social Insurance Institution) (2013) *Orzeczenia lekarzy orzeczników ZUS o niezdolności do pracy wydane w 2012 roku* [Certificates concerning work incapacity issued by SII practitioners in 2012], Warsaw: SII.

SII (2014) *Miesięczna informacja o wybranych* świadczeniach *pieniężnych wypłacanych przez ZUS* [Monthly information on selected cash benefits paid by the Social Insurance Institution], Warsaw: SII, www. zus.pl/default.asp?id=5&p=5

Smoczyńska, K. and Sijko, K. (2007) 'Wyniki badań pilotażowych nad aktywnością zawodową osób z ograniczoną sprawnością' [The results of pilot studies concerning vocational activity of disabled people], in A. Brzezińska, Z. Woźniak and K. Maj (eds) *Osoby z ograniczoną sprawnością na rynku pracy* [Disabled people in the labour market], Warsaw: Academica.

Sobczak, W. (2007) 'Postawy pracodawców wobec potrzeb osób niepełnosprawnych' [Attitudes of employers towards the needs of disabled people], in *Potrzeby osób niepełnosprawnych w zakresie aktywizacji zawodowej: Materiały konferencyjne* [The needs of disabled people concerning vocational activation: Conference materials], Warsaw: KIG-R.

Thornton, P. (1998) *Employment quotas, levies and national rehabilitation funds for persons with disabilities: Pointers for policy and practice*, Geneva, Switzerland: International Labour Office, www.ilo.org/skills/pubs/WCMS_106625/lang--en/index.htm

Thornton, P. and Lunt, N. (1995) *Employment for disabled people: Social obligation or individual responsibility?*, York: Social Policy Research Unit.

UN (United Nations) (2006) *Convention on the rights of persons with disabilities*, New York: UN.

Waszkielewicz, A. (2012) *Zabezpieczenie społeczne osób niepełnosprawnych* [Social security for disabled people], in A. Błaszczak (ed) *Najważniejsze wyzwania po ratyfikacji przez Polskę Konwencji ONZ o Prawach Osób Niepełnosprawnych* [The most important challenges for Poland after the ratification of UN Convention on the Rights of Persons with Disabilities], *Biuletyn RPO*, no. 10, Warsaw.

Wolski, P. (2010) 'Potrzeby osób z ograniczeniami sprawności w zakresie aktywizacji zawodowej' [The needs of people with disabilities concerning employment activation], *Polityka Społeczna*, special no., pp 27-30.

Yates, S. and Roulstone, A. (2013) 'Social policy and transitions to training and work for disabled young people in the United Kingdom: neo-liberalism for better and for worse?', *Disability & Society*, 28(4), pp 456-70.

Zub, M., Wolińska, I., Gierwatowski, T. and Omyła, M. (2008) *Ewaluacja zdolności absorpcyjnych system integracji zawodowej osób niepełnosprawnych: Raport końcowy.* [The evaluation of absorption abilities of the vocational integration system for disabled people: Final report], www.pfron.org.pl/portal/pl/70/77/Badania_i_analizy_PFRON.html

Disability and employment in the United States: the intersection of healthcare reform and welfare-to-work policy

Randall Owen, Robert Gould and Sarah Parker Harris

Introduction

Over recent decades, there have been significant policy changes to address the low employment rate of disabled people in the United States (US).[1] As with other liberal welfare states, such changes have been driven by government concerns with rapidly increasing expenditures on income support programmes. Concurrently, there has been increased recognition of the rights of disabled people. In attempts to reconcile these discourses, governments have turned to active social policies, encompassing the idea that rights come with responsibilities, in order to 'activate' people receiving various benefits and encourage labour market participation (Sainsbury, 2001; Humpage, 2007; Parker Harris et al, 2012). The right to access social security and social programmes has been replaced with the obligation to work and earn income as individuals are expected to meet their own needs (Gilbert, 2009). For disabled people in the US, the welfare-to-work agenda is a voluntary programme known as Ticket to Work (TTW). The voluntary nature of this programme is unique among liberal welfare states, which have typically introduced harsher reforms to welfare programmes for disabled people. In the US, disabled people have typically been treated as 'deserving' of welfare assistance. Moreover, healthcare coverage in the US has historically been tied to participation in the labour market (National Council on Disability, 2008). Many disabled people are forced to choose between employment in the labour market or the receipt of benefits, including healthcare, but having a low standard of living.

In 2010, the US adopted the Patient Protection and Affordable Care Act, commonly called the Affordable Care Act (ACA), which expanded access to healthcare services within the Medicaid programme and private insurance companies. The ACA has the potential to positively impact TTW to enable disabled people to participate in the labour market, and receive rights typically afforded on the basis of social citizenship. However, as argued in this chapter, there are several inherent flaws in the ACA's policy framework that limit its impact for disabled people.

Below, we describe the policy context in the US, focusing on neoliberal and rights discourses and their role in active citizenship. We analyse how these discourses have been applied in policy rhetoric of welfare and healthcare reform specific to the TTW and ACA. Finally, the interconnected impact of these reforms is explored, with emphasis placed on neoliberalism and rights within these reforms.

The policy context in the United States

This chapter focuses on the TTW and ACA reforms and how they intertwine. It is important to consider the broader policy context and competing sociopolitical discourses of neoliberalism and rights that have influenced the trajectory of these reforms. In practice, as seen in the discussion below, these discourses are not easily separated, and policies are influenced to some degree by both the rights agenda and the neoliberal agenda. In fact, each agenda uses much of the same rhetoric and has similar goals.

The rights agenda in the United States

In liberal welfare regimes, including in the US, civil rights provide the primary basis for preventing discrimination and ensuring that people are treated as equal citizens. In 1990, the US adopted the Americans with Disabilities Act (ADA), becoming the first country to specifically recognise the civil rights of disabled people and prevent discrimination in employment, public accommodations[2] and other areas. Subsequently, the ADA served as a blueprint for similar legislation in dozens of countries, including disability discrimination Acts in both Australia and in the United Kingdom, in addition to influencing international disability law (Jimenez, 2000). The ADA also informed the development of the United Nations' *Convention on the rights of persons with disabilities* (UN, 2006).

Despite the advanced legal and political rights afforded to disabled people in the US, issues of social rights have not received equal attention. The primary social programmes that disabled people use (for example, Medicaid and Social Security Income) are less a matter of rights than they are of entitlement/social assistance. Consistent with other liberal welfare regimes, the US has a minimal safety net in place, but few universal social programmes. Instead, individuals, including disabled people, qualify for these programmes through various income and asset tests. As Esping-Andersen (1990, 1996) argues, social policy in the US provides safety-net social programmes as a form of 'recommodification' to ameliorate the failures of the market, whereas countries that provide healthcare or income support not contingent upon one's level of employment tend to decommodify paid labour (see Sainsbury, 2001). People are required to meet eligibility criteria in order to receive benefits in the US, and frequently eligibility for mainstream entitlements (Medicare and Social Security Disability Insurance) is predicated on a historical record of contributing to these insurance-based programmes through paid employment.

The neoliberal agenda in the United States

Since the 1970s, the US has pursued a framework consistent with a neoliberal policy agenda: market-based policy solutions are preferred to publicly funded social systems. The goal is to minimise the role of the state and to transfer responsibility of social programmes from the government to the private sector through labour market participation (Peck, 2002; Swenson, 2008). This shift to 'active social policy' implies that people are expected to meet their needs through labour market participation. A minimal social safety net is available under a social contract based on the idea of 'rights and responsibilities'. People have rights to social programmes, but those rights come with responsibilities, namely the responsibility to participate in the labour market (Owen and Parker Harris, 2012).

Harvey (2006, p 145) defines neoliberalism as 'a theory of political economic practices which proposes that human well-being can best be advanced by the maximisation of entrepreneurial freedoms within an institutional framework characterised by private property rights, individual liberty, free markets and free trade'. The state's role is to preserve this framework and create markets where they did not exist before (for instance, by privatising public utilities). Martinez and Garcia (2000) identify five major tenets of neoliberalism:

- the rule of the free market;
- reductions in government expenditures for, and involvement in, social services;

- deregulation;
- privatisation;
- emphasising individual responsibility.

Neoliberalism diminishes the role of the state so that the free market takes a bigger role in public policy and service provision (Harvey, 2006).

Under neoliberal ideology, individual needs are best provided for by participating in the labour market so that individuals are held responsible for meeting their own needs. Many social needs and services, including disability services, have been transformed into a commodity that can be bought and sold like any other. Only people who are able to purchase and access those services can secure them. In brief, neoliberal policies have not provided equal access for everyone.

The sociopolitical shift towards neoliberalism is of particular concern for disabled people because existing economic and environmental barriers remain substantial obstacles to full participation in the open labour market. Currently, many disabled people are unable to obtain economic self-sufficiency through paid labour. Disabled people often require additional income to participate in traditional conceptions of work. This can include redistributive support to enter the paid labour market (that is, wage adjustments or physical accommodations) and traditional welfare provisions, such as supplementary income to pay for the extra costs of impairment and disability. The costs of living as a disabled person or in a family with a disabled person are substantially higher than those of the rest of the population (Fujiura, 2010). The neoliberal reduction of traditional welfare provision marks a significant barrier for disabled people who require financial supports to enter the paid labour market in a social climate that increasingly stigmatises welfare.

Links between the rights agenda and the neoliberal agenda

The rights agenda and the neoliberal agenda come together in contemporary discourses of social citizenship. The shift towards active social policy and the link between rights and responsibilities result in changing definitions of who 'qualifies' for equal citizenship. Welfare reforms since the mid-1990s have shifted rights-based policies so that the liberal conception of citizenship is often conditional on active and full participation in liberal society (Sainsbury, 2001). This shift is indicative of global trends of liberal welfare policy that have made workforce participation the central tenet of social citizenship. Such developments present numerous problems for disabled people who often do not participate as equal citizens in society. The goal of active citizenship in and of itself is not necessarily problematic. Disabled people have long struggled for an enhanced level of participation in all aspects of social living (see Parker Harris, 2007), and the social, attitudinal and physical barriers they face make the prerequisite of workforce participation in order to be perceived as a full citizen problematic (Zola, 1989).

Facilitating access to paid labour is often a vital policy goal for ensuring rights and equal participation in liberal society where there is a 'deeply rooted connection between the ability to exercise social citizenship and participation in waged labour' (MacGregor, 2012). The roots of continued marginalisation in employment and citizenship are often debated, but scholars seldom agree on how to best improve policy and practice. The notion of social citizenship offers a critical lens to understand why such marginalisation continues, even in the context of growing legal protection of rights-based legislation. Disabled people are seldom included as a marginalised group in the broader literature of citizenship (see, for example, Young, 1990; Fraser, 1997, 1998, 2003). The growth of policy that makes labour force participation the primary indicator of social citizenship reflects this exclusion, through the key policy reforms to employment and health policy.

Policy reforms in the United States

Welfare to work

In the US, welfare-to-work policy for the non-disabled population incentivises paid labour by limiting the availability of various publicly funded out-of-work social assistance programmes. Support for these reforms was based on the rhetoric of 'welfare dependence' among poor Americans and evidence of low labour force participation of impoverished individuals, particularly as a consequence of Reagan-era politics (Clarke and Piven, 2001). The discourse of welfare to work suggests that reducing publicly funded supplementary income support and other benefits (including healthcare), which are viewed as disincentives to enter the labour market, will enhance open labour market participation and stimulate economic self-sufficiency (Levy et al, 2013). The Clinton administration formalised the concept of 'welfare to work' in the mid-1990s by terminating the longstanding federal cash transfer, Aid to Families with Dependent Children (AFDC), with the goal of 'ending welfare as we know it' (Clinton, 2006). The Personal Responsibility and Work Opportunity Reconciliation Act

1996 (PRWORA) replaced AFDC and shifted control of many publicly funded welfare services from the federal system to individual states. Unlike AFDC programmes, PRWORA framed welfare programmes with time limits and work requirements. In order to maintain eligibility for benefits, recipients must participate in employment programmes and/or meet other requirements, such as applying for a certain number of jobs each week.

The PRWORA has had a limited impact on disabled people, partially because disabled people have been viewed as a special, separate and passive population of welfare recipients (Bagenstos, 2009) – part of the 'deserving poor' who merited the provision of aid as an act of charity (Diller, 1998). While some advocates see these depictions as necessary to protect basic social rights, these paternalistic ideas have contributed to an entrenched stigmatisation of disabled people. In contrast, the PRWORA primarily targeted marginalised groups, such as single black mothers, who faced growing levels of stigma for receiving welfare during the 1980s and 1990s (Gordon, 1994). It was not until the implementation of the Ticket to Work and Work Incentives Improvement Act in 1999 that welfare-to-work policy in the US was expanded to also include disabled people as a target population for increasing open labour market participation.

A key difference between 'mainstream' workfare (and welfare to work for disabled people in other countries) and the TTW programme is that the latter is voluntary. However, for people who choose to take advantage of the programme, the goals are the same as for mainstream workfare programmes – to promote economic self-sufficiency through transitioning from benefit programmes into paid participation in the labour market and to increase the available choices of service options (Livermore et al, 2012). These goals align neatly with the neoliberal agenda in the US.

The TTW programme is available to both Social Security Disability Insurance (SSDI) and Supplemental Security Income (SSI) beneficiaries. As the name implies, SSDI is a social insurance programme that provides income to disabled people with substantial work history to replace earnings that they have lost because they cannot work (Wittenburg and Favreault, 2003). SSI is an income related programme available to people, regardless of work history, on the basis of low income. From their inceptions, these programmes have made distinctions between people who have worked and people who have not (Clarke and Piven, 2001). This is an important development for current policy that favours people who have participated in the labour market as deserving of social assistance with more generous benefits. The SSDI and SSI programmes are based on a policy principle that assumes a permanent incapacity to work, and this 'all-or-nothing' nature creates challenges to promoting employment or welfare-to-work reforms (Golden et al, 2014).

Cultural barriers compound these policy challenges. Disabled people must engage with the contradictory position of seeking paid labour while combating the stigmatisation of receiving benefits, specifically the misconception of being unable to work (Bagenstos, 2009). At the crux of this paradox is the dominant discourse that open labour market participation is a central, necessary and desirable outcome of social citizenship.

In line with this discourse, TTW aims to:

- provide disabled people with more opportunities to participate in employment;
- reduce disincentives and inherent risks in transitioning from income support to employment;
- increase individual financial wellbeing, while decreasing dependence on welfare benefits.

TTW encourages disabled people to seek work by offering a virtual ticket to SSI and SSDI beneficiaries which can be redeemed for skills training, employment and benefits counselling, and transition services.

However, the design of TTW has kept it from being effective. For example, disabled people receive services through an Employer Network (EN), which consists of private organisations and state service providers that provide these services in return for reimbursement from the federal government. The reimbursement arrangements for ENs primarily reward outcomes. ENs receive increased and more timely reimbursements for working with an individual who achieves employment 'milestones' (National Consortium for Health Systems Development, 2009). Incentivised successful labour outcomes may appear preferential for those who want to enter the labour market, but there is limited room for ENs to be reimbursed for participants obtaining outcomes that disabled people prefer, including part-time employment (Stapleton et al, 2008). Hence, ENs forcibly engage with the goal of obtaining full-time employment for beneficiaries that they choose to work with.

The outcome-based payment structure impacts disabled people's choice and satisfaction. Participation in TTW is partially up to disabled people, but they also have to locate an EN willing to work with them. Thus, the degree to which TTW embodies the right's agenda (that is, choice) is limited by the neoliberal agenda. ENs have been criticised for only working with their conceptions of the most employable disabled people and ignoring people who may need additional supports to enter the open labour market (often referred to as 'creaming') (Altshuler et al, 2011; see also Chapter Four, this volume). Given the focus on full employment outcomes, ENs have little incentive to work with people who might take longer to become 'self-sufficient', or who may not want to transition from benefits entirely. Even after changes intended to address problems with this reimbursement process, there has not been a significant increase in TTW participants who achieve their work goals (Livermore et al, 2012).

In its 15 years of existence, TTW has achieved mixed results with regards to employment outcomes for disabled people and it has been difficult to draw overall conclusions. Early studies showed low enrolment, few positive outcomes and a dwindling number of participating ENs (Altshuler et al, 2011). Stapleton et al (2014) note that, since the 2008 changes, the only conclusive outcome data indicate that the increased mailing of tickets is gradually increasing service enrolment. Their study also found that there is little evidence to suggest increased employment outcomes, and only minimal evidence that enrolees spend more months off benefits. Poor employment outcomes may be attributed partially to the low use of TTW. As of December 2010, only about 2.4% of eligible SSI/SSDI beneficiaries had used their ticket (Prenovitz et al, 2012).

There is still the question of how TTW impacts the experiences of disabled people in terms of enabling their rights as citizens. The 2008 policy changes expanded the programme to include a wider range of people and addressed low enrolment by increasing financial incentive for ENs. Livermore et al (2012) reveal that, following the changes, new enrolees were less likely to be employed and more likely to have unmet service needs than previous cohorts of enrolees. The authors note several compounding factors that prevent attributing the lower participation rate entirely to the policy, including the increased support needs of enrolees (the programme expanded to people with more significant impairments who were less likely to have worked) and the broader effects of the post-2008 recession in the US. Although we cannot blame the inadequacy of TTW for the low employment participation rate of disabled people, it is still of note to consider the ongoing negative effects of the political economic system and the barriers it erects to full participation for disabled people.

Other factors not explored in longitudinal data on TTW outcomes can also help to explain the low rate of positive outcomes and satisfaction of disabled people with their TTW experiences. Qualitative research on welfare to work in the US supports many of the quantitative findings. Parker Harris et al (2013) conducted a series of focus groups with disabled people about the TTW programme. Most of the participants noted their frustration with employment accommodations and services, and the general lack of information available to themselves and potential employers. Nearly all of the participants mentioned their confusion with the myriad benefit programmes available and frustration trying to navigate them. While the confusion over the impact of employment on various benefits programmes is common in liberal welfare states, beneficiaries in the US have an added layer of complexity when it comes to the transition into employment because of the link between welfare programmes and healthcare (Parker Harris et al, 2012). This link is a substantial concern for people considering the transition into the labour market, with some choosing not to try to enter the labour market because of their fears about losing their healthcare benefits.

Healthcare reform

In the US, among people of working age (aged 18-64), 2.5 million (16.6%) of disabled people do not have health insurance (United States Census Bureau, 2012). Non-disabled people are more likely than disabled people to be uninsured (38.2 million people, or 21.5%). However, disabled people are more likely to be enrolled with public healthcare programmes, such as Medicaid (29.6%) or Medicare (23.4%) than non-disabled people (1% and 5.7% respectively) (Erickson et al, 2010). Together, Medicaid and Medicare provide health insurance to 100 million people. Recently, Medicaid outgrew Medicare and became the government insurance programme that covered the largest number of people (50.9 million people compared with 48.9 million for Medicare in 2011) (United States Census Bureau, 2012).

Medicare is a federally run programme and covers people over the age of 65 and some disabled people. People who receive SSDI are eligible for Medicare, which includes coverage for hospital attendance, medically necessary treatment and prescription drugs. In general, Medicare covers more services and pays providers higher rates than Medicaid, and its status as an 'earned entitlement' means that Medicare recipients are not stigmatised (Grogan and Patashnik, 2003). On the other hand, people who receive SSI are eligible for Medicaid, which is a network of health insurance programmes run by individual states. It is a programme for low-income individuals and families that covers a range of services, including medical services, equipment and nursing home costs. Unlike Medicare where benefits and services are consistent across the US, Medicaid's structure means that a health benefit or service covered in one state may not be in another. Medicaid is often referred to as 'welfare medicine' (Grogan and Patashnik, 2003; Stevens and Stevens, 2003), emphasising that the programme is one of assistance to poor people and is often stigmatised like other social assistance programmes.

In 2010, President Obama passed the Patient Protection and Affordable Care Act, the most significant reform to the healthcare insurance system to date. The ACA requires all people in the US to have health insurance and aims to improve access to health insurance through two primary methods. First, individual states can create 'health exchanges', which allow people to purchase a variety of private insurance plans with a federal subsidy. Second, states can expand their Medicaid programmes to include people who earn higher incomes (discussed below). While states can choose to expand Medicaid or not, the federal government encourages them to do so by covering a large portion of Medicaid expenses for the first two years for new enrolees. The ACA contains a detailed description of 'essential health benefits' that all insurance plans must offer and eliminates insurance companies' capacity to charge higher premiums or deny coverage because of pre-existing health conditions.

While it is too early to know how much of an impact the ACA will have, estimates prior to implementation suggested that 21.3 million people would benefit, including almost 10 million people who will become eligible for Medicaid (United States Census Bureau, 2012). It is difficult to forecast how many disabled people this includes and Kenney et al (2012) note the difficulty of identifying the overall population in the available data.

Healthcare reform and welfare to work

The ACA has the potential to remove many healthcare policy barriers that disabled people face and address concerns with access to healthcare that disabled people experience under welfare to work. These potentialities relate to the possibility of decoupling healthcare from participation in the labour market under the ACA. These include:

- expanding Medicaid eligibility;
- making health insurance available through health exchanges;
- promoting equal access to health insurance.

Expanding Medicaid eligibility

The ACA helps to improve access to healthcare by allowing individual states to offer Medicaid benefits to individuals who earn up to 138% of the federal poverty level (as opposed to the previous 100%). In the first few years of the programme, the federal government is to cover the additional costs of expanded Medicaid eligibility before costs begin to balance out between federal and state governments in later years. The implication for welfare to work is that people can now earn more money and maintain eligibility for Medicaid. Even for people participating in a Medicaid Buy-In programme (an option where working disabled people can purchase Medicaid services), they now have more flexibility, and do not have to monitor their monthly income as closely, to determine the impact of extra employment on Medicaid benefits.

Expanded Medicaid eligibility appears to align with the rights agenda and provide benefits to a wider range of individuals. However, the neoliberal agenda is also strongly influencing the process of expansion. In the US, devolution, which transfers power from a centralised government to state, and local control, is critical to neoliberalism (Peck, 2014). By giving states the option to extend Medicaid, the federal government transfers its power to provide healthcare to them. As of March 2014, 19 states had declined to expand Medicaid (Kaiser Commission on Medicaid and the Uninsured, 2014). Therefore, the expanded Medicaid eligibility is not available to all. The neoliberal shift to decentralise eligibility criteria creates challenges for disabled people who seek equal access to the open labour market. Grossman (2013; see also Shapiro, 2013), for example, suggests the fact that eligibility criteria for Medicaid services vary between states creates barriers to full and equal citizenship for disabled people. Their ability to work, seek better jobs and fully participate in the open labour market is diminished because of restrictions on moving between states.

Creating health exchanges

Other changes within recent healthcare reform are similarly framed within discourses that suggest a rights approach, but which also encapsulate neoliberal reform. To facilitate the individual purchase of healthcare plans, the ACA created health exchanges (also known as 'health marketplaces') where, as previously mentioned, individuals can purchase healthcare insurance from private providers. Health exchanges enhance access to healthcare provision, but also bring challenges for disabled people that are indicative of neoliberalism. For people earning up to 400% of the federal poverty level, federal subsidies to purchase insurance are available, which aim to ensure that all people have the opportunity to purchase affordable health insurance. The guarantee that health insurance will be available means that many people, notably disabled people, have additional flexibility with the choices that they can make. They no longer have to wait for jobs that include healthcare benefits, which may help to curtail many disabled people's fears of losing health benefits (see Parker Harris et al, 2012). TTW beneficiaries can arguably accept a wider range of jobs because they can find health insurance through a health exchange.

Similarly, and especially important for disabled people, this wider access to healthcare insurance helps to make full-time employment less of a concern and necessity. In the past, many disabled people only found it worthwhile to work if they were able to obtain a job that came with healthcare, which typically meant working full time. However, access to health exchanges and federal subsidies means people can accept part-time employment and still be assured access to healthcare. Further, the availability of the health exchanges gives disabled people more flexibility when it comes to switching employment and avoiding 'job lock'. Previously, disabled people with employer-sponsored healthcare found it difficult to leave paid labour, be temporarily employed, switch careers or move into part-time employment because they would lose that insurance. This aspect of the ACA offers a step towards advancing the rights of disabled people by increasing access to care and mobility within the labour market.

However, the mechanism used to promote these rights is again reticent of neoliberal reform. By creating a new market for people to buy healthcare insurance, as noted earlier as a hallmark of neoliberalism, the US is privatising responsibility for providing solutions to a social problem. The rhetoric of expanded choice and rights obfuscates the role of private insurance in the ACA.

Promoting equal access to health insurance

The ACA also includes an 'individual mandate' that requires all individuals to have health insurance. This mandate is strongly rooted in neoliberal discourse because the mandate is primarily met through involvement in markets (either the labour market or health exchanges). However, the mandate's impact also mirrors key concepts of rights and the language may not appear particularly neoliberal. Specifically, the mandate is predicated on increased opportunities for universal access, which reflects a principal goal of rights – equal opportunity and access to healthcare. Disabled people have more opportunities to choose alternative pathways to employment as healthcare becomes more decoupled from employment. While the ACA did not specifically aim for this decoupling, it is closely related to the ACA's primary goal of increasing access to health insurance. This benefits disabled people seeking careers, rather than just jobs. However, consistent with neoliberal discourse, disabled people are still presented with a choice between employment in the open labour market (so that they can afford the individual mandate to have health insurance) or receiving Medicaid (and, therefore, living at or below the poverty line).

Because of the mandate to have health insurance, and the importance of non-discrimination in general, the ACA prohibits the denial of such insurance on the basis of pre-existing conditions. This applies to the health exchanges and private insurance, including employer-based insurance. This provision should increase the number of disabled people with health insurance. Similar to the discussion in the preceding section, the individual mandate offers additional flexibility to disabled people who no longer need to rely on employer-sponsored healthcare. This provides more flexibility for disabled people to find new or alternative employment and not remain in their current employment situation because it provides health insurance.

Conclusion

The US continues to face complex policy challenges in attempts to bridge healthcare and employment policies for disabled people. The discourse of active citizenship resonates with recent attempts to improve the rights of disabled people by increasing access to a variety of employment and healthcare options. Concurrently, policy reforms present the active citizenship model through adherence to a neoliberal agenda that excludes universal healthcare and further entrenches market rationality and privatisation within public service provision. The ACA reforms are a necessary step towards decoupling healthcare benefits from labour market participation, but fall short of the provision of healthcare as a matter of right. This limits the impact that both welfare to work and health care reform has on disabled people. While it is likely that disabled people will have increased access to healthcare insurance following the ACA, it is not yet clear whether this will result in improved employment outcomes (if, indeed, that is even a desired goal for disabled people).

Similar to other liberal welfare regimes, the policy context in the US is embedded within competing policy ideologies. The US faces an additional policy challenge (healthcare) to welfare reforms, such as TTW. Historically, US policy forces disabled people to choose between welfare (and Medicaid eligibility) and work. If a person chooses work, they face an additional choice of the type/quality of employment available to them. The available employment situations generally fit one of three tiers:

1. work that offers employer-sponsored healthcare;
2. work that pays a decent wage but is not accompanied with healthcare;
3. a job that pays wages at a low level near the poverty line so that they qualify for Medicaid.

The rhetoric of both welfare to work and healthcare reform set the precedent of 'choice' under the guise of rights as one of their central components. However, in practice, the choices available to disabled people are restricted to the first and third tiers of employment. The second tier does not offer many opportunities for disabled people to obtain healthcare. Restrictions on pre-existing conditions and high premiums typically preclude them from private insurance. Hence, reforms in the ACA, especially the introduction of health exchanges and the elimination of discrimination on the basis of pre-existing conditions, have the potential to expand employment options for disabled people. Still, the influence of neoliberal discourse on the ACA makes it important to monitor its impact on disabled people.

Notes

[1] In May 2014, for example, the employment rate for working-age people was 25.8% for disabled people and 71.7% for non-disabled people (Bureau of Labor Statistics, 2014).

[2] 'Public accommodations' is an ADA term referring to places the public might visit (usually businesses, for example stores and restaurants). It includes places – such as websites – that people may visit virtually.

References

Altshuler, N., Prenovitz, S., O'Day, B. and Livermore, G. (2011) *Provider experiences under the revised Ticket to Work regulations*, Washington, DC: Mathematica Policy Research.

Bagenstos, S. (2009) *Law and the contradictions of the disability rights movement*, New Haven, CT: Yale University Press.

Bureau of Labor Statistics (2014) *Table A-6: Employment status of the civilian population by sex, age, and disability status, not seasonally adjusted*, Washington, DC: U.S. Bureau of Labor Statistics, www.bls.gov/news.release/empsit.t06.htm

Clarke, J. and Piven, F. (2001) 'United States: an American welfare state', in P. Alcock and G. Craig (eds) *International social policy*, New York, NY: Palgrave Macmillan.

Clinton, B. (2006) 'How we ended welfare, together', *New York Times*, 22 August, www.nytimes.com/2006/08/22/opinion/22clinton.html

Diller, M. (1998) 'Dissonant disability policies: the tensions between the Americans with Disabilities Act and federal disability benefits programs', *Texas Law Review*, 76(5), pp 1003-82.

Erickson, W., Lee, C. and von Schrader, S. (2010) *2008 disability status report: Illinois*, Ithaca, NY: Cornell University Rehabilitation Research and Training Center on Disability Demographics and Statistics.

Esping-Andersen, G. (1990) *The three worlds of welfare capitalism*, Cambridge: Polity Press.

Esping-Andersen, G. (1996) 'After the Golden Age? Welfare state dilemmas in a global economy', in G. Esping-Andersen (ed) *Welfare states in transition: National adaptations in global economies*, London: Sage Publications.

Fraser, N. (1997) *Justice Interruptus: Critical reflections on the 'postsocialist' condition*, New York, NY: Routledge.

Fraser, N. (1998) 'From redistribution to recognition? Dilemmas of justice in a post-socialist age', in A. Phillips (ed) *Feminism and politics*, Oxford: Oxford University Press.

Fraser, N. (2003) 'Social justice in the age of identity politics: redistribution, recognition, and participation', in N. Fraser and A. Honneth (eds) *Redistribution or recognition? A political-philosophical exchange*, London: Verso.

Fujiura, G.T. (2010) 'Aging families and the demographics of family financial support of adults with disabilities', *Journal of Disability Policy Studies*, 20(4), pp 241-50.

Gilbert, N. (2009) 'US welfare reform: rewriting the social contract', *Journal of Social Policy*, 38(3), pp 383-99.

Golden, T.P., Zeitzer, I. and Bruyère, S.M. (2014) 'New approaches to disability in social policy: the case of the United States', in T. Dereli, Y.P. Soykut-Sarica and A. Sen-Tasbasi (eds) *Labor and employment relations in a globalized world*, New York, NY: Springer International Publishing.

Gordon, L. (1994) *Pitied but not entitled: Single mothers and the history of welfare, 1890-1935*, New York, NY: Free Press.

Grogan, C. and Patashnik, E. (2003) 'Between welfare medicine and mainstream entitlement: Medicaid at the political crossroads', *Journal of Health Politics, Policy and Law*, 28(5), pp 821-58.

Grossman, B.R. (2013) 'Locked in state: how Medicaid creates barriers to cross-state movement for people with disabilities', presentation at the annual meeting of the American Sociological Association, New York, NY.

Harvey, D. (2006) 'Neo-liberalism as creative destruction', *Geografiska Annaler*, 88B(2), pp 145-58.

Humpage, L. (2007) 'Models of disability, work and welfare in Australia, *Social Policy and Administration*, 41(3), pp 215-31.

Jimenez, R. (2000) 'The Americans with Disabilities Act and its impact on international and Latin-American law', *Alabama Law Review*, 52, pp 419-23.

Kaiser Commission on Medicaid and the Uninsured (2014) *Current status of state Medicaid expansion decisions*, Oakland, CA: Kaiser Family Foundation, http://kff.org/health-reform/slide/current-status-of-the-medicaid-expansion-decision/

Kenney, G.M., Zuckerman, S. and Dubay, L. (2012) *Opting in to the Medicaid expansion under the ACA: Who are the uninsured adults who could gain health insurance coverage?*, Princeton, NJ: Robert Wood Johnson Founation.

Levy, A., Bruen, B. and Ku, L. (2013) 'The potential employment impact of health reform on working-age adults with disabilities', *Journal of Disability Policy Studies*, 24(2), pp 102-12.

Livermore, G., Hoffman, D. and Bardos, M. (2012) *Ticket to Work participant characteristics and outcomes under the revised regulations*, Washington, DC: Mathematica Policy Research.

MacGregor, M. (2012) 'Citizenship in name only: constructing meaningful citizenship through a recalibration of the values attached to waged labor', *Disability Studies Quarterly*, 32(3), http://dsq-sds.org/article/view/3282/3116

Martinez, E. and Garcia, A. (2000) *What is 'neo-liberalism'? A brief definition*, www.globalexchange.org/campaigns/econ101/neoliberalDefined.html

National Consortium for Health Systems Development (2009) *At-a-glance: The final Ticket to Work regulations*, Chicago, IL: HDA.

National Council on Disability (2008) *The state of 21st century financial incentives for Americans with Disabilities*, Washington, DC: National Council on Disability.

Owen, R. and Parker Harris, S. (2012) '"No rights without responsibilities": disability rates and neoliberal forms under New Labour', *Disability Studies Quarterly*, 32(3), http://dsq-sds.org/article/view/3283

Parker Harris, S. (2007) 'Searching for the absent citizen: enabling and disenabling discourses of disability', *Australian Journal of Human Rights*, 12(2), pp 1-25.

Parker Harris, S., Owen, R. and Gould, R. (2012) 'Parity of participation in liberal welfare states: human rights, neoliberalism, disability and employment', *Disability & Society*, 27(6), pp 823-36.

Parker Harris, S., Owen, R., Jones, R. and Caldwell, K. (2013) 'Does workfare policy in the United States promote the rights of people with disabilities?', *Journal of Vocational Rehabilitation*, 39(1), pp 61-3.

Peck, J. (2002) 'Political economies of scale: fast policy, interscalar relations, and neoliberal workfare', *Economic Geography*, 78(3), pp 311-60.

Peck, J. (2014) 'Pushing austerity: state failure, municipal bankruptcy and the crises of fiscal federalism in the USA', *Cambridge Journal of Regions, Economy and Society*, 7(1), pp 17-44.

Prenovitz, S., Bardos, M. and O'Day, B. (2012) *Ticket to Work after the release of the 2008 revised regulations: Progress and prospects*, Washington, DC: Mathematica Policy Research, Inc.

Sainsbury, D. (2001) 'Review essay: welfare state challenges and responses: institutional and ideological resilience or restructuring', *Acta Sociologica*, 44, pp 257-65.

Shapiro, J. (2013) *Why a young man died in a nursing home, a state away from his mom*, blog, www.npr.org/blogs/health/2013/01/15/169457118/why-a-young-man-died-in-a-nursing-home-a-state-away-from-his-mom

Stapleton, D., Livermore, G., Thornton, C., O'Day, B., Weathers, R. and Harrison, K. (2008) *Ticket to Work at the crossroads: A solid foundation with an uncertain future*, Washington, DC: Mathematica Policy Research, Inc.

Stapleton, D., Mamun, A. and Page, J. (2014) 'Initial impacts of the Ticket to Work program: estimates based on exogenous variation in Ticket mail months', *IZA Journal of Labor Policy*, 3(1), www.izajolp.com/content/3/1/6

Stevens, R. and Stevens, R. (2003) *Welfare medicine in America: A case study of Medicaid*, New Brunswick, NJ: Transaction Publishers.

Swenson, S. (2008) 'Neoliberalism and human services: threat and innovation', *Journal of Intellectual Disability Research*, 52(7), pp 626-33.

UN (United Nations) (2006) *Convention on the rights of persons with disabilities*, New York, NY: UN.

United States Census Bureau (2012) 'Health insurance status by sex and age: 2011', www.census.gov/population/age/data/2011comp.html

Wittenburg, D. and Favreault, M. (2003) *Safety net or tangled web: An overview of programs and services for adults with disabilities*, Washington, DC: The Urban Institute.

Young, I.M. (1990) *Justice and the politics of difference*, Princeton, NJ: Princeton University Press.

Zola, I.K. (1989) 'Toward the necessary universalizing of a disability policy', *The Milbank Quarterly*, 67(2, 2), pp 401-28.

EIGHT

Social dialogue, partnership and the Danish model of activation of disabled people: challenges and possibilities in the face of austerity

David Etherington and Jo Ingold

Introduction

The number of people claiming sickness benefits has risen considerably across countries of the Organisation for Economic Co-operation and Development (OECD) and employment rates for those with a disability average around half of those without (OECD, 2009). In response to the increasing numbers of older workers and those with long-term health conditions receiving out-of-work benefits and the accompanying increase in public expenditure, most developed countries have reformed their welfare states to 'activate' these groups and to facilitate their entry into the labour market. These policy shifts have been characterised as 'neoliberal workfare', whereby entitlements to benefits are restricted and benefit claimants are subject to tighter work-focused conditions (Peck, 2001).

In the 2000s, the Danish 'activation' model was transformed towards stronger 'work first' principles, but has retained key traditional elements of social dialogue, with a particular emphasis on trade union representation and negotiated rights and duties for unemployed people. In particular, the Danish welfare reforms of 2013 promote co-production and an increasing 'ownership' by people on sickness benefits through user involvement in multi-agency services (Bredgaard, 2013). In Denmark, local government (and the elected representative political process) is responsible for running jobcentres and activation programmes. Social dialogue and partnerships are regulated through local employment committees (*Lokal Beskaeftelses Rad* – LBRs) in the municipalities, which include employers, trade unions and disability advisers as social partners (Damgaard and Torfing, 2010). The role of LBRs is to advise and monitor jobcentre performance, providing a link between benefit recipients, trade union officials and disability organisations. The trade unions have traditionally been key actors in the Danish labour market model through their representation on tripartite bodies and through management of unemployment insurance (UI) funds (Bredgaard and Larsen, 2008; Etherington, 2008).

The aim of this chapter is to explore the influence of social dialogue on activation for disabled people, looking at the emerging tensions arising from an increasing orientation towards workfare, which poses challenges to corporatism and the influence of the social partners on policy. Specifically, the chapter will:

- outline the reforms of the 2000s, involving a more work-first orientated strategy for disabled people;
- analyse the devolution and municipalisation of activation and the shift to multi-agency approaches embedded in the 2013 reforms;
- assess the impact of austerity and more intensified work-first-based interventions on the Danish welfare 'consensus'.

Theoretical reflections on the Danish 'Nordic' model

The theoretical starting point draws on a Marxist perspective of the state as a social relation and state intervention as contingent on a balance of class and social forces (Etherington and Jones, 2004). In this respect, we conceptualise policy as a continually negotiated and contested process in which power interest groups and their actions influence outcomes. In this approach to the state, active labour market policies (ALMPs) are shaped by a number of functional imperatives in the reproduction of capitalism. Of importance is the requirement to manage a reserve army of labour to control labour supply and to secure its social reproduction. Key to this is 'the role played by the institutions and actors representing civil society in the priority-setting process and the historically-institutionalised agreements between them (consensus, conflict, cooperation, competitiveness)' (Revilla and Pascual, 2007, p 5). This focus on forms of political mobilisation and institutions also enables an understanding of the links between industrial relations and welfare systems (Trampusch, 2006; Clegg and van Wijnbergen, 2011). Contemporary moves towards 'workfare' can be seen as a further development in the process of managing the reserve army of labour, promising a more 'active' management of the labour market instead of – or in addition to – the relatively passive approach implied by the notion of 'social security'. It builds on the disciplinary aspects of social security to offer ways of not only bringing labour into employment but also developing labour to fit more closely with the specific needs of particular industrial sectors or local employers.

Jessop (2002) argues that there has been a decisive shift, involving the creation of a Schumpeterian 'workfare' state across the developed capitalist world. State restructuring involves 'rescaling': the national scale is no longer the sole source of political and policy power, and governance and policy formation is shifted upwards, outwards and downwards. This devolution to localities is important because ALMPs are increasingly designed in closer proximity to their sites of implementation, taking account of local labour market conditions and inherited institutional and governance structures and relations (Peck, 2002). Such scalar shifts often involve a reordering of relations between different levels and responsibilities for socioeconomic governance. However, in some contexts this can increase the centralisation and control functions of the state and undermine locally based innovations (Jessop, 2002). This process of state decentralisation within the context of a more neoliberal and market-based politics involves new forms of interventions and categorisation of marginalised groups, as well as the outsourcing of employment services (van Berkel and Borghi, 2007). This process of state restructuring involves tensions and conflict and the reordering of power geometries and structures of negotiation with respect to central and local actor relations.

Danish social democracy and the Nordic model were born of mass struggle at the end of the 19th century. This established the trade union movement's rights to association and representation in policy decision making through the creation of tripartite bodies, and led to a series of welfare reforms embracing social insurance, health and universal benefits (Lind, 1996; Etherington and Jones, 2004). Furthermore, the active role of the women's movement within the trade union and labour movements was crucial in defending redistribution, the universal components of social policies and the design of policies such as maternity rights and comprehensive childcare. The state's assumption of caring roles otherwise performed by the family (that is, women) has been crucial in facilitating women's access to the labour market. This strong basis for social solidarity within the welfare model has also informed policies for disabled people and the integration of occupational health within municipal social and health interventions (Etherington and Ingold, 2012).

Several institutional factors have contributed to the maintenance of relatively high levels of union membership and density (70-80% of employees) in the Nordic countries, even after the culmination of post-war unionisation in Europe in the 1970s. First, the presence and wide-ranging functions of unions in the workplace have facilitated acceptance and support of unions as a 'matter of fact' in Nordic working lives (Dølvik, 2008). Collective bargaining agreements cover wages and all issues around working conditions, with a co-determination system and co-determination committees at the occupational, as well as the local, level. Social partners establish general wage scales and terms and conditions at the overall level (state, region or municipalities), which are then integrated into individual agreements for different occupations (Mailand, 2012). Second, all the Nordic countries (except Norway) have unemployment benefit systems administered by the trade unions (the 'Ghent system'). In Denmark this has a long history – the trade unions have managed UI benefits since the 1930s, with benefits being based on individual contributions through employment. In the event of unemployment, claimants receive their benefit from the UI office, which tends to be run by the relevant trade union. Social assistance and disability benefits are managed by the municipalities, with the level negotiated by trade unions via the social partners at the national level.

Activation and institutional and policy changes

In Denmark, labour market policies have undergone a number of changes, which for the purposes of this chapter can be grouped into four key phases (summarised in Table 8.1):

1. the reforms of 1994;
2. the neoliberal turn in the 2000s;
3. the 2007–10 'municipalisation' of activation;
4. the reforms of the Social Democratic government since 2011.

A central strategic framework for Denmark's labour market policy has been the pursuance of 'flexicurity', based on securing the objectives of relatively generous social protection (income security), flexibility for recruitment and rationalisation of employment (in terms of workplace regulation), accompanied by strong ALMPs that assist in improving labour mobility (Bredgaard, 2012). The Danish model is considered to be a successful hybrid of the flexible labour markets of the liberal welfare states and generous social protection characteristics of the Nordic welfare regimes (Kongshøj Madsen, 2013a, 2013b).

Table 8.1: Development of activation programmes for people receiving sickness benefits in Denmark

Timeframe	ALMPs	Governance structures
Late 1990s	1998 – development of flex-jobs scheme for people on disability pension Subsidised employment with personal adviser support	Regional labour market councils involving social partners Coordinating committees at the local authority level for developing inclusive labour market policy for people in receipt of long-term benefits
2002–04	2002 – 'More People in Work' – strategy focused on long-term unemployed people and people with disabilities 2003 – introduction of the 'ability to work' assessment to determine eligibility for Disability Pension or Flex-Jobs/other employment initiatives	Danish Council for Disabled People joins National Labour Market Councils as a partner
2005–06	2006 – welfare agreement – 'New Roads to Employment' programme of initiatives targeting people with mental health problems Creation of fund for occupational health and prevention, and more intensive local authority casework support	
2007–12	2007 – municipal reforms in which local authority-run jobcentres are responsible for all active labour market programmes (in place by 2009) Increasing role of personal advisers and conditions on access to benefit Tightening of ability to work through categorisation of unemployed people	Regional Employment Council (steered by social partners) oversees running of local employment councils (also steered by social partners), monitors and advises Municipal jobcentres responsible for activation strategies for uninsured and insured unemployed people Increase in use of private contractors in delivery
2013	Scaling down of subsidised employment and greater reliance on conditionality and targeted service delivery for sickness benefit claimants	Focus on multi-agency coordination of support for sickness benefit recipients and increasing emphasis on involving recipients through co-production of rehabilitation plans

The labour market reforms of 1994

In 1994, the then Social Democratic government created a comprehensive programme of active labour market measures, involving leave schemes for both employed and unemployed people, and a range of activation programmes. The reforms were adopted with the full agreement of the trade unions as key social partners. Those claiming unemployment and social benefits, and employees were entitled to undertake either childcare, educational or sabbatical leave. This policy was combined with job rotation programmes, whereby unemployed people – including disabled people – could obtain short-term work experience by acting as substitutes to cover those on leave (Etherington and Jones, 2004). Local government (*Kommune*) was given responsibility for activating people on social assistance, while the public employment service (*Arbejdsformedlingen*) was charged with signposting insured people into leave schemes and activation policies. A major plank of the reforms was the decentralisation of labour market policy and an enhanced role for the social partners in the planning and delivery of policy via tripartite regional labour market councils (*Regional Arbejdsmarked Rad*). In essence, the 1994 reforms introduced conditionality into ALMPs, while at the same time providing rights for unemployed people (a condition of trade union agreement to the reforms) in the form of action plans and a wide choice of training and employment schemes. Those in receipt of long-term sickness benefits tended to be excluded from benefit conditionality, with an emphasis on social support and an enhanced role for occupational health as a way of facilitating employment opportunities. Towards the late 1990s, the trade unions made a concerted push to develop support and representation of social assistance and disability claimants via the government's 'Inclusive Labour Market' (*Rummeligearbejdsmarked*) through involvement in local coordinating committees, and developing counselling and advice services on a similar basis to those provided for UI claimants (Damgaard and Torfing, 2010).

The neoliberal turn in the 2000s

Although workfare has always been present to some extent within Danish ALMPs, in recent years it has become more explicit and integral to welfare policy (Rosdahl and Weise, 2001). In the 2000s, the Liberal-Conservative government introduced a series of measures that tightened conditionality for disabled people and long-term sickness benefit recipients. The first measure was tougher work assessments following the creation in 1998 of a special activation programme – 'flex-jobs' – involving subsidised employment. People on sickness benefit and Disability Pension had to undergo a 'work ability' assessment (introduced in 2003 as part of a wider pension reform – see Table 8.1) in order to qualify for benefits and assess their eligibility for flex-jobs, or sheltered employment. Flex-jobs are integral to the Danish occupational health intervention model for both employed and unemployed people whose working capacity is reduced by at least 50%. Within eight weeks of sick leave, the local authority verifies eligibility to sickness benefits and sets in motion appropriate measures and instruments to facilitate a speedy return to work. These include counselling, work capacity assessments, vocational rehabilitation, job training and a phased return to work. If ordinary work is not possible, a subsidised flex-job under special conditions is offered on a permanent basis, involving specific work tasks, in-work support and reduced working hours.

Those who are eligible for, but are waiting to join the scheme, receive an unemployment allowance equivalent to UI benefit, averaging around 80-90% of the highest rate of daily social security benefits. In 2011, 70,000 people were employed in flex-jobs, half in the public sector and half in the private sector (Gupta et al, 2013). Municipalities also operate a sheltered employment scheme for people with more severe disabilities. In 2013, less than 5,000 people were in such jobs (Statistics Denmark, 2014). However, flex-jobs continues to be the main activation programme for disabled people, combined with other support services, such as personal assistance, career counselling and access to training (Etherington and Ingold, 2012). Although intervention measures for disabled people are undertaken in liaison with relevant agencies and trade unions, in terms of social dialogue trade union influence, particularly at the national level, declined throughout the 2000s, with their role being reduced to merely commenting on policy proposals, rather than being involved in their development (Jørgensen and Schulze, 2012).

The 'municipalisation' of activation

In 2007, the Danish government undertook a major reorganisation of local government and welfare, which devolved responsibility for activation from the public employment service to local government (see Table 8.2). The reforms in effect abolished the public employment service, and the powerful and influential regional labour market councils, in which the trade unions and labour movement had a strong voice. However, this 'municipalisation of employment policy'

(2007–10) retained the role of the social partners through the creation of LBRs, whose role is to advise and monitor jobcentre performance, establish local priorities and pilot or develop projects in accordance with them. The central objective of the LBR is to use its capacities and resources to assist those most disadvantaged in the labour market. A key element of the reforms was the increasing inclusion of disability rights organisations and the allocation of specialist disability advisers within jobcentres. The pressure on municipal budgets and a complicated financial reimbursement model for activation led to pressures to signpost more disabled people into the 'open' labour market and reduce the disability benefit bill. This involved the use of stricter work-related conditions and sanctions and was underpinned by stricter performance measurement, outcome targets and an overall reduction in discretion for case workers (Østergaard Møller and Stone, 2013). The establishment of the local committees brought about a decentralisation of social dialogue and potentially closer contact between the trade unions and marginalised groups in the labour market (Bredgaard and Larsen, 2008). On the other hand, in terms of social dialogue the reforms weakened the role of social partners in shaping labour market policies at the national level (Jørgensen and Schulze, 2012, p 641).

Table 8.2: Social dialogue and governance of activation programmes in Denmark

Level	Administrative bodies
National	National Labour Market Authority (*Arbejdsmarkedstyrelsen*) – overall management of employment policy
	National Employment Council (*National Beskaeftelses Rad*) – advisory body of social partners to the Minister of Employment in relation to labour market policy
	Labour Directorate – supervision of UI funds and local authority administration of social benefits
Regional/city region	Employment regions – supervision of jobcentre performance
	Regional Employment Council (*Regional Beskaeftelses Rad*) – advisory body on policy and monitoring of regional labour markets
Local	Local authority *jobcentres* – employment services for insured and uninsured people on sickness benefit; payment of social assistance and unemployment benefit
	Local Employment Council (*Lokal Beskæftelses Råd*) – policy-making and supervisory role

The Social Democratic government's labour market reforms

The incoming Social Democratic government in 2011 implemented a package of austerity measures combined with a public investment package designed to stimulate the economy (Mailand, 2012). The actual relationship between the social partners and the nature of social dialogue displayed continuities with the previous centre-right government (Mailand, 2013; see also Jørgensen and Schulze, 2012). The new government implemented the previous government's plans to increase conditionality by (from 2013) reducing the duration for which UI benefit could be claimed from four to two years, tightening the criteria for re-entitlement and restricting access to Disability Pension.

Disability Pension is awarded to those of working age whose ability to work is considered on the basis of a medical assessment to be permanently reduced. Since 2013, eligibility has been restricted to those aged over 40, with those under 40 being targeted for specific interventions. This involves undergoing intensive health management, including engaging with a rehabilitation plan administered by inter-agency teams, and special measures, such as enhanced employment and training, support for self-health-management and access to subsidised employment to enhance 'employability'.

A significant new policy turn by the Social Democrats was to address the problems of the high numbers of people (around 240,000) in receipt of disability benefits and the high demand for flex-jobs by shifting the focus from flex-jobs and subsidised employment to a more coordinated rehabilitation model. Access to flex-jobs is to be rationalised, with the largest subsidies paid to workers with the least working capacity (Brix Pedersen, 2013). 'Mini flex-jobs' have also been introduced, giving more opportunities to people with reduced capacity to work up to 12 hours. A key emphasis of the reforms is for disabled people to have a voice in the planning process, reflecting the government's commitment to the co-production of services (Brix Pedersen, 2013). At the same time, there has been a raft of policies targeting older workers vulnerable to long-term sickness absence. So, for example, all unemployed people aged 55 years or over with UI have the right to make an agreement with an employer to be employed on a wage subsidy for up to six months.

A new committee of experts (the Koch Commission) was established in 2013 to review activation policies and recommend potentially far-reaching changes to the system, particularly in relation to the governance and role of education and training (Kongshøj Madsen, 2014). This includes more focused links between jobcentres and employers in relation to education and training, and the delivery of activation. The recommendations also promote co-production and an increasing 'ownership' of activation by insured unemployed people, principles which in the next phase of the Commission's work are anticipated to apply to uninsured unemployed people and other disadvantaged groups, including disabled people (The Danish Government, 2013; Kongshøj Madsen, 2014). There are also proposals to rationalise the institutional structures, creating more regional councils (from four to 8-12) to reflect regional labour market conditions, with representation from the social partners to address the weaknesses of the linkages between jobcentres and regions.

Discussion

In Denmark, changes to the governance of activation are clearly a terrain of political struggle. Van Berkel and Borghi (2007) contend that such changes involve a transformation of the way that roles and responsibilities relating to the delivery of activation are shared among:

- actors at different geographical levels (national/supranational/regional/local);
- social actors (social partners, civil society);
- economic actors (public/private);
- administrative actors (education, social, economic and finance departments).

In Denmark, state rescaling (Jessop, 2002) is also visible, whereby policies are devolved to municipalities, but accompanied by the centralisation of control. First, there has been an increasing control of municipal expenditure and the deployment of performance and expenditure targets on activation and other social and welfare services. Second, while the social partners have tended to be marginalised, the power of certain actors has increased through their involvement in shaping economic and social policy. So, for example, the key actor in relation to bipartite negotiations is the Danish Local Government Association (*Kommunerneslandsforegningen*) (Mailand, 2012).

The Danish collectivist tradition has been retained to a greater degree than expected given the economic downturn and successive waves of austerity. This is underpinned by a version of 'egalitarianism' (Kananen, 2012), a (relatively) strong welfare state and local governance structure and 'income security' designed to cushion against poverty (Daemmrich and Bredgaard, 2012). Nevertheless, the 'active line' has taken on a more workfarist orientation, illustrated by the increasing work-first policies for disabled people and other labour market groups, and restrictions placed on access to Disability Pension (Østergaard Møller and Stone, 2013). The actual impact of this shift towards work-first policies in terms of employment outcomes for disabled people is unclear. There may be a case to argue that the package of measures – subsidised jobs, employment support combined with counselling/signposting and occupational health – may have important impacts in terms of disabled people accessing sustained employment. Although there is a marked gap in employment rates between disabled (52.6%) and non-disabled people (75.4%) in Denmark, employment rates for the former are the second highest in the EU27 countries (Zaidi, 2011, p 26, table A.3).

One of the key changes in Danish activation policies is the increasing conditionality and changes to eligibility for UI benefit, which poses potentially serious challenges to trade union influence. This influence takes two key forms: (a) the Ghent system and (b) the retention of social partner involvement. In the Danish model the Ghent system provides a direct link between the trade unions and unemployed people, and is an important social solidaristic foundation for providing socially progressive and encompassing support to other groups, such as disabled people. Successive changes have reduced the numbers of people eligible to claim UI benefit, producing conflict between the social partners and government (Daemmrich and Bredgaard, 2012). Significant numbers of people who are long-term unemployed as a consequence of the economic crisis (Kongshøj Madsen, 2013a) will exhaust their right to UI benefit and face restrictions on re-entitlement. Such groups are likely to migrate to social assistance and potentially disability benefit. On the other hand, the retention of social partner involvement in the municipal-run LBRs presents both opportunities and challenges for trade union influence in programmes and services for vulnerable groups, including disabled people (Etherington and Ingold, 2012).

The Danish system of collective agreements has a major influence on trade union links with the activation system. The shift in focus away from subsidised employment to providing more intensive support for people in receipt of sickness benefits may be related to trade union criticisms of flex-jobs. These have focused on their displacement and substitution effects (Mailand, 2012, p 17) and the potential for 'parking' of disabled people in poor-quality workplace schemes that do not result in sustained employment in the open labour market. This tension has manifested in conflicts within the corporatist institutions (such as the regional and local labour market committees), with flex-jobs being perceived as potential threats to employment and collective bargaining.

Within the collective agreements between the local authority trade unions and the Local Government Association, an employer cannot recruit someone under the flex-jobs scheme without consulting the shop steward and the agreement states that the shop steward should take an active involvement in the recruitment process. Research undertaken for the public sector trade unions (Ipsen and Hansen, 2009) found that a third of shop stewards had not been involved and, where they had been consulted, in most cases decisions had already been made by department managers (FOA, HK and 3f, 2010). Nevertheless, in general, the trade unions have supported the principle of activation, as long as it does not negatively impact upon their members. Two aspects ensure some protection for vulnerable groups when accessing employment and activation programmes. First, trade unions are consulted (although this can be uneven) when activation placements are being established by the jobcentres. Second, employment placements provided under activation programmes are guaranteed at negotiated wage rates under sectoral collective agreements.

Conclusion

In this chapter we have seen that the exclusion of the social partners from meaningful dialogue with respect to influencing economic and social policy at the national level has been an important feature of changes and sources of tensions in the governance of activation in Denmark (Kongshøj Madsen, 2013b). In addition, the municipalisation of employment services is seen by the trade unions as a threat to the control of UI benefits. There is a view that the municipalities could take over their administration, which would weaken the links between the trade unions and ALMPs (Jørgensen and Schulze, 2012). Furthermore, the tightening of conditions in terms of access to benefits while employment policies take on an increasingly work-first orientation has, unsurprisingly, been met by a critical response from the trade unions as being 'substandard' and is viewed as potentially 'parking' disabled people into poorer-quality schemes (FOA, HK and 3f, 2010; Andersen, 2011).

This said, there is evidence that the trade unions and social dialogue still have an important role in terms of the retention of the redistributive element (that is, income security), which is crucial for marginalised groups in the labour market (Kongshøj Madsen, 2013b). The attempt by the Social Democratic government from 2011 to refocus policies for people in receipt of sickness benefits towards rehabilitation and supported employment has been matched with significant resources.

For example, €370 million (approximately £275 million) has been allocated until 2020, with an additional €500 million (approximately £371 million) on a longer-term basis (Brix Pedersen, 2013). The Koch Commission's recommendations for overhauling the activation system include the empowering of individuals, key institutional and governance reforms and an increased emphasis on education and training. The last of these has for a long period been the focus of campaigns by the trade unions. However, in the context of the recession, austerity and difficult labour market conditions, the calls from trade unions and other social movements for job creation programmes are likely to reinforce existing tensions around social dialogue.

The Danish model has focused on supporting disabled people to remain in or enter the labour market and this has undoubtedly been facilitated by social partner involvement. Furthermore, participation in flex-job programmes also means that wage rates are set by collective agreements and that disabled people will have access to trade union representation. In this respect, the model of collective bargaining where workplace conditions and wages are covered by agreements must be seen as an important factor in terms of the employment rights of people who are disabled and who live with long-term health conditions. However, the focus on labour market participation has to an extent been compromised by the shift towards workfare. The more recent moves towards the co-production of rehabilitation pathways is important, on the one hand, in incorporating the voice of disabled people, but, on the other hand, the potential for the creation of quality, sustainable jobs for disabled people in difficult labour market conditions remains a challenge.

References

Andersen, T. (2011) *A flexicurity labour market in the great recession – the case of Denmark*, Aarhus, Denmark: Aarhus University.

Bredgaard, T. (2012) 'Flexibility and security in employment regulation: what can be learned from the Danish case?', in H. Arthurs and C. Stone (eds) *Employment regulation after the standard employment contract*, London: Russell Sage.

Bredgaard, T. (2013) 'Flexibility and security in employment regulation: learning from Denmark', in K. Stone and H. Arthurs (eds) *Rethinking workplace regulation: Beyond the standard contract of employment*, New York, NY: Russell Sage Foundation, pp 213-33.

Bredgaard, T. and Larsen, F. (2008) 'Lokalbeskaeftigelsesrad I krydsfeltetmellem stat og commune', *Tidskrift for Arbejdsliv*, 10(3), pp 57-72.

Brix Pedersen, K. (2013) 'Replacing disability pension for young people under 40 with a rehabilitation model', presentation to the Organisation for Economic Co-operation and Development, New York, 17 April, www.oecd.org/els/emp/mentalhealthandworkseminar-countryreports.htm

Clegg, D. and van Wijnbergen, C. (2011) 'Welfare institutions and the mobilization of consent: union responses to labour market activation policies in France and the Netherlands', *European Journal of Industrial Relations*, 17(4), pp 333-48.

Daemmrich, A. and Bredgaard, T. (2012) 'The welfare state as an investment strategy: Denmark's flexicurity policies', in A. Bardhan, D. Jaffee and C. Kroll (eds) *The Oxford handbook of offshoring and global employment*, Oxford: Oxford University Press, pp 159-79.

Damgaard, B. and Torfing, J. (2010) 'Network governance of active employment policy: the Danish experience', *Journal of European Social Policy*, 20(3), pp 248-62.

Dølvik, J.H. (2008) 'Negotiated Nordic labour markets from bust to boom: background paper', paper for the conference 'The Nordic Models: Solutions to Continental Europe's Problems?', Center for European Studies, Harvard University, 9-10 May.

Etherington, D. (2008) *New welfare spaces: Labour market policies in the UK and Denmark*, Saarbrücken, Germany: VDM Dr Mueller.

Etherington, D. and Ingold, J. (2012) 'Welfare to work and the inclusive labour market: a comparative study of activation policies for disability and long term sickness benefit claimants in the UK and Denmark', *Journal of European Social Policy*, 30(1), pp 22-44.

Etherington, D. and Jones, M. (2004) 'Welfare-through-work and the re-regulation of labour markets in Denmark', *Capital and Class*, 83, pp 19-46.

FOA, HK and 3f (2010) *Aktiveringpåkommunalearbejdspladser – igår, i dag, ogimorgen,* Copenhagen, Denmark: FOA, HK and 3f.

Gupta, N., Larsen, M. and Thomsen, L. (2013) *Do wage subsidies for disabled workers result in deadweight loss? Evidence from the Danish Flexjob scheme,* Economic Working Papers 24, Aarhus, Denmark: Aarhus University, http://pure.au.dk//portal/files/56741447/wp13_24.pdf

Ipsen, S. and Hansen, H. (2009) *Aktiveringpåkommunalarbejdsplads – effekter, konsekvensogpraksis,* Copenhagen, Denmark: CASA.

Jessop, B. (2002) *The future of the capitalist state,* Cambridge: Polity Press.

Jørgensen, H. and Schulze, M. (2012) 'A double farewell to a former model? Danish unions and activation policy', *Local Economy*, 27 (5-6), pp 637-44.

Kananen, J. (2012) 'Nordic paths from welfare to workfare: Danish, Swedish and Finnish labour market reforms in comparison', *Local Economy*, 27(5-6), pp 558-76.

Kongshøj Madsen, P. (2013a) *Marginalisation, the Danish labour market and in-work poverty*, Brussels, Belgium: European Employment Observatory, www.eu-employment-observatory.net/resources/reports/DenmarkMarginalizationPovertyWorkingPoorFINAL.pdf

Kongshøj Madsen, P. (2013b) 'Shelter from the storm? Danish flexicurity and the crisis', *Journal of European Labour Studies*, 2(6), pp 2-19.

Kongshøj Madsen, P. (2014) Danish Flexicurity - still a beautiful swan? Peer Review on Adjustments to the Danish flexicurity model in response to the crisis, Copenhagen, 20-21 November, 2014.

Lind, J. (1996) 'Unions: social movements or welfare apparatus?' in P. Leinsink, J. Van Leemput, and J. Vilrokx (eds) *The challenges of trade unions in Europe: Innovations or adaptation*, Cheltenham: Elgar.

Mailand, M. (2012) *National report Denmark: Social dialogue and the public services in the aftermath of the economic crisis: Strengthening partnership in an era of austerity*, Copenhagen, Denmark: FAOS, University of Copenhagen.

Mailand, M. (2013) *Denmark: Social partners involvement in unemployment benefit regimes*, Brussels, Belgium: Eurofound, www.eurofound.europa.eu/eiro/studies/tn1206018s/dk1206019q.htm

OECD (Organisation for Economic Co-operation and Development) (2009) 'Sickness, disability and work: keeping on track in the economic downturn background paper', OECD High Level Forum, Stockholm, 14-15 May.

Østergaard Møller, M. and Stone, D. (2013) 'Disciplining disability under Danish active labour market policy', *Social Policy and Administration*, 47(5), pp 586-604.

Peck, J. (2001), *Workfare states*, New York, NY: Guilford Press.

Peck, J. (2002) 'Political economies of scale: fast policy, interscalar relations and neoliberal workfare', *Economic Geography*, 78, pp 331-9.

Revilla, J.C. and Pascual, A.S. (2007) 'Normative foundations of activation regimes', paper presented at the ESPAnet Conference, Austria, 20-22 September.

Rosdahl, A. and Weise, H. (2001) 'When all must be active – workfare in Denmark', in I. Lødemel and H. Trickey (eds) *'An offer you can't refuse': Workfare in international perspective*, Bristol: Policy Press, pp 159-80.

Statistics Denmark, www.statbank.dk

The Danish Government (2013) *The national reform programme: Denmark 2013*, http://ec.europa.eu/europe2020/pdf/nd/nrp2013_denmark_en.pdf

Trampusch, C. (2006) 'Industrial relations and welfare states: the different dynamics of retrenchment in Germany and the Netherlands', *Journal of European Social Policy*, 16(2), pp 121-33.

Van Berkel, R. and Borghi, V. (2007) 'New modes of governance in activation policies', *International Journal of Sociology and Social Policy*, 27(7/8), pp 277-86.

Zaidi, A. (2011) *The situation of working-age people with disabilities across the EU*, Research Note 5/2011, Brussels, Belgium: European Commission, www.euro.centre.org/data/1364397289_92141.pdf

Part Three
Assistance and access to paid work

NINE

Employment experiences and outcomes of young people in Scotland who are deaf or hard of hearing: intersections of deafness and social class

Mariela Fordyce and Sheila Riddell

Introduction

The financial crash of 2008 has had a particularly negative effect on young people born in the 1980s, especially those from poorer backgrounds (Hills, 2013). The consequences have been dire for young people living in poverty with additional support needs, which are often a consequence of social disadvantage. This chapter focuses on the employment experiences and outcomes of young people who are deaf or hard of hearing (DHH), who make up approximately 0.3% of the total population of young people in Scotland (Scottish Government, 2013). Whereas much analysis of the experiences of disabled people treats those with particular impairments as homogeneous groups, this chapter attempts to unpick the relationship between social class and labour market outcomes for people who are DHH.

Drawing on recent research into the post-school transitions of young people who are DHH (Fordyce et al, 2013a), we discuss the role played by social class in their employment outcomes as depicted by findings from interviews with young people who are DHH in Scotland.

The significance of educational qualifications in the labour market outcomes of disabled people

Young disabled people occupy an increasingly precarious position in the labour market due to their disability status (Meager and Higgins, 2011) and the generally high youth unemployment in recent years (Hills, 2013). Although the employment rates of disabled people have slightly increased in the last decade (Sayce, 2011), they still remain approximately 30 percentage points lower than those of non-disabled people (Office for Disability Issues, 2013). The reasons for this include:

- lower qualifications (Burchardt, 2005);
- lower participation rates in post-16 education, training and employment (Directorate-General for Education and Culture, 2012);
- employer discrimination (Jones and Sloane, 2010; Meager and Higgins, 2011).

Research suggests that the labour market penalty associated with lower qualifications is higher for disabled than non-disabled people. Berthoud (2007), for example, carried out a secondary analysis of data from the General Household Survey and found that between 1974 and 2003 the employment rates of disabled men with no qualifications decreased by half (from 77% to 38%), while those of non-disabled men with no qualifications decreased by only 10 percentage points (from 95% to 85%). In comparison, disabled men with post-secondary qualifications faced a less dramatic, albeit marked reduction in employment rates over the same years (from 93% to 75%). This indicates that higher educational qualifications have a mitigating effect on the disadvantage associated with disability. This finding is supported by Meager and Higgins' (2011) analysis of Labour Force Survey data. Meager and Higgins (2011) demonstrate that in 2010, disabled people with post-secondary qualifications were 3.6 times more likely to be in employment than disabled people with no qualifications (72% versus 20%), while the employment rate of non-disabled people with post-secondary qualifications was only 1.6 times higher than those of non-disabled people with no qualifications (88% versus 55%).

While there is no comparable research in Britain on the employment rates of people who are DHH in relation to their qualifications, studies conducted in Sweden and the United States (US) substantiate this finding. Rydberg et al (2011) compared the sociodemographic characteristics and employment rates of 2,144 people aged 25-64 who attended a Swedish school for deaf people with the general population, and found that for both groups a higher level of educational attainment was associated with higher employment rates. However, deaf people with low qualifications had markedly lower employment rates than their non-disabled counterparts (43% versus 65%), while the employment rates of deaf people with post-secondary qualifications were similar to those of the general population (83% versus 84%). In the US, Schley et al (2011) found that DHH people who had completed post-secondary education, including those with vocational qualifications, were less likely to claim unemployment benefits than DHH people with lower qualifications.

Social reproduction, disability and deafness

The influence of parental socioeconomic status on young people's labour market outcomes has been widely documented (see, for example, Iannelli and Smyth, 2008). Parental social background has been found to be a direct or indirect predictor (through education) of young people's employment outcomes and job satisfaction (Iannelli, 2003; Faas et al, 2012). There has been little research on the effects of socioeconomic background on the labour market outcomes of disabled people, although the relationship between social background and disability in relation to prevalence and educational outcomes has long been acknowledged (Elwan, 1999; Burchardt, 2005; Dyson and Kozleski, 2008). Theorists, such as Vernon (1999, p 394), have argued that 'class privilege is a powerful diluter of discrimination both economically and socially', but 15 years later there seems to be limited research evidence to substantiate this claim.

A longitudinal survey of the post-school transitions of young people with special educational needs in five European countries (Ebersold, 2012) revealed that young people from advantaged socioeconomic backgrounds had better post-school outcomes than those from poorer backgrounds. Ebersold (2012, p 69) suggests that the support and involvement of more highly qualified parents was the key factor in ensuring positive outcomes, and that parents with lower qualifications may lack the ability to 'overcome weaknesses of existing support'. Similarly, findings from the National Longitudinal Transitions Study in the US (Newman et al, 2011) show that eight years after leaving secondary education, young disabled people from high-earning households were significantly more likely to be employed than those from poorer households. Also in the US, this finding was replicated for young people who are DHH by Garberoglio et al (2014), who call for further research into the relationship between the post-school experiences of young deaf people and other indicators of socioeconomic status, such as parental education level.

Our study of the post-school outcomes of DHH young people in Scotland sought to investigate the influence of parental social capital on the education and employment outcomes of DHH young people (Fordyce et al, 2013a; Fordyce et al, 2014). Findings revealed that the social networks and advocacy skills of middle-class parents mitigated the negative consequences of deafness. This contrasted with the more troubled post-school experiences of DHH young people from less advantaged social backgrounds. At the same time, the study revealed that DHH university graduates, who were a socially advantaged group, had good employment outcomes, which were in stark contrast to the low employment rates of the working-age people who were DHH. The aim of this chapter is to explore the qualitative differences between the labour market experiences of young people with higher qualifications and from socially advantaged backgrounds, and those of young people with lower qualifications and socially disadvantaged backgrounds.

Method

The study of the post-school transitions of young people who are DHH combined a secondary analysis of survey and administrative data of post-school outcomes, and semi-structured interviews with 30 DHH young people. The interviews aimed to place young people's post-school transition experiences in the wider context of their life histories from primary school to the present. Using biographical research conventions (Merrill and West, 2009), the interviews elicited information on:

- their school background;
- post-school transition planning;
- experiences of post-16 education, training and employment.

This chapter focuses on findings related to employment outcomes as reflected in the semi-structured interviews.

Participants

The participants were 30 young people aged 18-24 with various degrees and types of hearing loss. Their degrees of hearing loss ranged from mild to profound, and the majority were in the severe to profound range. Eight participants were cochlear implant users. The participants were at various stages of their transitions from compulsory education to full-time employment. The majority were in higher and further education, training or employment (24), but the sample also included young people who were looking for paid work or were not in education, employment or training at the time of the interview (6). All participants were or had been in employment, on a full-time, part-time or temporary basis. Table 9.1 shows the number of participants by highest qualification.

Table 9.1: Number of participants by highest qualification

Scottish Credit and Qualifications Framework	Type of qualification	Number of participants
SCQF Level 11	Postgraduate Diploma	1
SCQF Level 10	Honours Degree	5
SCQF Level 9	Bachelors	2
SCQF Level 8	Higher National Diploma	2
SCQF Level 7	Scottish Vocational Qualification Level 3 Modern Apprenticeships Level 3 Advanced Highers	8
SCQF Level 6	Highers	3
SCQF Level 5	Scottish Vocational Qualification Level 2 Modern Apprenticeships Level 2 Intermediate 2	7
SCQF Level 4	Scottish Vocational Qualification Level 1 Intermediate 1	2
TOTAL		30

In order to ensure that the sample reflected the sociodemographic characteristics of the wider population of 18- to 24-year-olds who are DHH in Scotland, information was also collected on characteristics such as gender, ethnicity, socioeconomic status, urban/rural residence, preferred mode of communication, highest qualification and presence of other disabilities or support needs. The sample included young people from minority ethnic backgrounds, the most deprived areas in Scotland and remote rural areas, and young people who preferred to communicate orally, in British Sign Language (BSL) or Sign-Supported English. Some participants had additional disabilities or support needs.

Data collection and analysis

Most interviews were conducted face to face in spoken English or BSL. The interviews with young people who preferred to communicate in BSL were carried out by a deaf researcher.

An intersectional approach was adopted for data collection and analysis (Siltanen, 2004) in recognition of the fact that individual experiences are shaped by complex interactions between multiple structural dimensions, such as disability, social class, ethnicity and gender. Interview data were analysed horizontally (through thematic analysis) and vertically (as individual case studies). The case studies provided insights into how outcomes and experiences were influenced by the interplay between social class and disability. The Scottish Index of Multiple Deprivation (SIMD) is used as an indicator of social class. The SIMD is a measure of the relative level of deprivation of the areas where participants lived. It consists of a ranking of neighbourhoods based on seven different aspects of deprivation: employment, income, health, education, access to services, crime and housing (Scottish Government, 2012). In this chapter we used the quintile ranking, where the most deprived areas are in the first quintile and the least deprived are in the fifth quintile.

Ethical considerations

The research was carried out in adherence to university research ethics standards. Given the wide range of communication needs of the young people who took part in the study, an easy-read version and a BSL version of the project leaflet and consent form were made available. With participant permission, oral interviews were audio-recorded and transcribed, and BSL interviews were videotaped and translated into English by the deaf researcher who conducted the interviews. In this chapter, participants' names have been changed in order to protect their anonymity.

DHH young people's labour market experiences: evidence from the case studies

The case studies reveal that all participants believed that they experienced a certain degree of disadvantage when they were in employment or looking for work. However, there seemed to be qualitative differences in the difficulties they encountered, depending on their qualifications and socioeconomic resources. Given the discrepancy between the employment levels of graduates who are DHH and those of DHH people with lower qualifications (Fordyce et al, 2014), this chapter consists of a comparison between the labour market experiences of young people with higher school-level qualifications, most of whom were on degree programmes, and those with few or no qualifications, most of whom were in vocational education or training. It is important to emphasise that, apart from differences in qualifications and post-16 pathways, there were also marked socioeconomic differences between the two groups, in line with the research findings outlined in the previous section.

The interviews revealed that young people who were DHH encountered a series of barriers to securing and maintaining employment. Some were experienced by young people irrespective of their qualifications or socioeconomic backgrounds, while others were shared only by those who had lower qualifications and came from disadvantaged backgrounds. Table 9.2 provides an overview of these barriers.

Table 9.2 suggests that those who had lower qualifications suffered increased disadvantage in the labour market and had fewer resources to draw on in order to negotiate these difficulties. The combined influence of social capital and educational qualifications on the employment outcomes of young people who are DHH is illustrated in the case studies below.

Table 9.2: Perceived barriers to finding and staying in employment

All young people, irrespective of qualifications	Young people with lower-level educational qualifications
Lack of accessibility in applying for work Employers' and co-workers' lack of deaf awareness	Overt discrimination in recruitment practices Limited social networks Limited work experience

Lack of accessibility in applying for work

Some jobseekers encountered recruitment practices that were inaccessible to people with hearing loss. These included having to ask for job details over the telephone or being invited to have telephone interviews. Young people who communicated orally, such as Jack, whose case study is given below, also mentioned difficulties in taking part in group interviews or exercises, or the inability to take advantage of networking opportunities. There were differences in the way young people with different levels of qualifications negotiated these barriers. Karen, an 18-year-old college student from a deprived area, who at the time of the interview had been looking for work for six months, explained that she relied on her mother to telephone potential employers. On the other hand, young people with graduate qualifications were more likely to apply for work with larger companies, and notified potential employers in writing of their communication needs.

Case study 1: Jack

Jack had meningitis when he was two years old, and started using hearing aids when he was three. He has profound hearing loss in one ear, and severe hearing loss in the other. He lives with his family in a very affluent urban area (SIMD fifth quintile). He communicates orally. He went to a private mainstream school, which he left in his sixth year with Advanced Highers. He graduated with a degree in Business from an ancient university. At the time of the interview he was looking for work in the financial sector. He first described how, unlike his peers, he could not take advantage of university careers fairs:

> 'I went along to the careers fairs the university arranged and they were a bit of a disaster because the rooms were so packed and it was so noisy you couldn't speak, you couldn't network so you were just reduced to picking up the literature they had on the tables and trying to avoid speaking to people and looking like an idiot because you can't understand a word that they're saying. So that was a hindrance, especially when everyone says networking is so important and all that sort of thing.'

He also reported that he could not take full advantage of networking lunches and that he had difficulties in group exercises, which were part of the selection procedure. Nevertheless, Jack always disclosed his disability in job applications and asked for face-to-face interviews. He reported that companies were eager to oblige. In spite of this, he still encountered communication difficulties. He explained that in his first interview he failed to show enthusiasm because he struggled to hear the interviewers' questions. In spite of these difficulties, he was successful in obtaining a place on a graduate employment scheme.

Jack benefited from the fact that he applied for work with large companies that had commitments to equality and offered guaranteed interview schemes to disabled people. His experience is similar to that of many other graduates in the study, who were more likely to be aware of equality legislation than jobseekers with lower qualifications.

Employers' and co-workers' lack of deaf awareness

Many young people who were in employment or training mentioned that employers and co-workers were unaware of their communication needs. This was particularly problematic for young people who communicated orally, who were believed to be or wanted to be considered hearing in the workplace. Co-workers' lack of deaf awareness seemed to affect young people with lower qualifications to a larger extent, possibly because of poorer self-advocacy skills. Mia, a 19-year-old apprentice from a deprived rural area, recounted that that she struggled to hear at work and missed out at training courses, but did not ask for adjustments because she believed that she did not need any. However, the case study below suggests that even young people with good self-advocacy skills and knowledge of specialist employment support may suffer from the negative consequences of co-workers' lack of deaf awareness.

Case study 2: Emily

Emily was diagnosed with severe hearing loss when she was two years old. She communicates orally. She lives with her father in a relatively disadvantaged urban area (SIMD third quintile). She went to local mainstream schools. In spite of the fact that her secondary school had very low rates of progression to higher education, she achieved one Advanced Higher and went on to study Religious Studies at a pre-1992 university. After graduation she was offered a full-time permanent position in the public sector. She worked in a busy, open-plan office:

> 'The telephones rang a lot and I was expected to answer them. I was expected to take people at reception as well ... as well as all these other sort of admin duties.... It quickly became apparent though that the telephone was a big part of the job and so something was going to have to be done about that.'

Although she obtained an amplified telephone through the Access to Work[1] scheme, she continued to have difficulties using the telephone because of the background noise in her office. In time, she developed what she described as 'a phone phobia'. Her fear of making mistakes was augmented by the unsupportive attitude of some of her co-workers. After five months, Emily handed in her resignation. She was later diagnosed with anxiety and depression. At the time of the research interview she had completed a postgraduate diploma in Information

Technology and was looking for work. Commenting on her previous employment experiences, she explained that she found it difficult to make others aware of her communication needs, as they did not 'fit in a neat box'.

Discrimination in recruitment practices

Most young people feared discrimination in recruitment, irrespective of their qualifications. However, while graduate jobseekers always disclosed their disability in job applications and were aware that they could use equality legislation as a 'battering ram', DHH young people with lower qualifications were more likely to encounter potential employers who held openly negative views of deafness. Madhat, a 24-year-old beautician, recounted how some employers seemed to doubt her ability to work with the public. Many young people with lower qualifications believed that they were more likely to be offered an interview when they did not disclose their disability. The case study below is an example of a young person who believed she was discriminated against because she was a BSL user.

Case study 3: Leah

Leah is a full-time mother and communicates mainly in BSL. She was diagnosed with hearing loss when she was a toddler. She lives in an urban area of high social deprivation (SIMD first quintile) with her partner and baby daughter, who are also deaf. Her parents and siblings are hearing and she communicates with them orally, although she is most comfortable using BSL. Leah spent most of her school career in schools for deaf people. She left school at 16 with Intermediate 2 qualifications, and went on to a college of further education, where she obtained a vocational qualification in Beauty Therapy. She looked for work for a year. She believed that she had difficulties finding work because she was deaf and was a victim of discrimination:

> 'I received lots of rejections because I am deaf, have no telephone skills and no communication skills with the public.... It was interesting because I noticed that when I sent my CV to the employers with a statement about me being deaf, I never got a reply. I tried again with no mention about my deafness on my CV and I received replies! I have been invited to interviews but I had to let them know that I

need an interpreter for the interview. The interviews were then cancelled. This is discrimination!'

Equality legislation in the United Kingdom has sought to tackle prejudice and encourage positive attitudes towards disabled people. The General Equality Duty associated with the Equality Act 2010 aims to protect disabled job applicants by placing duties on employers not to discriminate in the way they offer employment. However, evidence suggests that smaller employers may be less likely to make reasonable adjustments (Fordyce et al, 2013a). Young people with lower qualifications, like Leah, are particularly at risk as they are more likely to apply for positions with smaller companies or businesses and at the same time may lack the knowledge or advocacy skills to request reasonable adjustments.

Social networks versus the jobcentre

A common and effective jobseeking strategy of DHH young people with graduate degrees and who came from socially advantaged backgrounds was to seek help from family, friends and wider social networks. Several young people reported that they found work through parents, other relatives or friends. This usually started with short summer jobs or internships, which later led to full-time employment. The case study below is an example of a young woman who benefited from her mother's social capital, which consisted of knowledge of employment opportunities and extended social networks. On the other hand, there was little evidence that jobseekers from poorer backgrounds could make use of parental social capital in finding employment. They mainly looked for work online or through Jobcentre Plus.[2] This may be a less effective strategy to secure paid work, as these young people were less successful in finding work.

Case study 4: Lucy

Lucy was diagnosed with profound hearing loss when she was four years old. Her mother is deaf and they both communicate orally. Lucy lives with her parents in an advantaged suburban area (SIMD fifth quintile). She went to local mainstream schools. She left school with Advanced Highers and went on to study Law at a pre-1992 university. In her final year at university, Lucy started working part time as a support worker for the third sector organisation where her mother worked.

Soon after graduation she was encouraged by her mother to send a speculative application to a similar organisation:

> 'So my mum said: "Why don't you hand in a speculative application?" As it turned out, I had done [this] at the right time because they were actually looking for relief workers.... And she would often say: "Why don't you try this?" She obviously knows other organisations that maybe other people wouldn't be aware of.'

Lucy was offered permanent full-time employment within the organisation. She was one of several graduates in our study to achieve full-time employment with the help of their parents. The interviews with young people from socially advantaged backgrounds revealed how they benefited from their parents' social capital and advocacy skills throughout their school career. They were more likely to receive a good level of support in school and to achieve qualifications, which enabled them to enter higher education. And, as illustrated in the above case study, middle-class parents were often instrumental in helping their young people find employment.

Limited work experience

There were also marked differences between graduates and young people with lower qualifications with regard to their work experience. Most graduates worked part time or had summer jobs when they were at university. Some even started to work for their current employers when they were students. This is, at least in part, a consequence of these young people's social capital, as most found their first part-time jobs with the help of their parents. On the other hand, jobseekers with lower qualifications, such as James (see case study 5 below), reported fewer part-time work opportunities, although work experience was sometimes required as part of their vocational education.

Case study 5: James

James had meningitis when he was 18 months old. He has profound hearing loss and communicates in BSL. He went to special schools for deaf people and mainstream schools with resource centres. At the time of the interview he lived with his partner in an area of social disadvantage (SIMD first quintile). James left school at 16 and went to a college of further education to train as a car mechanic. At the time of the research interview he had been looking for work for six months, but had never been offered a job interview. He blamed this on his lack of work experience, which was limited to one work placement arranged by the college.

Similar to other young people from poorer backgrounds, James used conventional jobseeking strategies, such a registering with the jobcentre. Similar to other jobseekers who had been referred to disability employment advisers, he believed that the specialist support provided by the jobcentre was not effective in helping him find employment.

The intersection between DHH young people's post-school outcomes and social class

There are limited data on the education and employment outcomes of disabled people in Scotland and Britain in relation to their socioeconomic characteristics. Secondary analyses of Scottish Government data on pupils in publicly funded schools has revealed that there is an association between the socioeconomic background of pupils who are DHH and their attainment levels, as well as their post-school destinations (Fordyce et al, 2014). School leavers who are DHH and come from the most disadvantaged areas in Scotland were more likely to be unemployed than both DHH school leavers from more advantaged areas and their non-disabled counterparts.

Like all Scottish young people from the most deprived backgrounds (Sosu and Ellis, 2014), school leavers who are DHH are more likely to enrol in further education courses compared with their peers (Fordyce et al, 2014). It is important to note that DHH students in further education may be enrolled on a range of Scottish Vocational Qualifications at different levels, or in extension (or 'special') programmes for disabled students, which focus on life skills. Riddell et al (2001) explored the experiences of learning disabled young people on extension programmes and concluded that they tended to lead into a revolving cycle of training, with little chance of moving into mainstream education or employment. In addition, there is evidence to suggest that there are inconsistencies in the level and quality of support offered to students who are DHH by various Scottish colleges (Fordyce et al, 2013a), and that in the first six months students who are DHH are more likely to drop out from further education courses compared with their peers in higher education (Fordyce et al, 2013b).

On the other hand, graduates who are DHH have good employment outcomes (Fordyce et al, 2014). This success is likely to be attributable both to their high skill levels, and also to their relatively high socioeconomic status, which provides access to social networks, facilitating entry to the professions via internment positions and work experience. An analysis of parental occupations of DHH students in higher education suggests that they are a relatively advantaged group, similar to their non-disabled peers: approximately 60% of students in both groups have parents in managerial and professional occupations (Fordyce et al, 2014).

Conclusions: the interplay between deafness, social class and employment

Evidence is mounting with regard to the importance of different types of social capital available to young people from more and less socially advantaged backgrounds as they negotiate the world beyond the school gates. Scottish Government survey and administrative data (see Fordyce et al, 2013b) indicate that school leavers who are DHH have lower qualifications and as a consequence their post-school trajectories are different from those of their non-disabled peers. The small proportion who have the necessary qualifications to enter higher education have very positive employment outcomes. However, DHH people with lower qualifications are very likely to be excluded from the labour market altogether or find themselves in low-level and insecure jobs. DHH people from poorer backgrounds may suffer a triple disadvantage. First, they have to compete for work with an increasingly overqualified workforce. Second, they may lack the resources to overcome systemic barriers in the labour market (such as parental social capital and extended social networks, which would give them access to gainful employment, and the ability to take advantage of social support mechanisms, like the employment protection legislation or employment support programmes such as Access to Work). And, finally, they may be more likely to be victims of employer discrimination. Due to their hearing loss and possible communication difficulties, they may be perceived by employers as lacking the soft skills that are increasingly important in the low-skills area of the labour market (Keep, 2012).

The case studies of young people who are DHH in Scotland reveal qualitative differences in the disabling barriers encountered by people with low and high qualifications. The magnitude of these barriers is amplified by the difference in social resources between those from more and less advantaged backgrounds. The Scottish Government recognises the need to improve transitions for school leavers with additional support needs. However, the latest report on the implementation of the Additional Support for Learning Act 2004 (Scottish Government, 2014), which covers the issue of post-school transitions, does not mention the increased risk of stalled transitions of DHH young people from disadvantaged backgrounds. In addition, there is a growing tension between government rhetoric of support for disabled people and the undertow of hostility towards those living with poverty and disability, who are increasingly likely to be stigmatised and excluded (Jones, 2011). Unless there are serious efforts to understand the relationship between poverty and disability, young disabled people, including those who are DHH, are likely to be the victims of the growing economic inequalities associated with late capitalist societies.

Notes

[1] Access to Work is a British government grant for disabled people in employment, towards extra costs such as specialised equipment and support workers.

[2] Jobcentre Plus is an executive agency of the British Department for Work and Pensions. It offers support to people who are looking for work and/or who are in receipt of benefits.

Acknowledgements

We are grateful to the National Deaf Children's Society for funding the research project with the title 'Post-school Transitions of Young People who are Deaf or Hard of Hearing', on which this chapter is based. We would also like to thank colleagues Rachel O'Neill, Elisabet Weedon and Audrey Cameron, who collaborated on the project.

References

Berthoud, R. (2007) *Work-rich, work-poor: Three decades of change*, Bristol: Policy Press.

Burchardt, T. (2005) *The education and employment of disabled young people: Frustrated ambition*, Bristol: Policy Press.

Directorate-General for Education and Culture (2012) *Education and disability/special needs policies and practice in education, training and employment for students with disabilities and special educational needs in the EU: An independent report prepared for the European Commission by the NESSE network of experts*, Brussels: European Commission.

Dyson, A. and Kozleski, E.B. (2008) 'Disproportionality in special education: a transatlantic phenomenon', in L. Florian and M. McLaughlin (eds) *Dilemmas and alternatives in the classification of children with disabilities: New perspectives*, Thousand Oaks, CA: Corwin Press, pp 170-90.

Ebersold, S. (2012) *Transitions to tertiary education and work for youth with disabilities*, Paris: OECD Publishing.

Elwan, A. (1999) *Poverty and disability: A survey of literature*, Washington, DC: The World Bank.

Faas, C., Benson, M.J. and Kaestle, C.E. (2012) 'Parent resources during adolescence: effects on education and careers in young adulthood', *Journal of Youth Studies*, 16(2), pp 151-71.

Fordyce, M., Riddell, S., O'Neill, R. and Weedon, E. (2013a) *Post-school transitions of people who are deaf or hard of hearing: Report commissioned by the National Deaf Children's Society*, Edinburgh: Centre for Research in Education, Inclusion and Diversity.

Fordyce, M., Riddell, S., O'Neill, R. and Weedon, E. (2013b) *Post-school transitions of people who are deaf or hard of hearing: Appendices*, Edinburgh: Centre for Research in Education, Inclusion and Diversity.

Fordyce, M., Riddell, S., O'Neill, R. and Weedon, E. (2014) 'Educational outcomes of young people in Scotland who are deaf or hard of hearing: intersections of deafness and social class', *International Journal of Inclusive Education*, published online 30 June, doi: 10.1080/13603116.2014.929749.

Garberoglio, C.L., Cawthon, S.W. and Bond, M. (2014) 'Assessing English literacy as a predictor of postschool outcomes in the lives of deaf individuals', *Journal of Deaf Studies and Deaf Education*, 19(1), pp 50-67.

Hills, J. (2013) *Winners and losers in the crisis: The changing anatomy of educational inequality in the UK 2007-2010 social policy in a cold climate: Research report 02*, London: Centre for Analysis of Social Exclusion.

Iannelli, C. (2003) 'Parental education and young people's educational and labour market outcomes: a comparison across Europe', in I. Kogan and W. Muller (eds) *School-to-work transition in Europe: Analyses of the EULFS 2000 qd hoc module*, Mannheim, Germany: MZES, pp 27-53.

Iannelli, C. and Smyth, E. (2008) 'Mapping gender and social background differences in education and youth transitions across Europe', *Journal of Youth Studies*, 11(2), pp 213-32.

Jones, M.K. and Sloane, P.J. (2010) 'Disability and skill mismatch', *Economic Record*, 86(1), pp 101-14.

Jones, O. (2011) *Chavs: The demonization of the working class*, London: Verso.

Keep, E. (2012) *Youth transitions, the labour market and entry into employment: Some reflections and questions: SKOPE Research Paper Number 88*, Cardiff: SKOPE.

Meager, N. and Higgins, T. (2011) *Disability and skills in a changing economy*, Briefing Paper Series, Wath Upon Dearne, UK: UK Commission for Employment and Skills.

Merrill, B. and West, L. (2009) *Using biographical methods in social research*, London: Sage Publications.

Newman, L., Wagner, M., Knokey, A.-M., Marder, C., Nagle, K., Shaver, D. and Schwarting, M. (2011) *The post-high school outcomes of young adults with disabilities up to 8 years after high school: A report from the national longitudinal transition study-2 (NLTS2) (NCSER 2011-3005)*, Menlo Park, CA: SRI International.

Office for Disability Issues (2013) *Disability equality indicators*, London: Office for Disability Issues, http://odi.dwp.gov.uk/disability-statistics-and-research/disability-equality-indicators.php

Riddell, S., Baron, S. and Wilson, A. (2001) '*Social capital and people with learning difficulties*', International Studies in Sociology of Education, 11(1), pp 3-23.

Rydberg, E., Gellerstedt, L.C. and Danermark, B. (2011) Deaf people's employment and workplaces–similarities and differences in comparison with a reference population, *Scandinavian Journal of Disability Research*, 13(4), pp 327-45.

Sayce, L. (2011) *Getting in, staying in and getting on: Disability employment support fit for the future*, London: Department for Work and Pensions.

Schley, S., Walter, G., Weathers, R., Hemmeter, J., Hennessey, J. and Burkhauser, R. (2011) 'Effect of postsecondary education on the economic status of persons who are deaf or hard of hearing', *Journal of Deaf Studies and Deaf Education*, 16(4), pp 524-36.

Scottish Government (2012) *Scottish Index of Multiple Deprivation 2012: A national statistics publication for Scotland*, Edinburgh: Scottish Government.

Scottish Government (2013) *Pupil Census Supplementary Data*, Edinburgh: SG, http://www.scotland.gov.uk/Topics/Statistics/Browse/School-Education/dspupcensus/pupcensus2012

Scottish Government (2014) *Implementation of the Education (Additional Support for Learning) (Scotland) Act 2004 (as amended): Report to Parliament 2013*, Edinburgh: Scottish Government.

Siltanen, J. (2004) 'Inequalities of gender and class: charting the sea change', in J. Curtis, E.G. Grabb and L. Guppy (eds) *Social inequality in Canada* (4th edn), Toronto, Canada: Pearson Education Canada.

Sosu, E. and Ellis, S. (2014) *Closing the attainment gap in Scottish education*, York: Joseph Rowntree Foundation.

Vernon, A. (1999) 'The dialectics of multiple identities and the disabled people's movement', *Disability & Society*, 14(3), pp 385-98.

TEN

Supply- and demand-side policies and the employment of learning disabled people in Britain

Sarah Woodin

Introduction

This chapter discusses the position of learning disabled people[1] in Britain in relation to the labour market, and supply and demand policies. Welfare policies in Britain have recently sought to reposition many disabled people as potential workers rather than welfare recipients (DWP, 2013b), but there has been much more reticence and ambivalence in relation to learning disabled people. Relatively recent acknowledgement that learning disabled people should be included in 'work-first' policies and evidence of the efficacy of some support programmes such as supported employment (OECD, 2010) have not resulted in a large increase in the numbers working, despite clear evidence that learning disabled people have long valued the opportunity to work and to earn money on the same basis as everyone else.

In this chapter, a description of the employment position of learning disabled people is followed by a discussion of the value of work. The chapter then focuses on labour market developments, including flexibility and commodification, and the implications of these for learning disabled people before moving on to consider supply- and demand-side policies. The chapter suggests that while supply-side policies have arguably become more benign and informed, emphasising co-production, inclusion and the importance of community connections, rather than 'readiness' to work, they often remain focused on increasing the capacity of individuals, rather than the creation of demand-led opportunities. Without seeking to undermine the importance of individually tailored support, the rest of this chapter discusses the contribution and limitations of demand-side strategies and the contribution of some user-led initiatives. The chapter is mainly concerned with the situation in Britain and with the employment situation of people with labels of 'moderate' and 'severe' learning difficulties, rather than, for instance, those who may have learning difficulties such as dyslexia (Office for Disability Issues, 2010).

Paid work and learning disabled people

The proportion of learning disabled people in paid work

Establishing the proportion of learning disabled people in paid work is difficult (Emerson et al, 2010). Available data tend to concentrate on the activities of services, rather than outcomes for learning disabled people and their families (Emerson and Hatton, 2008) and different definitions used lead to varying results. Bearing in mind these caveats, learning disabled people consistently have an employment rate – 7.1% in 2011-12 (Emerson et al, 2012) – that is lower than that of disabled people generally (46.3%) and non-disabled people (76.4%) (Office for Disability Issues, 2012). The employment gap between disabled people and non-disabled people, therefore, is a little over 30 percentage points, but a massive 69.3 percentage points between learning disabled people and non-disabled people. These differences have remained relatively stable over recent decades.

There are also considerable regional variations in employment rates for learning disabled people, ranging from 0% to 20.4%, with the highest rates recorded in the South East of England (Emerson et al, 2012). The employment rates of learning disabled people correlate with overall employment opportunities in an area and the existence of local initiatives that aim specifically to support learning disabled people into work (Broad, 2007; Beyer and Robinson, 2009; Greig et al, 2014). Therefore, it is clear that learning disabled people face a wide and persistent gap in employment compared with other disabled people and with non-disabled people.

Earnings

The earnings of learning disabled people are low. Employment is often distinguished from the welfare benefit system (Stone, 1986), but learning disabled people who do work are often not clearly positioned on one side or the other of the earnings/benefit divide. In brief, they often continue to receive benefits while working. It is also important to note that numerically, more learning disabled people work on a voluntary basis than do paid work (Boyce et al, 2008; Emerson et al, 2010; see also Chapter 12, this volume).

Of those who are paid, Emerson and Hatton's (Emerson et al, 2010) figures show a clustering of employment, where a large number (approximately 35% of people with 'mild' learning impairments and about 56% of those with 'severe' learning impairments) earned a very limited amount of money – less than £50 per week. Details of this are not elaborated on in the report but typically people on such low wages may be working for just a few hours per week and retaining welfare benefits under one or more of a number of regulations that allow small amounts to be earned without incurring a financial penalty through loss of benefits. Precise data on the hours worked are not available, although the issue is alluded to as a problem in the government strategy, *Valuing employment now*[2] (HM Government, 2009). In other instances, people may be working for much longer hours, but for very little pay. In Emerson and Hatton's (2010) study, at the other end of the earnings scale were those who earned enough to be better off through working, although they might retain non-means-tested benefits. Just 5% of people in the study labelled as having severe learning difficulties earned between £50 and £100 per week. The overriding picture is, therefore, one of low wages. Exceptions, however, have been noted where at least some benefit payments have been relinquished through being able to earn more money, indicating that working on the fringes of employment is not inevitable for learning disabled people. For example, McInally (2008) has described how a strong commitment from senior social work management, combined with a purposeful focus on full time work (as opposed to training in work programmes or part-time jobs) led to learning disabled workers being significantly financially better off (see also Beyer, 2007).

Types of jobs

Recent data on the types of jobs carried out by learning disabled people are scarce. What there is indicates that in the main, work available through supported employment opportunities tends to be relatively low skilled, including jobs such as cleaning, catering, routine office work and retail work (Wistow and Schneider, 2003; McInally, 2008). As discussed in the following section, while there is evidence that learning disabled people value these jobs, some are employed in professional jobs that are more skilled, such as in training and consultancy work, especially where they receive continuing organisational support from people in their workplace (for examples, see Fembeck et al, 2013). Learning disabled people have taken roles in advisory, advocacy and campaigning organisations, particularly those representing learning disabled people or involving disabled people in the running of services (Beresford and Hasler, 2009; Branfield, 2009; Fyson and Fox, 2014). Exact numbers are not available, but this kind of participation in service planning is for many voluntary rather than paid, again indicating the ambiguous position occupied by learning disabled people between work and welfare.

The value of work

The low rates of employment described above might be discouraging, but the majority (65%) of learning disabled people who are not working are consistently reported as wanting a job (Emerson et al, 2005). Reasons for wanting to work given by learning disabled people include money, social contact and being perceived as competent (Andrews and Rose, 2010). Researchers have reported benefits from work in developing countries (Lamichhane, 2012) and more affluent ones alike (Skellern and Astbury, 2012), which are said to include greater autonomy, emotional wellbeing and an improved sense of control over the wider world (Jahoda et al, 2008). Improvement of social status and opportunities to form friendships are also reported, especially where employment is more individualised (Jahoda, 2008).

Conversely, a rather less benign approach has been evident historically, where disabled people have been expected to work for their own 'good' and to reduce their 'dependency' on charity or the state (Wolfensberger, 1975; Ryan and Thomas, 1980). This perspective downplays the value and contribution of work carried out by disabled people in favour of an approach that assumes they will be improved, made less dependent and possibly made more 'normal' through work. While such views have also been expressed about the general population (Bambra, 2011), the consequences for learning disabled people have been more serious. The tasks carried out in hospital occupational therapy units and in day centres in the 20th century are examples of this reasoning (Mitchell, 1998), even if work periods were short and the overriding picture in institutions became increasingly one of wasted time and inactivity (Wolfensberger, 1975; Mansell and Beadle-Brown, 2012). Similar work (repetitive light industrial work for very small token payments, often a standard £4 per week) characterised day centre services in Britain in the 1970s and 1980s, until replaced by models emphasising the value of therapies and/or education. Reasons for the limited ability of day centres to help learning disabled people to find paid work are beyond the scope of this chapter. However the need for change became evident from the 1980s onwards, due to a lack of progression out of these services. As a consequence, more optimistic models were developed as alternatives (Porterfield and Gathercole, 1984; WHO, 2011).

Disabled people were traditionally seen as 'deserving' under the Poor Laws and exempted from expectations that they should work in the open labour market. However, as with all disabled people, more recently they have been subject to more stringent reassessments to determine their fitness for work. Accompanying these developments there are elements of an ideology that casts disabled people receiving benefits as 'shirkers', actively avoiding paid work (Garthwaite, 2012; Briant et al, 2013). Where learning disabled people fit in this classification is not clear as, on the one hand, they are caught in the net of increased work expectation, but, on the other hand, they are more likely to still be thought of as being a long way from the employment market by service providers and in need of specialised employment support services (DWP, 20113a; see also Chapters Four and Five, this volume).

In summary, therefore, the majority of learning disabled people express interest in working in the same kinds of jobs, with the same terms and conditions, as non-disabled people. In practice, the support they receive to do so is limited by the resources allocated by society to enable learning disabled people to participate (Gold, 1980) and the organisation of almost all of the labour market, which assumes a certain type of non-disabled worker (Finkelstein, 1980). In the following section, recent labour market developments are considered.

Changing labour markets in Britain

Western capitalist societies are increasingly characterised by a globalised economy and the further commodification of all aspects of the economy. More unstable and uncertain working conditions are the norm for a growing number of workers employed in a market increasingly characterised by part-time, temporary work in private sector jobs. At the same time, changing conditions may offer new unforeseen opportunities as older labour patterns are disrupted. In this context, this section discusses two important issues – flexibility and commodification – that impact on learning disabled people.

Flexibility

In the 1970s and 1980s, neoliberal policies found a political voice in the Thatcher governments in Britain and the Reagan administrations in the United States. Economic growth was to be maximised through increased national and personal competition and secure employment conditions were challenged (and continue to be) on the basis that they inhibited the employment flexibility that was necessary for economic growth. This flexibility has centrally involved employers' freedom to hire, and especially fire, workers as they wish (numerical flexibility), as well as to move workers around into different positions within organisations (functional flexibility). The increasingly uncertain and insecure position of many workers has been implicated by some authors in the growth of a new group who are precariously employed in traditionally white- and blue-collar jobs (Wolff, 2010; Standing, 2011).

There is some evidence that disabled people have welcomed flexibility in that it can offer more possibilities for carrying out work in conditions that may better suit their needs and that offer a more conducive working environment (Adams and Oldfield, 2011). For example, the 'reasonable adjustments' provided for in the United Kingdom's Disability Discrimination Act 1995 were introduced with the explicit intention of introducing these flexibilities. Advances in technology may be advantageous for some (Roulstone, 1998) and similar developments for learning disabled people may lead to opportunities to work in new ways. It can mean that job carving – a practice where employees and employers negotiate a specific set of duties suited to each party's job requirements – may appear more usual and part of accepted practice.

The ways that flexible working arrangements have been implemented, however, have not been wholly advantageous for employees in general. For instance, critics point to the introduction of zero-hours contracts (contracts that require workers' availability but with no guarantee of hours offered) as an example of an arrangement that is designed to suit the needs of the employer, not the employee. The term 'flexploitation' (Gray, 1998; Dean, 2008) has been used to describe situations where people do not have a strong bargaining position to secure flexible working arrangements on their own terms. Flexibility is often designed to meet the needs of short-term contracts, as well as offer a means to limit employment rights of workers. Employees may not be consulted, but expected to move from one set of tasks to another after a relatively short period of time and this presents difficulties for learning disabled people who need longer and more help to learn specific jobs.

The critique of 'flexploitation' has also been elaborated in tandem with the policy of 'flexicurity'. Originating in Denmark and adopted by the European Union (EU) as part of the Lisbon Strategy, under the policy, governments are encouraged to increase labour market flexibility and active labour market policies, while strengthening social protection measures to ensure the wellbeing of workers who have to move jobs at regular intervals. Combined with the provision of lifelong learning opportunities, the intention of the policy was that employees should be provided with a safety net to offset the results of employers' flexibility measures. Flexicurity has been less prominent in Britain than in some other EU countries and some authors have questioned the degree to which it has remained influential following the 2008 economic crisis (Heyes, 2013). For example, Britain has not strengthened, but weakened eligibility for social protection in recent years (Clegg, 2010).

These issues are important in any consideration of how to assist learning disabled people to gain employment. Competition for scarce employment opportunities, for instance, means that very few organisations regularly provide the degree of information in terms of the timeliness, relevance and strength that are needed for people with labels of 'severe' learning difficulties to succeed in employment (Gold, 1980; Callahan and Mank, 1997). Increased demands for flexibility of employees exacerbate this problem because of the need to continually learn new skills, deal with new colleagues and changing contexts for exchanging information. That a few workplaces do manage to offer the conditions needed for learning disabled people to succeed indicates that learning disabled people are able to hold down challenging and interesting jobs in such professions as training and consultancy when conditions are conducive (Fembeck et al, 2013). However, the reality of such a low rate of employment for learning disabled people points to the lack of leverage that they have to influence employment conditions in this direction on any meaningful scale.

Commodification and service work

With the relocation of manufacturing jobs to developing countries, Western economies have in recent decades moved from primary production economies, where agriculture and manufacturing provided the bulk of jobs, to post-primary production economies, where human services form a major source of employment (Wolfensberger, 1989). This shift has important implications for disabled people and learning disabled people in particular, because the way human service industries have developed contributes in various ways to their commodification. In brief, it is argued that disabled people have an economic value for organisations that provide services to them.

Authors have argued (see, for example, Wolfensberger, 1989) that services designed to make people more independent may in fact have a vested interest in keeping disabled people dependent because it is only in such a state that they are a source of value (income) to the enterprises delivering services. While, for instance, the number of people in receipt of 'care' services in Britain is now falling (HSCIC, 2013), over a million people received some sort of such service in the community in 2012–13 and an additional quarter of a million received residential services. This represents an important source of income to a large sector of the economy. Despite tightening eligibility criteria, the value of the 2011–12 social care market in England was estimated at nearly £7.8 billion, across all adult age groups (HSCIC, 2013).

While it may be argued that learning disabled people choose to have and need this kind of assistance, they may also not have an option but to use mainstream services, which often screen them out. Where they are included, for example, disabled people are a potential commodity for employment services providers that are contracted to run 'welfare-to-work' schemes in Britain. However, because of the way that employment services are paid (primarily by results – see Chapters Four and Five, this volume) and because demand for assistance outstrips its supply, the evidence suggests that disabled people are often disadvantaged in gaining access to employment assistance services. The commodification of disabled people in this instance means a poor and exclusionary service.

The changing nature of the labour market presents both problems and opportunities for learning disabled people. To understand how the potential of learning disabled people to take up these opportunities has been facilitated in Britain, the focus in the following section is on employment policies.

Labour market policies

In Britain, a plethora of policies have sought to ameliorate the lack of employment and consequent poverty of learning disabled people, while at the same time exclusionary forces, many also part of the policy implementation process, have served to push learning disabled people away from the paid labour market. This ambivalence has created complex systems of opportunity and protection that are difficult for learning disabled people to negotiate in practice. At various times, work has been seen not as an end in itself in terms of offering routes to self-fulfilment and financial independence, but as something that might serve the useful function of ameliorating impairments, as something good for those seeking work. More recently, recognition has grown that learning disabled people want to work on the same terms as other people, but that opportunities lag behind. Employment policies have been implemented on both the supply and demand side of the economy, to which we now turn.

Supply-side policies

Supply-side employment policies essentially focus on the individual – for example, their educational qualifications and skills, and their attitudes to paid employment. Recent developments in work and welfare policies for disabled people have been structured by an almost exclusive focus on the supply side. Learning disabled people have not been excluded from this focus. This is important because while almost all young learning disabled people leaving school express an interest in doing paid work, most, in fact, do not get access to help to enter the labour market. Instead, many go to college, and while this mirrors the greater participation of learning disabled people in education generally, from here there may be an uncertain path into employment, if one at all (Smyth and McConkey, 2003; Kaehne and Beyer, 2009).

Most interventions have traditionally focused on the needs of unemployed people to learn about the world of work and have emphasised the development of skills to meet employers' needs, often before people have entered work. However, for a number of reasons, such efforts have been limited in their success for learning disabled people. Payment by results provides an incentive to select people who most closely fit employers' requirements, especially during periods of high unemployment. So, for example, an internal evaluation of Work Choice, a programme designed, among other things, to assist learning disabled people to access support to get paid employment, found that contracted agencies excluded and 'parked' (accepted on the programme but did not provide a service to) learning disabled people (Thompson et al, 2011).

That learning disabled people are frequently seen by mainstream employment services as 'not ready' for work, or as being a long way from the employment market (see Newton et al, 2012), is also reflected in the categories used for Employment and Support Allowance (ESA), Britain's primary out-of-work welfare benefit for disabled people. The ESA provides financial support on the basis of an assessment (the Work Capability Assessment [WCA]) in relation to judged ability to participate in paid work and different employment-related requirements are set depending on levels of impairment and perceived distance from the labour market. Some learning disabled people are defined as fit for work by the WCA, while others are deemed to be unlikely to work in the future (those placed in the support group) and some (those placed in the work-related activity group) are considered capable of making efforts to (re-)enter paid work as soon as possible. Many learning disabled people, placed in the support group, have not been considered able to work. The relationship between welfare benefits and employment is beyond the scope of this chapter (for further discussion, see Grover and Piggott, 2012), but the expectation of being not able to work can provide a powerful disincentive to participate in mainstream services that those people in the support group can do on a voluntary basis.

Learning disabled jobseekers are more likely to be successful when they have dedicated assistance to determine a job choice, find employment and have additional support after starting employment (Beyer and Robinson, 2009; OECD, 2010; WHO, 2011). Supported employment services have been developed in many areas in Britain and many are able to provide this kind of personalised assistance, especially as they are founded on assumptions of employability and eligibility. However, overall, investment in such services is small and, as discussed above, the numbers of learning disabled people in paid employment remain small. The strategy, *Valuing people now* (DH, 2009), included a commitment to narrow the gap between the employment rate of learning disabled people and that of disabled people as a whole by 2025. To this end, a number of initiatives established by the previous New Labour government in some localities were continued by the coalition government for a while, but no commitment was made to fund these after the pilot phases. Local authority targets (Public Service Agreements), which included some for supported employment, were abolished in June 2010 and a policy of localism has required local authorities to make decisions about what initiatives to prioritise in the context of severe central government funding cuts. A pattern of reduced expenditure combined with some uncertainty by service commissioners has been reported (Greig et al, 2014).

Supply-side interventions represent the vast majority of policy effort related to the employment of learning disabled people. While effective strategies, such as supported and customised employment services, are understood and used in many areas, they are not available on a sufficiently large scale in Britain.

Demand-side policies

Demand-side policies broadly refer to those policies that are aimed at the employers', rather than job applicants' or workers', side of the employment relationship. Demand-side interventions are visible at various levels. For example, they may range from concerted efforts to influence employers individually, such as through awareness campaigns, to macro-level interventions to influence the nature of the employment market. Demand-side policies, therefore, are part of the usual business of government, and they often entail such things as encouraging investment and economic growth and regulating taxes (Weisbrot and Jorgensen, 2013).

In relation to disabled people, and even more for learning disabled people, macro-level policies have been next to non-existent in recent years and this largely results from the strength of organised capitalism and the labour market situation described above (Barnes and Mercer, 2005; Standing, 2011). However, some notable measures were taken in the past and these are worth reviewing briefly. After the Second World War, when a labour shortage saw disabled people and women drafted into employment, the Disabled Persons (Employment) Act 1944 provided designated categories of employment for disabled people, sheltered employment and quotas. At various times in the period after the Second World War, all of these were abolished. In reality, however, they were not measures that provided many opportunities for people with labels of 'severe' learning disability as they were intended to prevent the destitution of men who had sustained injuries during war.

A more recent measure (also now abolished) involved the provision of subsidies to employers for taking on learning disabled workers. Originally called 'Sheltered Industrial Groups', the measure became the 'Sheltered Placement Scheme', indicating a move from an enclave model to one of individual placement (Department of Employment, 1990; Hyde, 2000). Following an assessment of the productivity of a worker, companies were awarded a certain amount of funding to offset an assumed lower productivity rate. While aimed at helping people to move out of sheltered workshops and into more inclusive settings, the scheme attracted criticism from many quarters for its pessimistic view of the capability of workers and the stigma it drew to people employed in this way (Barnes, 1992).

Problems with these types of demand-side interventions relate to when their intersection with prevailing attitudes and assumptions about the capabilities of learning disabled people (Staniland, 2009) leaves little room for demonstrating capabilities and contributions. Each of the measures used a deficit model to highlight a difference in the capacities of disabled people including learning disabled people, and non-disabled people (Barnes, 1992).

A more recent attempt to begin with a presumption of capacity may be seen in a demand-side policy introduced in the 1990s, which required user involvement in the development of public services (House of

Commons Public Administration Select Committee, 2008). Although not an employment measure, it has had important implications for employment. Public involvement was seen as a social good, in part motivated by a desire to strengthen democratic participation in the legitimation of political bodies. This initiative also involved disabled people, developing the argument that disabled people were 'experts by experience' (DH, 2001a) and that they had contributions to make by virtue of their identity. User involvement has taken different forms and success has been patchy (Arnstein, 1969; Barnes and Mercer, 2006; Woodin, 2006), but such opportunities have opened up chances for some advantaged and articulate learning disabled people to take part in decision-making bodies. For an even more fortunate few, they resulted in paid jobs that were focused on service improvement and advocacy. However, most positions and opportunities have been voluntary. There are also some indications that they have been particularly vulnerable to cutbacks in expenditure (Woodin, 2011), but this indication warrants further research. Nevertheless, the increased visibility and impact have been important for learning disabled people and have led to calls for greater recognition and challenges to the organisation and meaning of work for such people.

The organisation of work

The problems faced by disabled people in securing work have led some authors to call for a reconfiguration of the meaning of work (Barnes, 2003). For example, Prideaux et al (2009; see also Chapter Fourteen, this volume) argue that disabled people who employ personal assistants (PAs) should be recognised as employers, rather than welfare recipients. This would necessitate a change in attitudes to encompass a broader definition of work, as well as involving a questioning of the binary divide between work and welfare. These are important arguments in favour of the reconceptualisation of work and they also point the way for learning disabled people. Managing PAs needs to be understood as involving work and not just receiving assistance. However, not all learning disabled people operate PA systems of their own and the fact that many people who receive self-directed support rely on help from others for the management of assistance (Hatton, 2014) suggests that a reconceptualisation of work may not be to the advantage of all learning disabled people. This is particularly the case as user-led peer support organisations of learning disabled people are still underdeveloped. Hence, different approaches to paid work are also needed, including flexibility on workers' terms through, for instance, job carving, and the acknowledgement of new workplace relationships that recognise the value of co-working and joint contribution, as well as more specifically agreed arrangements between employers and workers.

Conclusion

This chapter has presented a brief overview of some of the issues influencing the employment opportunities of learning disabled people in Britain. It has been selective in highlighting key aspects of supply- and demand-side policies and it needs to be recognised that there are very many pertinent issues beyond those presented here. The main points to be drawn from this account are that policies have consistently been concerned with the very low employment rates of learning disabled people. To address this, effort over very many years has been put into vocational rehabilitation services that one way or another have sought to bring learning disabled people closer to the requirements of employers. The failure of these efforts is borne out by the continuing very low rates of employment experienced by learning disabled people. Successful efforts have been developed, in particular supported employment, which by increasing the level of assistance at all stages has helped a large number of individuals to find and keep work. However, the level of resources to develop jobs for all has not been forthcoming and, as has been shown in this chapter, there are indications that in Britain they are not likely to be. On the contrary, priorities by national governments are to encourage growth and competitiveness in the context of a free market. It follows, therefore, that there is a need to supplement supply-side efforts with attention on the demand side also. Just as there is a need to maintain opportunities for learning disabled people to compete in competitive employment where they wish and choose to do so, a way forward must involve developing and supporting new demand-side initiatives that help to challenge limiting beliefs, structures and opportunities through the development of collaborative or responsive ways of working.

Notes

[1] The term 'learning disabled' is used here to provide consistency with other chapters and in recognition of an international readership. The term 'people with learning difficulties' is preferred in Britain by People First, the representative organisation of learning disabled people, and is widely used in Britain.

[2] *Valuing people* (DH, 2001b) and *Valuing people now* (DH, 2009) are strategy documents concerned with learning disabled people developed by the-then New Labour

governments. Commitments were made to social inclusion for learning disabled people, including the development of employment opportunities (for further details, see Fyson and Ward, 2004). The programme ended in 2011.

References

Adams, L. and Oldfield, K. (2011) *Opening up work: The views of disabled people and people with long-term health conditions*, London: Equality and Human Rights Commission.

Andrews, A. and Rose, J. (2010) 'A preliminary investigation of factors affecting employment motivation in people with intellectual disabilities', *Journal of Policy and Practice in Intellectual Disability*, 7(4), pp 239-44.

Arnstein, S. (1969) 'A ladder of citizen participation', *Journal of the American Institute of Planners*, 35(4), pp 216-24.

Bambra, C. (2011) *Work, worklessness and the political economy of health*, Oxford: Oxford University Press.

Barnes, C. (1992) 'Disability and employment', http://disability-studies.leeds.ac.uk/files/library/Barnes-dis-and-emp.pdf

Barnes, C. (2003) '"Work" is a four letter word? Disability, work and welfare', invited presentation at 'Working Futures: Policy, Practice and Disabled People's Employment', University of Sunderland, Marriot Hotel, Seaburn, 3 December.

Barnes, C. and Mercer, G. (2005) 'Disability work and welfare: challenging the social exclusion of disabled people', *Work, Employment & Society*, 19(3), pp 527-45.

Barnes, C. and Mercer, G. (2006) *Independent futures: Creating user-led disability services in a disabling society*, Bristol: Policy Press.

Beresford, P. and Hasler, F. (2009) *Transforming social care: Changing the future together*, Uxbridge: Centre for Citizen Participation, Brunel University Press.

Berthoud, R. (2011) *Trends in the employment of disabled people in Britain*, ISER Working Paper Series, no 2011-03, Colchester: Institute for Social and Economic Research, www.iser.essex.ac.uk/files/iser_working_papers/2011-03.pdf

Beyer, S. (2007) *An evaluation of the costs and financial benefits of supported employment in North Lanarkshire*, Cardiff: Welsh Centre for Learning Disabilities.

Beyer, S. and Robinson, C. (2009) *A review of research literature on supported employment: a report for the cross-government learning disability employment strategy team*, London: Department of Health.

Boyce, M., Secker, J., Johnson, R., Floyd, M., Grove, B., Schneider, J. and Slade, J. (2008) 'Mental health service users' experiences of returning to paid employment', *Disability & Society*, 23(1), pp 77-88.

Branfield, F. (2009) *Developing user involvement in social work education*, London: Social Care Institute for Excellence.

Briant, E., Watson, N. and Philo, G. (2013) 'Reporting disability in the age of austerity: the changing face of media representation of disability and disabled people in the UK and the creation of new "folk devils"', *Disability & Society*, 28(6), pp 874-89.

Broad, M. (2007) 'Employment barriers for people with learning disabilities', *Community Care*, 30 May, www.communitycare. co.uk/2007/05/30/employment-barriers-for-people-with-learning-disabilities/

Callahan, M. and Mank, D. (1997) *Choice and control of employment for people with disabilities*, Gautier, MS: Marc Gold and Associates, www. marcgold.com/Publications/White%20Papers/Choice%20and%20 Control%20of%20Employment%20for%20People%20with%20 Disabilities.pdf

Clegg, D. (2010) 'Labour market policy in the crisis: the UK in comparative perspective', *Journal of Policy and Social Justice*, 18(1), pp 5-7.

Dean, H. (2008) 'Flexibility or flexploitation? Problems with work-life balance in a low-income neighbourhood', in T. Maltby, P. Kennett and K. Rummery (eds) *Social policy review*, Bristol: Policy Press, pp 113-32.

Department of Employment (1990) *Employment and training for people with disabilities*, London: Department of Employment.

DH (Department of Health) (2001a) *The expert patient: A new approach to chronic disease management for the 21st century*, London: DH.

DH (2001b) *Valuing people: A strategy for learning disability services in the 21st century*, London: DH.

DH (2009) *Valuing people now: A new three-year strategy for people with learning disabilities*, London: DH.

DWP (Department for Work and Pensions) (2013a) *Evaluation of the Work Choice specialist disability employment programme: findings from the 2011 Early Implementation and 2012 Steady States waves of the research*, Sheffield: Department for Work and Pensions

DWP (2013b) *Disability and health employment strategy: The story so far*, London: DWP.

Emerson, E. and Hatton, C. (2008) *People with learning disabilities in England*, Lancaster: Centre for Disability Research.

Emerson, E., Hatton, C., Robertson, J., Baines, S., Christie, A. and Glover, G. (2012) *People with learning disabilities in England*, London: Department of Health.

Emerson, E., Hatton, C., Robertson, J., Roberts, H., Baines, S. and Glover, G. (2010) *People with learning disabilities 2010*, London: Department of Health.

Emerson, E., Malam, S., Davies, I. and Spencer, K. (2005) *Adults with learning difficulties in England 2003-4*, Lancaster: Lancaster University.

Fembek, M., Butcher, T., Heindorf, I. and Wallner-Mik, C. (2013) *Zero Project report 2013*, Klosterneuburg, Austria: The ESSL Foundation.

Finkelstein, V. (1980) *Attitudes and disabled people*, New York, NY: World Rehabilitation Fund.

Fyson, R. and Fox, L (2014) 'Inclusion or outcomes? Tensions in the involvement of people with learning disabilities in strategic planning', *Disability & Society*, 29(2), pp 239-54.

Fyson, R. and Ward, L. (2004) *Making valuing people work: Strategies for change in services for people with learning disabilities*, Bristol: Policy Press.

Garthwaite, K. (2012) 'The language of shirkers and scroungers? Talking about illness, disability and coalition welfare reform', *Disability & Society*, 26(3), pp 369-72.

Gold, M. (1980) *Did I say that? Articles and commentary on the Try Another Way System*, Champaign, IL: Research Press Company.

Gray, A. (1998) 'New Labour – new labour discipline', *Capital and Class*, 22(2), pp 1-8.

Greig, R., Chapman, P., Eley, A., Watts, R., Love, B. and Bourlet, G. (2014) *The cost effectiveness of employment support for people with disabilities*, Bath: NDTi.

Grover, C. and Piggott, L. (2012) 'Employment and Support Allowance: capability, personalization and disabled people in the UK', *Scandinavian Journal of Disability Research*, 15(2), pp 170-84.

Hatton, C. (2014) 'Trends and variations in self-directed support and direct payments for adults with learning disabilities', *Tizard Learning Disability Review*, 19(1), pp 35-8.

Heyes, J. (2013) 'Flexicurity in crisis: European labour market policies in a time of austerity', *European Journal of Industrial Relations*, 20(2), pp 71-86.

HM Government (2009) *Valuing employment now: Real jobs for people with learning disabilities*, London: Department of Health.

House of Commons Public Administration Select Committee (2008) *User involvement in public services: Sixth report of session 2007-08*, London: The Stationery Office.

HSCIC (Health and Social Care Information Centre) (2013) *Personal social services: Expenditure and unit costs, England, 2011-12, final release*, London: HSCIC, https://catalogue.ic.nhs.uk/publications/social-care/expenditure/pss-exp-eng-11-12-fin/pss-exp-eng-11-12-fin-rpt.pdf

Hyde, M. (2000) 'From welfare to work? Social policy for disabled people of working age in the United Kingdom in the 1990s', *Disability and Society*, 15(2), pp 327-41.

Jahoda, A., Kemp, J., Riddell, S. and Banks, P. (2008) 'Feelings about work: a review of the socio-emotional impact of supported employment on people with intellectual disabilities', *Journal of Applied Research in Intellectual Disabilities*, 21, pp 1-18.

Kaehne, A. and Beyer, S. (2009) 'Views of professionals on aims and outcomes of transition for young people with learning disabilities', *British Journal of Learning Disabilities*, 37(2), pp 138-44.

Lamichhane, K. (2012) 'Employment situation and life changes for people with disabilities: evidence from Nepal', *Disability & Society*, 27(4), pp 471-85.

McInally, G. (2008) 'Supported employment for people with learning disabilities: the case for full-time work', *Tizard Learning Disability Review*, 13(3), pp 42-6.

Mansell, J. and Beadle-Brown, J. (2012) *Active support: Enabling and empowering people with intellectual disabilities*, London: Jessica Kingsley.

Mitchell, D. (1998) 'Learning disability nursing: reflections on history', *Journal of Learning Disabilities for Nursing, Health and Social Care*, 2(1), pp 45-9.

Newton, B., Meager, N., Bertram, C., Corden, A., George, A., Lalani, M., Metcalf, H., Rolfe, H., Sainsbury, R. and Westo, K. (2012) *Work Programme evaluation: Findings from the first phase of qualitative research on programme delivery*, DWP Research Report no. 821, Sheffield: Department for Work and Pensions.

OECD (Organisation for Economic Co-operation and Development) (2010) *Sickness, disability and work: Breaking the barriers: A synthesis of findings across OECD countries*, Paris: OECD Publishing.

Office for Disability Issues (2010) *Equality Act 2010: Guidance*, London: HM Government.

Office for Disability Issues (2012) *Disability facts and figures*, London: Department for Work and Pensions.

Porterfield, J. and Gathercole, C. (1984) *An ordinary working life: Vocational services for people with mental handicap*, London: The King's Fund.

Prideaux, S. J., Roulstone, A., Harris, J. and Barnes, C. (2009) 'Disabled people and self directed support schemes: re-conceptualising work and welfare in the 21st Century', *Disability & Society*, 24(5) pp 557-69.

Roulstone, A. (1998) *Enabling technology: Disabled people, work and new technology*, Buckingham: Open University Press.

Ryan, J. and Thomas, F. (1980) *The politics of mental handicap*, Harmondsworth: Penguin.

Skellern, K. and Astbury, G. (2012) 'Gaining employment: the experience of students at a further education college for individuals with learning disabilities', *British Journal of Learning Disabilities*, 42(1), pp 60-7.

Smyth, M. and McConkey, R. (2003) 'Future aspirations of students with severe learning disabilities and of their parents on leaving special schooling', *British Journal of Learning Disabilities*, 31(1), pp 54-9.

Standing, G. (2011) *The precariat: The new dangerous class*, London: Bloomsbury Academic.

Staniland, L. (2009) *Public perceptions of disabled people: Evidence from the British Social Attitudes Survey 2009*, London: Office for Disability Issues.

Stone, D. (1986) *The disabled state*, Philadelphia, PA: Temple University Press.

Thompson, A., Trenell, P., Hope, M. and McPhillips, A. (2011) *Work Choice evaluation: Commissioning and transition of clients to the programme*, DWP In-House Research no. 6, London: Department for Work and Pensions.

Weisbrot, M. and Jorgensen, H. (2013) *Macroeconomic policy advice and the Article IV consultations: Comparative overview of European Union member states*, Geneva: International Labour Organization.

WHO (World Health Organization) (2011) *World report on disability*, Geneva, Switzerland: WHO.

Wistow, G. and Schneider, J. (2003) 'Users' views on supported employment and social inclusion: a qualitative study of 30 people in work', *British Journal of Learning Disabilities*, 31(4), pp 166-73.

Wolfensberger, W. (1975) *The origin and nature of our institutional models*, Syracuse, New York, NY: Human Policy Press.

Wolfensberger, W. (1989) 'Human service policies: the rhetoric versus the reality', in L. Barton (ed) *Disability and dependence*, Lewes: Falmer.

Wolff, C. (2010) 'IRS flexible working survey 2010: combating the recession', *IRS Employment Review*, www.xperthr.co.uk/survey-analysis/irs-flexible-working-survey-2010-combating-the-recession/100963/

Woodin, S. (2006) *Mapping user led services: User-led services and centres for independent/integrated/inclusive living: A literature review prepared for the Department of Health*, London: Department of Health.

Woodin, S. (2011) *Fundamental Rights Agency (FRA) study on the fundamental rights of persons with intellectual disabilities and persons with mental health problems: Case study report*, Vienna: Fundamental Rights Agency.

ELEVEN

How can integrated services help sick and disabled people remain in employment? Findings from an evaluation of an in-work support service in the North of England

Jon Warren, Kayleigh Garthwaite and Clare Bambra

Introduction

The main focus of recent debates around disability, chronic illness and work has centred on access to paid work. Over the past two decades this has also been at the heart of the social policy agenda in Britain, with concerted efforts to maximise labour market participation, embodied in initiatives such as the New Deal programmes, which were aimed at various groups (for example, young people, single parents and disabled people) who were seen as being marginalised by the labour market. Additionally, schemes, such as Work Trials and Pathways to Work, were available to disabled people and those with long-term health issues. Initiatives such as these have been underpinned by a political commitment to the idea that work in any form is always preferable to welfare (Warren, 2005) and also by a large body of medical evidence that supports the idea that work is good for individuals and has positive health benefits (see, for example, Black, 2008; NICE, 2009). However, such claims are problematic because, as we shall see, the type of work and the context within which it takes place are important. In brief, 'good work' is good for health, while 'bad work' is not (see Chapter One, this volume).

Nevertheless, work has been seen as 'the answer' for disabled people and those with chronic health problems, in terms of offering both a higher degree of economic autonomy and potential health benefits, and, despite challenges from commentators such as Roulstone and Barnes (2005), this has remained a dominant and persistent theme. As a result, numerous activation policies and interventions to increase the employment of people in receipt of benefits due to ill-health or disability have been initiated in recent decades. These policy strategies have been directed at the supply side – enhancing the ability of individuals with a disability or chronic illness to be employed – and the demand side, notably increasing the desirability to employers of recruiting and retaining this particular group of workers (Bambra, 2006; see also Chapter 10, this volume).

Supply-side strategies are concerned with increasing the availability and work-readiness of individuals with a disability or chronic illness. They are designed to overcome some of the employment barriers that people with a disability or chronic illness face, particularly in terms of a lack of skills or work experience, and financial uncertainty about the transition into paid employment (Gardiner, 1997). British supply-side interventions have included:

- *education, training and work placement schemes*, which aim to increase employment rates by providing vocational skills, work experience and exposure to employers, or recognised qualifications
- *vocational advice and support services* designed to help movement into employment by enhancing job search skills, matching individuals to jobs, arranging access to training and education schemes, offering information about in-work benefits and providing other forms of individualised vocational advice and support
- *vocational rehabilitation*, a long-established form of return-to-work policy in many developed countries – rehabilitation (both medical and vocational) is particularly used to help people who develop a disability or chronic illness while they are in work retain their employment (Bloch and Prins, 2001)
- *provision of benefits for people in paid work* with the aim of increasing employment by overcoming the problems and the financial disincentives related to taking low-paid and often casualised jobs, such as the additional costs (like transport), the financial difficulties that the initial loss of benefits can create and the potential loss of future benefit entitlement if people become out of work again.

Demand-side interventions focus on increasing the demand for disabled workers among employers. They tend to focus on reducing the costs or perceived risks to employers of employing a disabled person or placing requirements on employers in their recruitment and retention of disabled people (Bambra, 2006). They are attempts to combat the other type of employment barriers that disabled people face: employer uncertainty and the physical difficulties of workplaces (Gardiner, 1997).

In Britain there have been three demand-side approaches in recent decades:

- *financial incentives for employers*, which aim to encourage recruitment by offering wage subsidies to cover the initial costs of employment or to compensate for any reduced productivity associated with employing someone with a disability or chronic illness
- *employment rights legislation* such as the Equality Act 2010 (and its predecessor, the Disability Discrimination Act 1995 [DDA]) to increase the employment of people with a recognised disability – since 2006, all European Union (EU) member states are obliged to have such legislation (OECD, 2009)
- *accessibility interventions*, designed to facilitate employment by reducing physical workplace barriers, for instance by providing specialist ergonomic equipment, for people with a disability or chronic illness.

With the forming of a Conservative–Liberal Democrat coalition government in 2010, the social policy agenda in Britain shifted. There is now more emphasis on how getting more individuals into work and off benefits would be beneficial to the state and society by reducing the cost of the welfare bill and the fiscal deficit. While such concerns were a feature of previous Labour governments (1997-2010), they also emphasised how work might be beneficial for individuals. This emphasis has arguably been lost with the formation of the coalition government. The recasting of disabled people and those with chronic health problems as 'scroungers and shirkers' (Garthwaite, 2011) has been the result of the coalition's welfare reforms. However, is simply getting more disabled and chronically sick people into work really the answer?

Numerous evaluations have examined the impact of these 'welfare-to-work' interventions on employment rates in Britain (Bambra et al, 2005; Bambra, 2006; Clayton et al, 2011; see also Chapter Four, this volume). With regard to supply-side interventions, the evidence suggests that vocational advice, and employment and training interventions, have positive impacts on employment rates, ranging from 11% to 50% depending on the characteristics of participants, such as 'job-readiness' or type of illness, as well as the local labour market context (Bambra et al, 2005). There is little evidence that in-work benefits have been effective in increasing employment rates (Bambra, 2006).

In terms of demand-side interventions, British evidence suggests that such interventions have a very limited impact. For example, financial interventions designed to incentivise employers have been found to be ineffective because they do not adequately offset the perceived risks and costs of employing disabled people (Bambra, 2006). The employment rights approach was similarly found to be ineffective in increasing the employment rates of people with a disability or chronic illness. Evidence from Britain suggests that legislation such as the DDA had no effect on employers' recruitment decisions, with the majority of employers unaware of the DDA's employment provisions (Roberts et al, 2004). In fact, the employment gap between those with and those without a health condition or disability actually increased after the introduction of the DDA (Pope and Bambra, 2005). In the case of demand-side interventions, only accessibility interventions – such as Access to Work[1] – appear to have a positive employment impact.

A major factor in the rather limited success of active labour market policies for disabled and chronically ill people is that they focus almost exclusively on employability. Little attention has been paid to the health needs of this population, who, after all, are workless in the first place as a result of ill-health. Recognising the importance of sickness as a barrier to employment would result in more innovative 'health first' approaches (Bambra, 2008). While such medical and psychosocial rehabilitation has been a common feature of interventions in the Nordic countries, more recently they have been applied in Britain. Recent evidence-based guidance produced by England's National Institute for Health and Care Excellence (NICE; NICE, 2009), for example, has recommended a 'health first' case management approach to improving the health and employment of people with a chronic illness.[2] It recommends that integrated programmes that combine traditional vocational training approaches, financial support and health management on an ongoing case management basis should be commissioned to help Incapacity Benefit (IB) recipients and those receiving Employment Support Allowance enter or return to work (Gabbay et al, 2011).

There are examples of services that emphasise addressing health prior to employment. A good example is the Condition Management Programme, provided by primary health care trusts and Jobcentre Plus as part of the Pathways to Work programme before its withdrawal in 2010–11. A case management initiative[3] evaluated by Warren et al (2013) showed that this type of intervention had the potential to make a positive impact on mental health for those people on ill-health-related benefits.[4] It is important to emphasise that the majority of these initiatives were focused on getting people into the labour market.

In contrast, maintaining people within the workplace has not been a high priority, and entering the labour market is too often seen as the end of the employment journey, rather than a staging post. Maintaining individuals in work and addressing the barriers and issues that they face within the workplace, and also in their wider lives, is arguably a logical extension of employment-related interventions for chronically sick and disabled people. It also ties in with the broader occupational health agenda in Britain (Black, 2008; Black and Frost, 2011) and is economically logical. If workers can remain in the workplace then welfare costs are minimised and the barriers to re-entering paid work do not have to be crossed anew.

This chapter explores the potential of the 'health first' approach using evidence collected through a mixed methods evaluation of an in-work support service in the North of England. The service was available to assist employees and employers with job retention. Usually, the problems experienced by employees were health related, but many individuals were also experiencing wider socioeconomic difficulties, such as debt, which led to the creation of new health problems and the exacerbation of existing conditions. The chapter draws on a survey and a series of qualitative interviews undertaken with service users and practitioners who delivered the service. It places the research within the broader British policy context and explores whether the expansion of such services for disabled people and those with chronic health problems might allow individuals to be better supported, and to remain in work for longer, and whether making such forms of support available to all workers may reduce barriers within workplaces to people maintaining their employment.

The In Work Support Project

The In Work Support Project (IWSP) began in 2010. It was originally put forward as a 'Fit for Work' pilot scheme for which the British government invited bids in 2009. Although commended, the project did not secure funding from it. Instead, the project was commissioned by a public sector partnership representing five local authorities and the local primary care trust. The project had a broad remit. Its primary goal was to provide case management in order to support individuals who were at risk of dropping out of paid work to remain in employment. It also sought to provide help and support to small- and medium-sized employers that did not have dedicated human resources or occupational health resources of their own.

This wide sphere of activity meant that the project dealt with service users with a very broad spectrum of issues. These ranged from individuals with health problems that impacted on their work performance, to employees who were struggling to pay their travel-to-work costs after leaving out-of-work benefits and still awaiting their first wage packet. The interventions and support provided to individual service users therefore varied depending on their specific circumstances. Service user problems also varied in complexity. Some users had simple problems that were easily dealt with, while others had multiple problems that required specialist help and took much longer to resolve. The project was also able to offer short-term financial help in the form of supermarket vouchers for people who were struggling financially.

Initially, the criteria for accessing the service were fairly minimal. Potential service users had to be in work and resident in one of the areas covered by the five local authorities funding the project. From April 2011, a minimum qualifying criterion for accessing the service was introduced whereby people were required to have been in employment for at least 13 weeks.

More broadly, the background to the project was the national Fit for Work agenda, which developed after the publication of Black's (2008) report on workplace health and the subsequent introduction of 'fit notes' into the general practice-managed system of sickness absence certification. The 'sick note', which was traditionally used to medically certify sickness absence from work, operated on a zero-sum basis. In other words, an individual was either too sick to work or well enough to work. This was replaced in 2010 with a 'fit note', which is intended to assess fitness for work, as opposed to sickness. The fit note adds the option of being partially fit for work if certain issues are taken into account, including a phased return to work, altered hours, amended duties and workplace adaptations. The intention of the fit note is to reduce the number of people on short-term sickness absence who then lose their employment and become long-term benefit recipients. It is also intended to address concerns that general practitioners were too close to their patients and too keen to sign people off as being unable to work, particularly in areas and/or times of high unemployment (Black, 2008). It was within this context of the concern with individuals' 'fitness to work' that the IWSP was developed to provide interventions that would help to retain people within work.

Evaluation plan and methods

The primary purpose of the evaluation was to assess whether the service had any health impacts. Other objectives included assessing the views and experiences of service users and providers. A mixed methods evaluation was undertaken that involved three key components: a longitudinal survey of service users, and qualitative interviews with service users, and project workers and managers. The study received ethical approval from the ethics committee of the Department of Geography at Durham University, UK.

Quantitative data collection

The aim of the survey of service users was to compare baseline measures with follow-up measures taken when involvement with the service was complete. The questionnaire captured information about the demographics, employment situations, health and expectations of service users and, if applicable, their households. Service users completed the questionnaire, which was administered by their project officer, when they first accessed the service and again upon their exit from the programme. A total of 72 baseline and 56 follow-up questionnaires were completed (a 77% follow-up rate). This represented all those who participated in the service and agreed to take part in the evaluation ($N = 72$) for a nine-month period between June 2011 and March 2012. As part of the initial questionnaire, service users were asked about whether they expected the service to improve their health. At exit the questions were repeated and participants were asked whether they felt the service had improved their health. Participants completed the EuroQol EQ-5D and EQ-5D-VAS validated health measures as part of the questionnaire. It was therefore possible to look at changes to health between the two time points.[5]

Qualitative data collection

The aim of the qualitative interviews with service users and project workers was to capture wider views and experiences of the service, with the intention of informing future discussions of improving the effectiveness of the project. Semi-structured interviews were undertaken with 10 service users, four project workers and two managers. Service users were asked open-ended questions about their health, experiences of the service and how the service could be improved. Project workers were asked open-ended questions about their roles, relations with other agencies and expectations of the service. Interviews were undertaken between December 2011 and March 2012. Service users who had recently exited or who were about to exit the service were asked by project workers if they would be interested in taking part in the research. If they were, contact details for service users were forwarded to the research team who then contacted them. All of the project workers and managers were invited to participate in the interviews and all did, with the exception of one who was not available due to sickness.

Survey results

The survey revealed useful information about those who accessed the service. However, numbers were low, with 72 completing the initial questionnaire and 56 completing the exit questionnaire. The service was accessed by more women (69.4%) than men (30.6%) and reached people from a wide age range (18 to 62 years). The service was accessed as much by owner occupiers (50.4%) as those living in rented accommodation (49.6%) and was used almost as much by those in unskilled (20.8%) and semi-skilled work (27.8%) as those in skilled manual work or higher occupational groups (51.4%). Over three quarters (76.8%) of service users regarded themselves as having health problems. The most prevalent health problems were mental health issues (43.9%), which were more than twice as numerous as the next most commonly reported problems of musculoskeletal issues (19.3%).

For the 56 service users who completed the exit questionnaire, their situation had generally improved. After accessing the service only 63.6% regarded themselves as having health problems. This had fallen from 76.8% (73.6% when the initial figure was adjusted for drop-out). The service had an impact on the reported EQ-5D and EQ-5D-VAS scores of service users. The average EQ-5D score improved to 0.77859 from 0.7331 (0.74246 when the initial figure was adjusted for drop-out). This improvement in the score, which meant it was moving towards the UK population norm, was not statistically significant. Average EQ-5D-VAS scores did show a statistically significant improvement, with a final figure of 73.32 compared with an initial figure of 59.63 (59.34 when the initial figure was adjusted for drop-out). As the evaluation was not able to utilise a controlled design, it is not possible to conclude that the health improvement was due to participation in the IWSP.

Qualitative results: service users

Health issues

Over half of the participants described having mental health issues that had led them to access the service. In some instances, these mental health problems were long term, while for others they were an acute response to a stressful situation that individuals were currently dealing with. For Cheryl,[6] aged 29, a combination of physical problems and mental health problems led to her reaching a crisis point:

> 'It sounds awful but I could have gone in the kitchen and ended me life, that's how bad I felt. I was suffering from bad back pains and all of that just seems to have gone, I was being sick and everything and I was going to the doctors saying I was being sick and I had a pain in me chest and I had blood tests and nothing could be found, they must have thought "What's she on about?" but obviously it was the stress.'

For many who used the service, work was not the solution. Work often combined with pre-existing health conditions and wider social problems such as debt to produce a toxic set of circumstances, as Cheryl outlined:

> 'I felt really depressed to the point where I didn't want to be here actually, it was really that bad. Since I started going to see the counsellor I do feel a lot better already, just knowing that I was actually going to get some help I think. I was stuck in a rut with the little one, and me husband was always shouting at me in front of her and it was getting really bad. I had problems with me stomach, I was being sick all the time and they were telling me I had a stomach ulcer. At the time when I was going [to the IWSP] I just felt so poorly, I felt so depressed really but yeah ... once I started going there I felt completely better.'

In addition to health problems, participants described other barriers that were affecting their ability to sustain or regain employment. Billy, aged 37, was doing three jobs and decided to seek help as a result of his debt problems:

> 'Well the biggest thing I have to be honest, the underlying reason why I'm working three jobs is 'cos I'm so damn deep in debt. If you could alleviate the debt problem I could try and slow down and feel the benefit of the work I'm doing rather than just treading water.'

One of the key issues highlighted was a lack of employer support. Both Sandra and Anna, aged 27, described how their employers were less than supportive when it came to managing their health conditions in the workplace. Sandra stated: "It was really disheartening and it was really, really depressing and it makes you feel you're worthless. You think they just don't care, not even enough to pick up the phone or email saying how was I doing." Similarly, Anna said she "went off sick, then I asked him [boss] to reduce my hours and he said no and if I phoned him he would never phone me back".

Key strengths of the service

Health improvement, job retention and return to work were considered to be the major strengths of the service for the majority of participants, who attributed these to a variety of factors, including:

- the personality of the project officer;
- having someone who listens to them;
- the holistic approach of the IWSP;
- the engaging of employers by IWSP staff.

Daniel, aged 42, commented on how working with the service alleviated problems he was having at work in relation to changing his working hours. Following intervention from his project officer, Daniel's hours were changed to suit his needs:

> 'I do like 6am to 2pm and 6am to 3pm and one late night, so now I do like four early shifts and one late one, and I do one Sunday a month so now I can care for my dad, spend more time with me family. Everything's sorted at work now so I don't have to worry about that, I can concentrate on me family and me dad now.'

The holistic nature of the service was often cited as being one of the most important factors. Participants described how project officers would attend Jobcentre Plus appointments with them, seek out services such as counselling, and engage with employers. For Harriet, aged 30, the holistic nature of the service meant that she did not have to worry about her finances as much: "He [project worker] gave me a couple of £20 gift vouchers to put some leccy [electric] and gas on, I was like 'Are you sure you can do this?' It was just such a relief to know I'd have some gas and leccy."

For Daniel and Harriet, the support of the IWSP meant that their circumstances, including their work situation, which had been threatening their health and therefore their ability to work, had been eased. This increased their likelihood of remaining in work.

Improvements to the service

Participants had a small number of suggestions for improvements to the service. The key improvement suggested was better advertising:

> 'The service I got was fantastic and I think why does no one know about this? There must be thousands of people out there and they said they'd advertised in the local paper but no one wants to take it up. I think the problem comes down to communication, whatever wording they're putting in there ... if it said "If you have a disability or an ailment that's making it difficult for you to remain in work, why don't you ring us up?" (Billy, aged 37)

Qualitative results: project workers and managers

Practice

All of the project officers recognised the diverse needs of their client group. Often, the issue a service user initially presented to project officers was just the "tip of the iceberg":

> 'You find with clients it's not just one thing, it's multiple things. With debt, it's been a major source of problems, that's where I've helped them with food vouchers and that's where I've explained that this is only a short-term fix. It's not going to help address the problem that's got them into this situation.'

Clients with multiple and complex issues were a familiar theme within all the interviews with project officers. Often, an initial issue led to a "domino effect" of problems. The complexity of some of the cases that the project officers encountered was commented on by the service managers:

> 'I think what has happened is that they've had individuals who have needed that support and really needed one point

of focus. I think lots of individuals have come onto the programme with issues which, in terms of sorting out the problem, are quite simplistic. And once that's been sorted out, the individual's gained the trust of that person and it's opened a can of worms and got a thousand and one other issues. They're the actual problems rather than the initial smaller ones.'

Project officers pointed out two problem areas – mental health problems and issues related to personal debt – that arose frequently: "I have more people with mental health issues than anything else. Nearly 80-90% have mental issues, maybe with something else. But a lot of mental health issues. I have them from all backgrounds and walks of life."

The project workers were keen to support service users as much as they could and find appropriate services for them. This was possible due to the wide scope of the project. This also meant that the project officers were working to the edge of their abilities. Often, service users' issues were a combination of factors and individuals only sought help from the service as a last resort. As one project officer, for example, told us: "It surprised me, the amount of stuff that people put up with without seeking help, and then when they do seek help, it's like oomph ... big avalanche."

The complexity of problems was combined with the reality of paid work that was often poorly paid, insecure and inflexible. As another of the staff told us: "People are potentially scared to admit to going on the sick because they know that their job, there are 80 people knocking on the door to take that job. I think people are scared to go on leave."

Future recommendations

Project officers pointed to the successful relationships that they had developed with welfare-based organisations, in particular those from the third sector:

'I found that linking in with third sector groups and networks is much more fruitful in terms of generating mutual referrals, because I'm then finding out more about what they can offer. Likewise, staff from those organisations need help when individuals have self-referred or been referred by someone else. And also when they're referring clients or people they're coming into contact with.'

There was also a feeling that a service like the IWSP could be successful if it was promoted more widely within National Health Service (NHS) settings, in particular in general practitioner (GP) surgeries. There are issues, for example, regarding how to get GPs to engage with, promote and refer individuals to any service. An initiative evaluated by Warren et al (2014a) had assumed that GP referral would be a major route into the intervention, yet it was not. The underlying issue that this point raises is that of branding: essentially to be identified as 'NHS' was seen as being advantageous as it was felt that it would put to rest any doubts that potential clients, and also employers, had about the service.

It was also felt that a clearer identity would allow a service such as the IWSP to engage better with other organisations, employers and employees and may consequently lead to a greater number of referrals. As such, project workers felt that a more NHS-based identity would be a key part of any future strategy: "The biggest thing that helped me was stopping saying I was from the In Work Support Project. I just started saying my employer was the council and the NHS. That gets you in."

Discussion

Both service users and project workers identified multiple and complex issues that needed to be addressed as part of the IWSP. The programme assisted with job retention by tackling health issues and, more broadly, by tackling issues such as debt, confidence and flexible working arrangements. The holistic nature of the programme was a key feature for service users who felt that this, coupled with the personalities of the project officers in assisting them through their service user journey, allowed them to retain employment or address wider social needs. Project officers felt that improvements could be made by creating a different focus and establishing a clear identity. This point was reinforced by service users who felt that better advertising was needed in order to promote the service.

It is known that case management can be beneficial for those with long-term health conditions, particularly in terms of mental health (Warren et al, 2013). Earlier evaluations have found that interpersonal relationships in case management programmes (Davis et al, 2012) and the pattern of interaction between the case managers and their co-workers (McEvoy et al, 2011) can be considered to be a key driver to health improvement. Previous research suggests that case management services provided after individuals find jobs do not seem to have produced positive results, primarily as a result of unsatisfactory implementation (for example, limited employment services, case workers carrying very large caseloads and services being poorly targeted; Holzer and Martinson, 2005).

Ultimately, many of the problems faced by service users in our study stemmed from the poor working conditions they had to tolerate in insecure, badly paid jobs. Research shows that poor work – low-quality, insecure employment that fails to provide labour market security or progress – can indeed be bad for health (Marmot, 2010; Bambra, 2011; Butterworth et al, 2011). Certainly for Patrick (2012, p 13), instead of promoting paid work for all, the government should concentrate on how best to improve the quality of work available, alongside reducing the extent of inequalities within the working-age population: "Were the reality of human interdependence to be acknowledged, as well as efforts to redefine our understanding of work taken seriously, the dualisms and dichotomies between workers and non-workers – the responsible and irresponsible – would be far less potent and might collapse entirely."

Poor work and economic marginality – rather than either regular employment or permanent unemployment – is said to have become more common in recent decades for larger numbers of workers at the bottom of the labour market (McKnight, 2002; Byrne, 2005). Therefore, not only a reconsideration of what work actually is, but also that paid work – any paid work – does not necessarily represent work that is good for you should also be considered. Indeed, such concerns led to some of the service practitioners in the present study questioning whether their efforts might have been better spent finding service users alternative employment, rather than seeking to maintain them in their current jobs.

Conclusion

The quantitative analysis found that service users reported fewer health issues after accessing the IWPS and the validated measures recorded a positive change in general health. The qualitative analysis showed the experience of service users and project workers to have been overwhelmingly positive. Any future initiative of this type should consider how it positions itself in relation to employees and employers, given the evidence to support the view that employees would access such a service better via referrals from health and welfare settings and organisations. Case management approaches can offer a supportive environment in which the health needs, as well as wider societal needs, of those in work who are trying to sustain their employment, can be addressed. It is also clear that such a service could also be beneficial to all individuals in employment as the ability to access such a service at an early stage may prevent the onset of workplace-related health problems. Consequently, this approach could be part of a wider occupational health strategy. The effectiveness and cost-effectiveness of case management-based approaches has been advocated by NICE (2009) and has been further evidenced by more recent evaluations of interventions (Warren et al, 2013, 2014a, 2014b).

This study, however, also highlights how this type of intervention is limited. Many of the underlying problems stemmed from insecure, poorly paid employment and workplaces that either ignored or were ignorant of employment regulations. Such problems need to be addressed systematically and upstream by legislation and better enforcement. Such measures will improve the chances of retaining work not only for disabled people and those with long-term health conditions, but also for the workforce as a whole.

Notes

[1] Access to Work is focused on people's specific needs. It offers help with things such as special equipment; fares to work for those who cannot use public transport; a support worker or job coach; disability awareness training for colleagues; communicators at job interviews; and the cost of moving equipment due to a change of location or job (see Beinart et al, 1996; Hillage et al, 1998).

[2] Guidance produced by NICE in England is followed in Wales, while in Northern Ireland, under an agreement of 2006, the Department of Health, Social Services and Public Safety (DHSSPS) examines any guidance issued by NICE to decide its relevance for Northern Ireland. If NICE guidance is found not to be relevant, or if the DHSSPS decides that it is only partly relevant, it advises on any changes that need to be made.

[3] A primary care trust commissioned an external agency to provide a 'health first' case management approach for long-term (three years or more) IB recipients. This pilot programme used telephone and face-to-face case management approaches to identify and address individual health needs (including health behaviours) and any other related barriers to employment (such as debt or housing). The scheme was intended to complement mainstream services, with case managers signposting patients to the NHS, the Department for Work and Pensions and other health and welfare services. They also referred patients to a physiotherapy service and a counselling service, which they provided as part of the service. Patients were referred onto the programme by other NHS services (such as the Alcohol Service), their general practitioner or they could self-refer. The length of engagement with the service varied according to the needs of each service user. Participants were discharged when they were assessed as

being able to enter mainstream services, such as Pathways to Work, vocational services or community health services.

[4] Starting from comparatively poor initial levels, the case management group of participants saw generic (EQ-5D, EQ-5D-VAS) and mental health (HADS-A, HADS-D and SF8-MCS) measures improved within six months to similar levels found in the comparison group. Musculoskeletal (Nordic 2) and health behaviours did not improve.

[5] The EQ-5D questionnaire asks participants about their mobility, ability to self-care, ability to carry out their usual activities, pain and discomfort, and anxiety and depression on the day when they are interviewed. The responses are converted to a value between 0 and 1. The higher the value is, the better the state of health. The Visual Analogue Scale (VAS), often known as a 'Health Thermometer', involves participants rating their health on the day they are interviewed on a scale between 0 and 100, with 0 representing the worst health state the participant can imagine and 100 representing the best health state they can imagine. Fifty represents the midpoint.

[6] All interviewees' names have been changed in order to preserve their anonymity.

Acknowledgements

The authors would like to thank the staff and service users of the In Work Support service for their help and cooperation with this study.

References

Bambra, C. (2006) 'The influence of government programmes and pilots on the employment of disabled workers', in K. Needels and B. Schmitz (eds) *Economic and social costs and benefits to employers for retaining, recruiting and employing disabled people and/or people with health conditions or an injury: A review of the evidence*, DWP Research Report no. 400, London: Department for Work and Pensions.

Bambra, C. (2008) 'In sickness or in health? Incapacity Benefit reform and the politics of ill health', *British Medical Journal*, 337, p a1452.

Bambra, C. (2011) *Work, worklessness and the political economy of health*, Oxford: Oxford University Press.

Bambra, C., Whitehead, M. and Hamilton, V. (2005) 'Does "welfare to work" work? A systematic review of the effectiveness of the UK's welfare to work programmes for people with a chronic illness or disability', *Social Science and Medicine*, 60(9), pp 1905-18.

Beinart, S., Smith, P. and Sproston, K. (1996) *The Access to Work programme: A survey of recipients, employers, employment service managers and staff*, London: Social and Community Planning Research.

Black, C. (2008) *Working for a healthier tomorrow*, London: HMSO.

Black C. and Frost D. (2011) *Health at work: An independent review of sickness absence*, London: HMSO.

Bloch, F. and Prins, R. (2001) *Who returns to work and why?*, London: Transaction.

Butterworth, P., Leach, L., Strazdins, L., Olesen, S., Rodgers, B. and Broom, D. (2011) 'The psychosocial quality of work determines whether employment has benefits for mental health: results from a longitudinal national household panel survey', *Occupational and Environmental Medicine*, published online first, March, doi: 10.1136/oem.2010.059030.

Byrne, D. (2005) *Social exclusion*, Maidenhead: Open University Press.

Clayton, S., Bambra, C., Gosling, R., Povall, S., Misso, K. and Whitehead, M. (2011) 'Assembling the evidence jigsaw: insights from a systematic review of UK studies of individual-focused return to work initiatives for disabled and long-term ill people', *BioMed Central*, 11, p 170.

Davis, E., Tamayo, A. and Fernandez, A. (2012) '"Because somebody cared about me: that's how it changed things": homeless, chronically ill patients' perspectives on case management', *PLoS ONE*, 7(9), pp 1-7.

Gabbay, M., Taylor, L., Sheppard, L., Hillage, J., Bambra, C. and Ford, F. (2011) 'NICE's guidance on long term sickness and incapacity', *British Journal of General Practice*, 61, pp e118-e124.

Gardiner, K. (1997) *Bridges from benefit to work*, York: Joseph Rowntree Foundation.

Garthwaite, K. (2011) '"The language of shirkers and scroungers?" Talking about illness, disability and coalition welfare reform', *Disability & Society*, 26, pp 369-72.

Hillage, J., Williams, M. and Pollard, E. (1998) *Evaluation of Access to Work*, Brighton: Institute for Employment Studies.

Holzer, H. and Martinson, K. (2005) *Can we improve job retention and advancement among low-income working parents?*, Low-Income Working Families Paper 3, Washington, DC: The Urban Institute.

McEvoy, P., Escott, D. and Bee, P. (2011) 'Case management for high-intensity service users: towards a relational approach to care co-ordination', *Health and Social Care in the Community*, 19(1), pp 60-9.

McKnight, A. (2002) 'Low-paid work: drip-feeding the poor', in J. Hills, J. Le Grand and D. Piachaud (eds) *Understanding social exclusion*, Oxford: Oxford University Press, pp 98-117.

Marmot, M. (2010) *Fair society, healthy lives*, The Marmot review executive summary, London: The Marmot Review.

NICE (National Institute for Health and Care Excellence) (2009) *Public health guidance 19: Managing long-term sickness absence and incapacity for work*, London: NICE.

OECD (Organisation for Economic Co-operation and Development) (2009) *Sickness, disability and work: Background paper*, Paris: OECD, www.oecd.org/dataoecd/42/15/42699911.pdf

Patrick, R. (2012) 'Work as the primary "duty" of the responsible citizen: a critique of this work-centric approach', *People, Place & Policy Online*, 6(1), pp 5-15.

Pope, D. and Bambra, C. (2005) 'Has the Disability Discrimination Act closed the employment gap?', *Disability and Rehabilitation*, 27, pp 1261-6.

Roberts, S., Heaver, C., Hill, K., Rennison, J., Staffors, B. and Howat, N. (2004) *Disability in the workplace: Employers' and service providers' responses to the Disability Discrimination Act in 2003 and preparations for the 2004 changes*, London: Department for Work and Pensions.

Roulstone, A. and Barnes, C. (2005) 'Work is a four letter word', in A. Roulstone and C. Barnes (eds) *Working futures? Disabled people, policy and social inclusion*, Bristol: Policy Press, pp 315-27.

Warren, J. (2005) 'Disabled people, the state and employment: historical lessons and welfare policy', in A. Roulstone and C. Barnes (eds) *Working futures: Disabled people, policy and social inclusion*, Bristol: Policy Press, pp 301-14.

Warren, J., Bambra, C., Kasim, A., Garthwaite, K., Mason, J. and Booth, M. (2014a) 'Prospective pilot evaluation of the effectiveness and cost utility of a "health first" case management service for long-term Incapacity Benefit recipients', *Journal of Public Health*, 36(1), pp 117-24.

Warren, J., Garthwaite, K. and Bambra, C. (2013) '"It was just nice to be able to talk to somebody": long-term Incapacity Benefit recipients' experiences of a case management intervention', *Journal of Public Health*, 35(4), pp 518-24.

Warren, J., Wistow, J. and Bambra, C. (2014b) 'Applying qualitative comparartive analysis (QCA) in public health: a case study of a health improvement service for long-term Incapacity Benefit recipients', *Journal of Public Health*, 36(1), pp 126-33.

Part Four
Alternatives to, and validated lives beyond, paid work

TWELVE

Thinking differently about 'work' and social inclusion for disabled people

Edward Hall and Robert Wilton

Introduction

Paid employment is the primary marker of social exclusion and inclusion in Western neoliberal states, including the two nations – Britain and Canada (Roulstone and Prideaux, 2012) – that we focus on in this chapter. Those not in receipt of income from work and reliant on welfare benefits, including disabled people, are being placed under increasing pressure to participate in state programmes of 'reactivation' to move from welfare into employment, as part of a broader transformation of the welfare state and government budget cuts (see, for example, Duncan Smith, 2014, in Britain). For some disabled people (in particular, those already in some form of work, or with higher skill levels and experience), there are new opportunities for access into and maintenance of employment. For many, however, gaining access to, and staying in, paid employment is extremely challenging.

There are numerous barriers to employment for disabled people, including:

- a lack of qualifications and experience;
- attitudes of employers;
- absence of adequate support from agencies;
- physical access to the workplace;
- a lack of appropriate job opportunities (Thornton, 2009; Crawford, 2012).

People can also face difficulties at work that include:

- the attitudes of fellow employees and supervisors;
- expectations in terms of behaviour and appearance;

- pay and conditions, including hours and flexibility (Roulstone et al, 2003; Wilton, 2004).

For these reasons, the proportion of disabled people in paid employment has plateaued at a level far below that for non-disabled people. Furthermore, as austerity measures tighten, many disabled people are finding themselves in a double bind. They are unable to secure a paid job *and* are denied adequate benefit payments to support themselves, with a resultant decline in wellbeing. Moreover, the rhetoric of welfare reform in both Britain and Canada is becoming increasingly sharp.

In Britain, popular and political discourses increasingly contrast those understood as 'strivers' (who take an active approach to gaining employment) with those seen as 'skivers' (in receipt of welfare benefits, and who make little effort to find work). The Canadian landscape is more uneven because social welfare is a provincial policy matter, but there too there has been a prevailing trend towards emphasising individual responsibility and (a lack of) motivation, while downplaying the 'complex and deeply-rooted social and systemic inequalities' that shape the employment prospects of disabled people (see Gewurtz et al, 2014, p 1; also Prince, 2012).

Given the difficult and constrained landscape of paid employment and a hardening of attitudes in relation to welfare payments and the perceived inactivity of disabled people (and many others), it is perhaps unsurprising that many disabled people have become increasingly disenchanted with mainstream employment and the claimed connection between being in work and securing broader social inclusion. Some are also vehemently protesting against current welfare changes and negative media portrayals of disabled people in receipt of welfare benefits (Briant et al, 2011; *The Guardian*, 2012; ODSP Action Coalition, 2014). However, there are alternative ways in which disabled people (and others excluded from mainstream paid employment) can become involved in 'work', conceived here in the broadest sense: undertaking a meaningful activity that is recognised by others as making a socially valuable contribution (in some cases paid, in many cases unpaid). In this chapter, we argue that there are a range of alternatives to mainstream paid employment that provide opportunities for many more disabled people to be involved in 'work' and so achieve an enhanced sense of social inclusion. We also suggest that these alternatives encourage a broader reimagining of the relationship of disabled people to the local places in which they live, and the networks in which they are embedded (Gibson-Graham, 2006).

The chapter comprises of three main sections. We look first at the nature of disabled people's current position in relation to paid employment, arguing that significant barriers to their expanded participation remain. We then consider the potential of two alternative forms of 'work'. The first of these centres on employment within the social economy as an alternative to the market economy. The second focuses on unpaid work, in particular volunteering and participation in the creative arts, which have the potential to generate social participation and inclusion, but without generating an income for disabled people. It is important to recognise that for both 'alternatives', there is the potential for the exploitation of disabled people's labour and for the perpetuation of dependent economic roles. However, the chapter argues that if these challenges are properly addressed, there is much to be gained by disabled people and those in wider society. Throughout, we present data and examples from Britain and Canada, drawing on our own research.

Disabled people and paid work

Despite the seemingly improved conditions in the labour market in Britain in 2013 and 2014, with the number of people registered as unemployed falling, and those in employment at an all-time high (BBC News, 2014; ONS, 2014), the position of disabled people vis-à-vis paid work has remained largely unchanged. Of the seven million people of working age (16–64 years) in Britain with a disability, 46.3% are in employment. This compares with 76.4% for non-disabled people (Berthoud, 2011; ONS, 2012). In Canada, approximately 50% of disabled adults of working age are in paid work, compared with 66.1% of non-disabled adults (Fawcett and Marshall, 2014). While there are undoubtedly more disabled people in work now than a decade ago, and the gap between disabled and non-disabled employment rates has therefore fallen, a significant difference remains (Sayce, 2011).

There is a dominant notion that 'some disabled people are unequivocally capable of work, while others are wholly incapable' (Berthoud, 2011, p ii). The reality, as Battams (2013, p 3) notes, is that 'the relationship between disability and employment is complex'. There is a 'sliding scale of employment probabilities' determined in part by the nature and severity of impairment (Berthoud, 2011, p ii). For example, data for the United Kingdom show that people with diabetes have an employment rate of 62%, and those with hearing difficulties 52%, compared with just over 12% for people with mental health conditions and learning disabled people (Sayce, 2011). In addition, there is a clear gradient in employment opportunity related to the severity of impairment (Statistics Canada, 2008; Berthoud, 2011). Further, recognising the ways in which disability intersects with gender, age and, in particular, educational level, clear patterns of participation emerge, with men, younger people and those with degree-level qualifications much more likely to be in paid employment (ONS, 2010; see also Chapter Ten, this volume).

These figures reveal the complex relationship between disabled people and employment, with some limited opportunities for younger disabled people with high-level qualifications, but many more challenges for those who are older and, in particular, for those without qualifications (Berthoud, 2011; Ziebart, 2014). As the labour market becomes ever-more fragmented, with at one end, professional-level jobs requiring high-level skills, and at the other end, low-skill jobs needing people who can work long hours on flexible contracts, there is concern that for many disabled people there is a mismatch between what they have to offer and what is available.

In both Britain and Canada, disabled people confront a dilemma around mainstream paid work. Many express a desire to engage in paid employment, and there is increasing sociocultural, political and financial pressure to move from receipt of benefits into paid work. However, for many this is not possible. The majority of jobs available and workplaces are not accessible and appropriate for many disabled people, most of whom are without high-level qualifications and skills, and do not fit with the often demanding needs and expectations of the contemporary workplace. Concurrently, British and Canadian government initiatives also favour those with the most skills and employability. In Britain, for example, the Access to Work programme supports disabled people already in employment or very close to being in employment (for instance, having a job interview) through the provision of equipment, travel costs and a support worker (Sayce, 2011). Meanwhile, the Work Choice programme uses a supported employment 'place, train and retain' model to get someone into a mainstream workplace and keep them there (DWP, 2014). Evidence suggests that the latter programme best serves those who are most able to secure employment and progress (Hall and McGarrol, 2012).

In both Britain and Canada, the 'supported employment' model is now widely seen as the best vehicle to get disabled people into employment in mainstream or 'open' workplaces (Kirsh et al, 2006; Wistow and Schneider, 2007). At the same time, 'sheltered' employment factories in Britain run by 'Remploy', which employed over 10,000 people at 94 sites, are being closed (*The Guardian*, 2013a), with the organisation now adopting the supported employment model, seeking to place individuals in mainstream employment. While supported employment settings can offer opportunities for some, those with more significant impairments, lower-level skills and fewer qualifications (that is, the majority who were employed at Remploy sites) will find it challenging to access employment in mainstream work contexts. The closure of sheltered workplaces and the focus on supporting individuals in open employment do not address the mismatch between the (lack of) skills of disabled people and the (lack of) access in mainstream employment.

It can be argued, therefore, that mainstream paid employment and workspaces, whether accessed directly or through supported employment programmes, are appropriate for only a limited group of disabled people. There are many others for whom such options are neither possible nor desirable. Challenging the dominant notion of paid employment as *the* route to social inclusion and wellbeing, we argue that there are substantive and hopeful alternatives to paid employment. We offer two examples: work in social enterprises and other forms of 'working' (volunteering and creative arts practice).

Alternative spaces of 'work' I: social enterprises

Recent scholarship has argued that the social and spatial organisation of work under capitalism has been based on a non-disabled norm, with the consequence that 'mainstream' labour processes, work environments and organisational cultures are designed to privilege certain types of bodies and minds over others (Wilton, 2004). As a result, it may be more realistic to imagine that truly accommodating job opportunities will be created in work environments that exist beyond these mainstream settings. Such environments can be conceptualised as what Leyshon et al (2003, pp 4-5) have called 'alternative economic spaces', settings in which individual and collective actors 'imagine and, more importantly, perform ... economic activities in a way that marks them out differently from the dictates and conventions of the mainstream economy'. There are a number of different types of 'alternative economic spaces' that could be considered in the context of a discussion about disability. Here, we focus on social enterprises as one part of a broader social economy (Noya and Clarence, 2007), thinking specifically about the extent to which such enterprises have the capacity to provide accommodating employment opportunities for disabled people (Kirsh et al, 2006).

In this section, we draw on data gathered in recent interviews with key informants from Canadian social enterprises. This research involved interviews with managers and directors of 46 organisations in eight different Canadian provinces.[1] In total, these organisations were operating 67 different social enterprises, employing more than 1,000 people (Wilton and Evans, 2014). These enterprises were engaged in a broad range of activities, including gardening and landscaping, janitorial services, food services and catering, packaging, painting and decorating, and textile/garment manufacturing. Some of the enterprises were run by larger service organisations, while others were started and run by groups of people with mental health issues. The specific focus of the research was driven by the recognition that people with such issues have some of the lowest rates of employment within the larger disabled population (Gewurtz et al, 2014).

Social enterprises are typically organisations with some degree of entrepreneurial orientation, but their economic objectives are connected to, and tempered by, a strong social mission (Amin, 2009; Hudson, 2009). They vary considerably in terms of their size and scope, organisational philosophy, division of labour and funding sources. However, they share in common the fact that 'their prime interest does not lie in profit-maximisation, but in building social capacity (e.g. through employing or training socially disadvantaged groups) and responding to under-met needs … and in the process creating new forms of work' (Amin et al, 2002, p 1). Existing research has suggested that there is a need to approach social enterprises critically. For example, scholars have cautioned that such organisations can be co-opted by the state, effectively serving as a means to prepare unemployed and marginalised groups for transition to mainstream labour markets, while managing those who fail to make this transition (Amin, 2009; Hudson, 2009). Moreover, the recent interest in 'entrepreneurial' activity must also be understood in light of increasing pressure on voluntary organisations to reduce dependence on state funding (Sepulveda et al, 2013). Notwithstanding these concerns, the potential of such organisations lies in their capacity to strike a different balance between the demands of an employer and the specific needs of disabled workers with respect to accommodation and the appropriateness of work.

Data from the interviews suggested that social enterprise staff typically had a wealth of knowledge and experience concerning accommodation and the creation of employment opportunities for people with mental health issues. Organisations varied in their specific approach to accommodation policies, but most offered a broad range of supports that related to the specific demands of work, as well as to the broader social environment of the workplace. The two most common forms of workplace accommodation were flexibility and security. Flexibility covered a range of issues, including pace, hours, training and work tasks. For example, the manager of a market garden talked about the importance of flexibility in training:

'Something I ask in the interview [is] "How do you best learn?".... Then they're able to tell me actually if you break things down to step by step and give me one step ... then everything works out great. So it's about being flexible and understanding that someone's medications or their illness may have an effect on how they learn.' (K28, Ontario)

Many respondents were also attentive to the fact that when people were hired there was often a need to negotiate their suitability for specific work tasks and positions. As one manager from an organisation that ran several enterprises explained:

'We had one man who was working in a cafe who was really quite obsessive about money and it became a bit of an issue. He'd start closing early because he got overly worried about the money. So we found there was probably a better fit for him working with the newspapers. Right now, he's employed with the newspapers and he really enjoys it.... We just try to fit everybody to the business so they're gonna be successful.' (K38, Nova Scotia)

The idea of finding a position that will fit a person's abilities and strengths stands in stark contrast to expectations in many mainstream workplaces that people will adapt themselves to the requirements of the job and the broader demands of the business.

Alongside flexibility, job security was also a critical consideration. This was true both for short-term absences from work, as well as longer-term absences prompted by fluctuations in mental health. As one respondent explained, the willingness to provide job security in the face of declining mental health meant understanding, and making accommodations for, difficult behaviour:

'Sometimes if they're ill and they get really angry, we'll become the enemy and so sometimes they leave for that reason. It's not unusual for them to come back six months later and say: "I'm really sorry I was kind of off my lid. Would it be okay to be back?" Unless it was a serious incident, we almost always let them come back.' (K03, Ontario)

Again, the degree of job security provided in these organisations stands in stark contrast to the precarious nature of many jobs in mainstream workplaces, particularly the kinds of service sector and low-end manufacturing jobs that may be open to people recovering from significant mental illness. Also significant is the fact that the vast majority of social enterprises saw their role as the provision of long-term, stable employment rather than as training or transitional work placements. This model of long-term employment reflects a conception of the social economy as an alternative to, rather than intermediate labour market for, the mainstream economy (Hudson, 2009). This is significant not least because a commitment to long-term employment allows for the ongoing provision of workplace accommodations in these social economy spaces. This approach can also challenge broader assumptions about 'mainstream employment' as the sole route to social inclusion and meaningful activity.

Beyond specific forms of accommodation, enterprises implemented other strategies to build inclusive and enabling work settings. A key component of these efforts centred on disclosure and openness about mental health. There is ample evidence that stigma surrounding mental illness and the subsequent pressure to avoid disclosure constitute major sources of stress for workers. In social enterprises, shared identification and experience often contributed to a sense of the workplace as a 'safe space'. As one manager, himself a disabled person, said: "Really what it is, it just gives that feeling where it's like, disclose or don't disclose, everyone's cut from the same cloth. So that's very comfortable for some people including myself like I was, it was huge for me in the beginning, you know" (K09, Ontario).

Linked to the sense of shared identification, respondents talked about the significance of organisations as spaces for social connection. The nature and extent of such connections varies between organisations and among workers, but it is interesting to think about how the culturally valued status of the workplace promotes formation of social ties. As a coffee shop manager said:

'People that started working here, they became friends, they'd get together after work and go to a movie or that kind of thing whereas before they led pretty isolated lives. Even though they had the opportunity to have that social connection at the day programme, it was like being in the workplace, they thought of it differently.' (K12, Alberta)

Such observations speak to the multiple benefits arising from people's participation in paid work (Butcher and Wilton, 2008).

It is clear, however, that social enterprises face challenges and dilemmas in their efforts to sustain these work environments. For example, the expectation that social enterprises should/will achieve financial self-sufficiency must often be balanced against a desire to improve the wages of workers within the enterprise. How organisations resolve such ethical dilemmas relates to a broader question about the extent to which they are able to create and sustain what Hudson (2009, p 509) describes as 'something genuinely different' beyond the mainstream economy. In the context of this chapter, such a 'genuine difference' might be understood in terms of organisations' capacity to sustain settings that enable people with mental health problems (and other disabled people) to realise their productive potential.

One such dilemma concerns the decisions that organisations make about hiring policies. For some social enterprises, hiring begins with the needs of the organisation. This means that managers may be more selective in whom they hire, looking for specific skills or experiences that fit with the needs of the enterprise. The logic of this approach is that careful hiring ensures the wellbeing and long-term success of the enterprise. At the same time, respondents recognise that this approach risks 'creaming off' (their term) the most able members of a larger population of job candidates. For example:

'Some people have applied for a number of businesses over time but because of the competitive process you take the person who's the best fit for the business. That's one of the problems … people who have higher needs often are not the ones that are successful in the interview process.' (K38, Ontario)

Others respondents explicitly rejected this approach to hiring, arguing that it would undermine the very reason for their existence. As one respondent explained: "We don't really have a selection process.... We're here to reintegrate people with mental illness and if we start saying, 'OK, I'm going to select', I put all the chances of success on my side, but what chances am I putting on their side?" (K17, Quebec).

These statements reflect differences among organisations in terms of the balance struck between economic imperative and social mission.

They also reflect important contextual variations. In Quebec, for example, there are stronger and more formalised ties between social enterprises and the provincial government, which provides core funding for employees' wages. In this context, pressure to 'cream off' more productive workers is greatly reduced.

Alternative spaces of 'work' II: what it can mean to work without pay

Social enterprises offer opportunities of an alternative form of employment for some, although as the section above makes clear, tensions remain in their operation and employment strategies. However, there remain significant numbers of disabled people, including many learning disabled people, people with mental health issues and people with severe and complex needs, for whom, and for various reasons, even social enterprise employment may not be an option. Other options might include alternative ways of being in 'work', involving physical, mental and social participation that is socioculturally recognised by the majority population as a valued contribution, but which lies outside the competitive labour market and economy. Gibson–Graham (2006) argue that there are many ways in which people make 'non-economic' contributions – they cite childcare and volunteering – without which the mainstream economy would flounder and through which those involved can gain a sustained sense of value and inclusion (see Chapters One and Fourteen, this volume). It can be argued that removing the issue of monetary compensation allows for greater attention to the nature of the 'work' being done and the relationships that are formed in the process, leading to a broader sense of wellbeing. In this section, we consider volunteering and creative arts practice as alternative forms of 'work'.

While little research has been carried out on disabled people as volunteers (exceptions include Balandin et al, 2006; Farrell and Bryant, 2009), findings suggest that disabled people can gain a sense of self-confidence, status in their local community and society more widely, as well as opportunities for interaction with other disabled and non-disabled people, and improved health and wellbeing through volunteering (Bates and Davis, 2004; FreshMinds Research, 2011). The facilitating organisation, Access to Volunteering, found that volunteering activity can have significant mental, physical and social wellbeing benefits:

> I'm a bit more confident when it comes to speaking to people, because before I wasn't. I think the volunteering helped me with that.
>
> I'm meeting people. It is nice to be around people and share ideas and views and listen to others' views.
>
> I would say I get more exercise in coming out, up and down and walking around.... My surgeries and volunteering activity are helping me to cope better with my pain.
>
> I'm a lot more stable than I've been in ages. It's taken a while – gradual change to start with, but when I started getting to know people I was more confident.... when I've been really depressed, you feel like you can't do anything and you lose faith in your abilities especially when you've had a manic episode and feel like you can do anything. Picking up new skills has been great, I feel more confident and about the future because I know I can actually do the work even if I can't get a job. (Anonymous volunteers, FreshMinds Research, 2011, pp 69-70)

In some cases, the skills gained through volunteering 'work' – in particular, self-confidence, work skills, 'soft' skills of communication and dealing with people, and networking and knowledge of the 'real world' – can be a stepping stone into paid employment:

> I think it has [made me want to work] because it's made me think I'd love working in a [sports] arena.
>
> Since I've been here I've had full admin office training to go for these kinds of jobs.... Now I'm applying to West Lancashire [Borough] Council for a job as a full time administrative assistant. (Anonymous volunteers, FreshMinds Research, 2011, p 62)

However, for many other disabled people, in particular those with more severe impairments for whom employment is an unrealistic aim, for reasons of impairment and/or a perception that mainstream workplaces are not accommodating, volunteering can offer a viable and attractive form of 'work' (Trembath et al, 2010):

> I don't really see the point [in applying for jobs] – I've got a bad criminal record and my illness [bipolar] and not worked before. (Anonymous volunteer, FreshMinds Research, 2011, p 57)

I don't think there is much out there for registered blind people – ordinary sighted people having a problem, it is very difficult at the moment. If you could be swallowed up somewhere it would be lovely – it did knock me back losing my job, because I thought that would never happen, because I can't see well enough. I feel more comfortable doing it this way [volunteering] because I don't want to be rejected. Rejection is awful. I used to get a lot out of my job and to be knocked back like that when it's something out of your control. I couldn't go through that again. (Anonymous volunteer, FreshMinds Research, 2011, p 57)

Miller et al (2003), in a study of young learning disabled people, found that a 20-week programme of volunteering led to increases in pride, empowerment, social interactions and communication. Significantly, Trembath et al (2009) noted that, in another study of disabled adults participating in voluntary activities, all referred to it as their 'work', even though it was unpaid. There is a further significance to disabled people doing voluntary work. For many, the reversal of roles from that of the receiver to the giver of assistance and support, is hugely empowering (Balandin et al, 2006).

The rate of regular volunteering among disabled people is significantly lower than that for the population as a whole (Cabinet Office, 2008; Human Resources and Skills Development Canada, 2010).[2] Much of this difference can be attributed to the same barriers that exist for disabled people in paid employment (that is, employer/ organiser attitudes and assumptions, and inappropriate working practices/accommodations). Balandin et al (2006) found that while a fifth of those seeking to become volunteers through Australia's network of volunteer resource centres were disabled people, coordinators often found it 'difficult to refer' disabled people to positions, due to lack of resources to provide necessary support and improve access, and sometimes fears of negative attitudes towards disabled volunteers in communities (see also *The Guardian*, 2013b).

This barrier has been further raised as many voluntary organisations have become involved in the delivery of public services under contract to local or central governments and, as a result, have had to professionalise their activities and the training of volunteers. The skills and capabilities – including in some cases health and fitness – of volunteers are often assessed. There is evidence that some voluntary agencies see disabled applicants in much the same way as many employers do – as unreliable, lacking in skills and unable to cope

(Balandin et al, 2006). To encourage disabled people to participate in voluntary work, charities and organisations need to be more flexible and supportive (Institute for Volunteering Research, 2007). Beyond this, for many disabled people, volunteering in smaller, less professionalised organisations may offer more opportunities for involvement and making a valued contribution (Fyfe and Milligan, 2003).

Successive governments have portrayed volunteering as a route into paid employment (and off welfare benefits) for 'excluded' social groups, including disabled people. While this may be the outcome for some, it is important to understand the wider (and deeper) benefits of taking part in non-paid work in local communities. For individual disabled people, it can mean an enhanced quality of life, self-confidence and wellbeing (Corden and Ellis, 2004). More broadly, making connections with others through formal and informal volunteering (that is, helping friends and neighbours) can build positive perceptions of the roles and abilities of disabled people within society.

A second area beyond paid employment where disabled people have found opportunities to build self-confidence, interact with others and gain skills, is in creative arts activities (Hall, 2013). The British government identified the 'arts' – including theatre, dance, art classes and museums – as a mechanism through which excluded groups can enhance their wellbeing and move towards social inclusion, including employment (Jermyn, 2004). There is a lot of evidence of the benefits of participating in arts activities. For example, Hacking et al (2008) found that participation in creative arts by people with mental health conditions boosted confidence, self-esteem and mixing with others. For learning disabled people, creative arts have been shown to provide opportunities for enhanced social and emotional experiences, contact, expression and the development of mental and physical skills (Jindal-Snape and Vettraino, 2007). There is something 'special' about creative arts in their ability to release potential within people, such as learning disabled people, who are assumed to be without ability and agency.

Drawing on evidence gathered in Edinburgh in 2009, in a project with the 'Lung Ha's Theatre Company', a learning disability arts organisation, we illustrate how the (unpaid) 'work' undertaken by the disabled artists is hugely beneficial to them, and to those they encounter.[3] For example, through the social interaction of rehearsal and the improvising of performances, they experience and reflect on intense feelings of togetherness, friendship and happiness:

Int:[4]   'What is it about drama?'
Jillian: 'It's just being with other people. I like going.'

Int: 'Do you know each other well?'

Mary: 'Yes. You know in theatre, you've got to have team work. If you've not got team work, what's the point?'

...

Int: 'What brings you back every week? You've been coming for 20 years.'

Lorna: 'Make good friends.'

...

Int: 'Do you think you get confidence from Lung Ha's?'

Mary: 'Community. Sometime in the meeting [rehearsal] sometimes sad, sometimes happy. People are upset, people are sad, people are angry.'

Int: 'If people are angry or sad, how do you help each other?'

Mary: 'Understand each other's point.'

However, this is only one part of the process. While those involved gain hugely from the process of producing the performances, in terms of confidence and skills, often over many months, there is another perhaps more significant gain. Lung Ha's seeks out audiences for its work, performing in mainstream theatres in Scotland and Europe. Through this, the actors receive praise and strengthened self-confidence and, further, an opportunity to 'articulate their world view' (Rose, 1997, p 3) and their abilities. Moreover, the strength and quality of the performances can begin to challenge and shift deep-seated attitudes about learning disability (even though Lung Ha's productions never directly address disability, allusions are made to broader notions of difference and othering):

Int: 'What is the reaction of the audience to your shows?'

Jillian: 'People say it's really good. People say nice comments. People you don't know. We go to Glasgow, to "Platform" [a theatre venue]. I was really fascinated when we were there last year; the audience was shouting out. It felt really good.'

...

Int: 'Do people think differently about [learning] disabilities because of seeing Lung Ha's?'

Stephen: 'They see us on stage and after we've done the show, we don't try to, but hopefully we change people's perceptions on the way they see disabled actors.'

Lung Ha's is a charity, funded by Creative Scotland (the Scottish government's arts body). It employs a small number of staff, and the actors are unpaid. While this may seem unfair and even exploitative, as people attending the shows pay for tickets, there is a practical reason for this – welfare benefits can be reduced or even lost if an income is received. However, there is a far more important argument for keeping Lung Ha's and other similar arts organisations separate from the competitive economy. The unpaid nature of the 'work' carried out by the actors in Lung Ha's – and they do see it as their 'work' – disentangles the experience of inclusion from the task of paid employment. In this sense, social inclusion can be thought of as something different from getting a paid job. For most of the actors in Lung Ha's, many of whom have significant impairments, paid employment in a mainstream setting is not likely. Indeed, for many, 'working' for Lung Ha's provides most of the claimed benefits of paid employment – enhanced self-confidence, social relationships and satisfaction – without the common problems of discriminatory attitudes, stress and poor access in mainstream workplaces.

Conclusion

In this chapter, we have argued that it has become necessary to think beyond mainstream paid employment, focusing on two examples within the broader realm of 'work'. First, social enterprises are a radical alternative to the dominant labour market, offering flexibility and accommodation in working practices, and an appreciation of the complex challenges of impairment. For many disabled people, in particular people with mental health problems, such a working environment is hugely beneficial, providing opportunities not available in the mainstream labour market. Second, we took the argument a step further, drawing on Gibson-Graham's (2006) contention that non-paid work both underpins the social fabric and offers the potential for many more people to make a contribution to the broader socioeconomy. The cases of volunteering and creative arts illustrated how, for many disabled people, unpaid work can provide many of the personal and social benefits of paid employment without the everyday experiences of discrimination *and*, through contributing something of social value, challenge dominant assumptions about the place of disabled people in society.

Together, these examples provide a valuable opportunity to reflect on the ways in which work is understood and valued in contemporary Western societies, and highlight very clearly why seeing paid employment as a straightforward route to social inclusion is mistaken. Different forms of 'work' – labouring, participating, contributing, making and giving – can generate both objects and actions of social value *and* emplace disabled people (and many others) in new social relations and contexts where their presence is valued and they can build a sense of belonging. This form of 'inclusion' – feeling part of something bigger than oneself – is on a different register from the claimed social inclusion of paid employment. If we think about 'work' differently, as this chapter suggests, then opportunities open up for many more disabled people to play a significant and respected role in society.

It is important to acknowledge that these alternatives to paid employment, with low or no income, will never give disabled people the financial and material security they require. Indeed, social enterprises, volunteering and creative arts could be seen as exploitative, and even supportive of the mainstream low-wage economy. However, for the many disabled people who are finding it increasingly difficult if not impossible to get a paid job in often hostile workplaces, these forms of 'work' offer possibilities of being valued and feeling included. As such, they need to be encouraged as alternative spaces of 'work' where it is not the profit motive that determines the contribution that disabled people can make.

Notes

[1] This research was conducted as part of a project on employment, mental health and the social economy, funded by the Social Sciences and Humanities Research Council. The research was evaluated and approved by the Research Ethics Board of McMaster University, Canada and followed institutionally approved guidelines with respect to informed consent, confidentiality and the right to withdraw. In this section, interview extracts are followed by interviewee code and province of Canada.

[2] In Britain, approximately 28% of disabled adults volunteer compared with 45% of the overall population (Cabinet Office, 2008); in Canada, the figures are 34% and 47% respectively (Human Resources and Skills Development Canada, 2010).

[3] The project was funded by the Nuffield Foundation (2008-10). The research was approved by the Research Ethics Committee of the University of Dundee, UK.

[4] All names used are pseudonyms.

References

Amin, A. (2009) 'Extraordinarily ordinary: working in the social economy', *Social Enterprise Journal*, 5(1), pp 30-49.

Amin, A., Cameron, A. and Hudson, R. (2002) *Placing the social economy*, London: Routledge.

Balandin, S., Llewellyn, G., Dew, A. and Ballin, L. (2006) '"We couldn't function without volunteers': volunteering with a disability, the perspective of not-for-profit agencies', *International Journal of Rehabilitation Research*, 29(2), pp 131-6.

Bates, P. and Davis, F. (2004) 'Social capital, social inclusion and services for people with learning disabilities', *Disability & Society*, 19(3), pp 195-207.

Battams, N. (2013) 'Disability and employment in Canada', *Fascinating Families*, 54, June, www.vanierinstitute.ca/modules/news/newsitem.php?ItemId=525#.VIWOZ8mlrwU

BBC News (2014) 'UK unemployment rate falls to five-year low', 14 May, www.bbc.co.uk/news/business-27406457

Berthoud, R. (2011) *Trends in employment of disabled people in Britain*, ISER Research Report 2011-03, Colchester: Institute of Social and Economic Research.

Briant, E., Watson, N. and Philo, G. (2011) *Bad news for disabled people: How the newspapers are reporting disability*, Glasgow: Strathclyde Centre for Disability Research and Glasgow Media Unit, University of Glasgow.

Butcher, S. and Wilton, R. (2008) 'Stuck in transition? Exploring the spaces of employment training for youth with intellectual disability', *Geoforum*, 39, pp 1079-92.

Cabinet Office (2008) *Helping out: A national survey of volunteering and charitable giving*, London: Cabinet Office.

Corden, A. and Ellis, A. (2004) 'Volunteering and employability: exploring the link for incapacity benefits recipients', *Journal of Poverty and Social Justice*, 12(2), pp 112-18.

Crawford, C. (2012) *Understanding effective practices in employment programs for people with disabilities in Canada*, Toronto: Institute for Research on Inclusion and Society.

Duncan Smith, I. (2014) 'Jobs and welfare reform: getting Britain working', speech delivered at the Centre for Social Justice, London, 8 April.

DWP (Department for Work and Pensions) (2014) *Work choice: official statistics*, London: DWP.

Farrell, C. and Bryant, W. (2009) 'Voluntary work for adults with mental health problems: a route to inclusion? A review of the literature', *British Journal of Occupational Therapy*, 72(4), pp 163-73.

Fawcett, G. and Marshall, C. (2014) 'People with mental/psychological disabilities: results from the 2012 Canadian Survey on Disability', paper presented at the Canadian Disability Studies Association meeting, St. Catherine's, Ontario, Canada.

FreshMinds Research (2011) *Evaluation of the Access to Volunteering Fund*, London: FreshMinds Research.

Fyfe, N. and Milligan, C. (2003) 'Space, citizenship and voluntarism: critical reflections on the voluntary welfare sector in Glasgow', *Environment and Planning A*, 35, pp 2069-85.

Gewurtz, R., Cott, C. and Kirsh, B. (2014) 'How is unemployment among people with mental illness conceptualised within social policy?', *Work: A Journal of Prevention, Assessment and Rehabilitation*, doi: 10.3233/WOR-141843.

Gibson-Graham, J.K. (2006) *A postcapitalist politics*, Minneapolis, MN: University of Minnesota Press.

Hacking, S., Secker, J., Spandler, H., Kent, L. and Shenton, J. (2008) 'Evaluating the impact of participatory art projects for people with mental health needs', *Health and Social Care in the Community*, 16(6), pp 638-48.

Hall, E. (2013) 'Making and gifting belonging: creative arts and people with learning disabilities', *Environment and Planning A*, 45, pp 244-62.

Hall, E. and McGarrol, S. (2012) 'Bridging the gap between employment and social care for people with learning disabilities: local area co-ordination and in-between spaces of social inclusion', *Geoforum*, 43, pp 1276-86.

Hudson, R. (2009) 'Life on the edge: navigating the competitive tensions between the "social" and the "economic" in the social economy and in its relations to the mainstream', *Journal of Economic Geography*, 9, pp 493-510.

Human Resources and Skills Development Canada (2010) *Federal disability report*, Gatineau, Quebec: HRSDC.

Institute for Volunteering Research (2007) *Volunteering for all? Exploring the link between volunteering and social exclusion*, London: Institute for Volunteering Research.

Jermyn, H. (2004) *The art of inclusion*, London: Arts Council England.

Jindal-Snape, D. and Vettraino, E. (2007) 'Drama techniques for the enhancement of social-emotional development in people with special needs: review of research', *International Journal of Special Education*, 1, pp 107-17.

Kirsh, B., Krupa, T., Cockburn, L. and Gewurtz, R. (2006) 'Work initiatives for persons with severe mental illnesses in Canada', *Canadian Journal of Community Mental Health*, 25, pp 173-91.

Leyshon, A., Lee, R. and Williams, C. (2003) *Alternative economic spaces*, London: Sage Publications.

Miller, K., Schleien, S., Kraft, H., Bodo-Lehrnan, D., Frisoli, A. and Strack, R. (2003) 'Teaming up for inclusive volunteering: a case study of a volunteer program for youth with and without disabilities', *Leisure/Loisir*, 28(1-2), pp 115-36.

Noya, A. and Clarence, E. (eds) (2007) *The social economy: Building inclusive economies*, Paris: Organisation for Economic Co-operation and Development.

ODSP Action Coalition (2014) *Income adequacy for people with disabilities*, Toronto: The Coalition, www.odspaction.ca/resource/adequate-incomes-people.odsp

ONS (Office for National Statistics) (2010) *Labour Force Survey*, London: ONS.

ONS (2012) *Labour Force Survey*, London: ONS.

ONS (2014) *Labour market statistics*, May, London: ONS.

Prince, M. (2012) 'Canadian disability activism and political ideas', *Canadian Journal of Disability Studies*, 1, pp 1-34.

Rose, G. (1997) 'Spatialities of "community", power and change: the imagined geographies of community arts projects', *Cultural Studies*, 11, pp 1-16.

Roulstone, A. and Prideaux, S. (2012) *Understanding disability policy*, Bristol: Policy Press.

Roulstone, A., Gradwell, L., Price, J. and Child, L. (2003) *Thriving and surviving at work: Disabled people's employment strategies*, York: Joseph Rowntree Foundation.

Sayce, L. (2011) *Getting in, staying in and getting on: Disability employment support fit for the future*, London: Department for Work and Pensions.

Sepulveda, L., Syrett, S. and Calvo, S. (2013) 'Social enterprises and ethnic minorities: exploring the consequences of the evolving British policy agenda', *Environment and Planning C*, 31, pp 633-48.

Statistics Canada (2008) *Participation and activity limitation survey: Labour force experiences of people with disabilities*, Ottawa: Statistics Canada.

The Guardian (2012) 'How the Spartacus welfare cuts campaign went viral', 17 January, www.theguardian.com/society/2012/jan/17/disability-spartacus-welfare-cuts-campaign-viral

The Guardian (2013a) 'Remploy factories shut up shop: the end of an era for disabled workers', 30 October, www.theguardian.com/society/2013/oct/30/remploy-factories-close-disabled-workers

The Guardian (2013b) 'Is it too difficult for people with disabilities to find volunteering roles?', 14 August, www.theguardian.com/voluntary-sector-network/2013/aug/14/disabilities-difficult-volunteering-roles

Thornton, P. (2009) 'Disabled people, employment and social justice', *Social Policy and Society*, 4(1), pp 65-73.

Trembath, D., Balandin, S., Stancliffe, R. and Togher, L. (2009) 'Volunteering and paid work for adults who use AAC', *Journal of Development and Physical Disabilities*, 22, pp 201-18.

Trembath, D., Balandin, S., Stancliffe, R. and Togher, L. (2010) 'Employment and volunteering for adults with intellectual disability', *Journal of Policy and Practice in Intellectual Disabilities*, 7(4), pp 235-8.

Wilton, R. (2004) 'From flexibility to accommodation: disabled workers and the reinvention of paid work', *Transactions of the Institute of British Geographers*, 29, pp 420-32.

Wilton, R. and Evans, J. (2014) *'A different way of seeing productivity': A report on the role of social enterprises in creating employment for people living with mental illness*, Hamilton, Ontario, Canada: McMaster University.

Wistow, R. and Schneider, J. (2007) 'Employment support agencies in the UK: current operation and future development needs', *Health & Social Care in the Community*, 15(2), pp 128-35.

Ziebart, C. (2014) 'Young adults with disabilities: an examination of social assistance, education and employment trends in Canada', paper presented at the Canadian Disability Studies Association meeting, St Catherine's, Ontario, Canada.

THIRTEEN

A right not to work and disabled people

Chris Grover and Linda Piggott

Introduction

In Britain and many other countries across the developed world, there have been changes to social security systems in recent decades that have attempted to commodify the labour power of disabled people. In Britain, a tripartite approach has been taken. This includes:

- the development of active labour market policies that are enforced through increasingly strict conditionality regimes;
- the replacing in 2008 of Incapacity Benefit (IB) with Employment and Support (ESA), the structural features of which are supposed to engender a closer relationship between disabled people and labour markets;
- an attempt through legislation, such as the Equality Act 2010 and its predecessor (the Disability Discrimination Act 1995), and policies (such as Access to Work), to reduce the discrimination faced by disabled people in accessing paid work.

In this chapter, we are not particularly concerned with the detail of these policies, but with the general thrust of policy that has focused primarily on placing greater pressure on disabled people to sell their labour power in open markets. The central issue considered is whether, given the material (the impoverishment of disabled people) and psychosocial (for instance, the creation of fear, anxiety and distress) effects that this process has caused, there might be an alternative to forcing disabled people to compete for wage labour alongside their disabled and non-disabled peers.

Disability and capitalism: some tensions for the social model of disability

Central to the social model of disability is the idea that disability is a form of social oppression, rather than being the consequence of an individual having a particular impairment or combination of impairments. In particular, the social model of disability suggests the material disadvantage that disabled people face is the consequence of the ways in which societies, and particularly their economies, are structured. In this context, it is argued, following Marxian ideas on the chronology of economic organisation, that the rise of industrial capitalism from the late 18th century resulted in the exclusion of disabled people from the one activity – wage labour – through which the basis of capitalism is expressed.

Finkelstein (1980) and others (for example, Gleeson, 1999; see also Chapter Fourteen, this volume) have argued that the way in which pre-industrial Feudal societies were organised allowed for the *social* use of the skills and capacities of disabled people. However, industrial societies, where the concern is not so much social use value, but *productive* value, demanded new forms of (wage) labour in new places of labour and to new rhythms and patterns of paid work (for example, Thompson, 1967; Ryan and Thomas, 1987). In this shift, Finkelstein (1980, p 10) argues that disabled people came to be seen 'as passive, needing others to do things for and to them; as disabled!'. While many Western societies are now described as post-industrial, the arrangements for the wage labour are similar; that the rhythms and patterns, and arguably the intensification, of paid work act to disadvantage many disabled people. Changing forms and practices of paid employment of the so-called knowledge-based economy, for instance, may eliminate some forms of participation through the use of technologies that are disabling (see Weber, 2006), while Sapey (2000) demonstrates that traditional industries are more likely to employ disabled people than are the new 'informational sectors'.

Calls for disabled people to have greater access to paid employment have occurred within this context of the way in which the capital accumulation process is organised; that if the basis of wage labour, along the lines of social model of disability's concern with barriers, could be reorganised, then the disadvantage of disabled people in labour markets could be addressed. While the materialist approach of the social model of disability is criticised by those who argue that it ignores the cultural and the more affective dimensions of disabled people's oppression (for a discussion, see Oliver, 2009), historical materialism remains nevertheless central to it. Indeed, access to wage labour is held to be central to the reduction of the disadvantages faced by disabled people. 'Ordinary employment', for instance, was a fundamental principle of the Union of Physically Impaired Against Segregation (UPIAS; UPIAS, 1976). UPIAS (1976, p 5) argued that for working-age people, 'financial and other forms of help must above all be geared to the retention or achievement of integrated employment: dependence on the State must increasingly give way to the provision of help so that a living can be earned through employment'.

The view of the importance of paid employment freeing disabled people from social oppression essentially came from the social model of disability's roots in historical materialism; that, as a socially embedded process, capital accumulation was organised in such a way it disabled people by excluding them from the activity – wage labour – through which people were expected to secure their income (Finkelstein, 1980; Oliver and Barnes, 1998). However, while this view undoubtedly drew on Marxist political economy, it arguably did not engage with Marxist views on the nature of labour in capitalist societies. Most notably, Marx distinguished between work as an activity (labour) and the capacity of people to work (labour power) (Peck, 1996). In capitalist societies it is the latter that is of importance, for capitalism requires commodified labour power to turn a profit. Under capitalism, labour power must be made to appear like any other commodity and, therefore, subject to the rules – particularly those framed by supply and demand – of markets. While it is not the only institution involved, the state is central to the commodification of labour power through what Offe (1984) described as 'active proletarianisation'.

These observations have important implications for disabled people. First, the main concern of proletarianisation is with the capacity to work. With or without workplace adaptions, this focus disadvantages disabled people because they are often considered as being less productive and, therefore, less valuable to capitalist enterprises than non-disabled workers (Grover and Piggott, 2013a). In such circumstances, the ability of enterprises to extract a surplus value from such workers has been through either the subsidisation of their employment (see, for example, Greaves and Massie, 1979, on sheltered employment and Barnes, 1992, on the Sheltered Placement Scheme) or directly through the subsidisation of the wages of disabled people (as, for instance, various in-work benefits and tax credits now available in Britain[1]).

It might be argued, therefore, that the social model of disability is reliant on an activity – wage labour – that by its very nature is exploitative, to address the disadvantage of disabled people. Carter and Jackson (2005, p 90; see also Carter and Jackson, 2007), for instance, argue that the 'core principle of busyness [to which paid employment is central] is exploitation and exploitation to exhaustion'. In other words, wage labour can be considered to be disabling. This view of wage labour – what Waddell and Burton (2006, p 2) describe as 'work as a potential hazard' in traditional conceptualisations of occupational health and safety – is very different from the view that governments, including Britain's, choose to construct. In Britain, for example, wage labour is held to offer a range of benefits to people who are not in paid employment. So, for example, ignoring important caveats – even Waddell and Burton (2006, p 34, original emphasis), for instance, note that 'work is good for your health and well-being, *provided* you *have a good job*' – the coalition's government's Minister for Welfare Reform, David Freud, has argued that: 'Quite simply good work is good for you'.[2]

A right to work?

Parker Harris et al (2012, p 826; see also Chapter Seven, this volume) argue that employment is 'a central piece to both human rights and neoliberal policy shifts ... each can claim increased labor market participation of people with disabilities as one of its goals'. In the case of neoliberalism, we can point to Clarke's (2004, p 90) observation that it involves '"putting people to work": expanding the range and variety of labour power that can be used in the continuing expansion of capitalist production and accumulation'. The emphasis on the employment of disabled people has certainly been influenced by such economic concerns and, as has been observed, such an approach has been informed by orthodox economic analysis concerned with the supply of labour and wage inflation (Grover and Piggott, 2005, 2007).

In the case of human rights, Parker Harris et al (2012) argue that some of the developments in recent social welfare policy for disabled people in various countries have been a reaction to developments in international human rights conventions. Since the 1940s, Article 23 of the Universal Declaration of Human Rights has noted that: 'Everyone has the right to work, to free choice of employment, to just and favourable conditions of work and to protection against unemployment'.[3] However, it was only in more recent years (in 2008) that through the United Nations' *Convention on the rights of persons with disabilities* (UNCRPD; UN, 2006) specific reference to the wage work rights of disabled people was recorded. Article 27 of the UNCRPD notes that: 'People with disabilities have the right to work, including the right to work in an environment that is open, inclusive and accessible'.[4] The discourse of a 'right to work' for disabled people in Britain has been adopted by some of the organisations that reportedly represent the interests of disabled people[5] and, perhaps unsurprisingly, those contracted to get disabled people into paid work.[6]

The notion of the 'right to work', however, is limited by the fact that, first, it is a contested concept. In the United States, for instance, the right to work has been used as an anti-trade union measure, to 'outlaw the union shop, a contract provision that requires employees to financially support the union' (Moore, 1998, p 445; see also Moore and Newman, 1985). Second, the idea of the right to work does not mean that states have a duty to provide wage labour for their (wage) workless populations. Indeed, Hepple (1981) argues that in free market economies the most that can be asked for from the right to work is a right not to be discriminated against. It is this approach that seems to have been accepted by those arguing for a right to work for disabled people, particularly those informed by the social model of disability's focus on employer barriers to paid work (Grover and Piggott, 2013a).

Alternatives to a right to work

In many ways, the tensions that we have seen frame the desire to address the disadvantages of disabled people through an activity (wage work) that can be considered exploitative and disabling reflect tensions in heterodox political economy, most notably between the exploitation of wage work and the strength of the working class (and hence the driver for social change) that comes from its participation in an activity that is exploitative. This tension has been recognised for many years, and to various degrees has involved a critical questioning of the nature of wage work and its place and role in various societies. As we shall see, for some analysts the solution to this tension has been to argue for less wage work or to demand the end to it (see also Chapter Fourteen, this volume).

Less wage work and its abolition

Perhaps the most well-known example of the call for people to engage in less wage work is in Marx's son-in-law, Paul Lafargue's (1883) essay, *The right to be lazy* (for a discussion, see Darier, 1998). Lafargue's (1883, p 9) work was not only a challenge to the architects and regulators of capital – 'the priests, the economists and the moralists [who] have cast a sacred halo over work' – but also to the working class. According to Lafargue (1883, p 13), the working class had 'let itself be perverted by the dogma of work'. This perversion, Lafargue (1883, p 16) argued, was best summed up in the actions of the French proletariat who, following the 1848 revolution, 'proclaim[ed] as a revolutionary principle the Right to Work', rather than 'forg[ing] a brazen law forbidding any man to work more than three hours a day' (1883, p 56).

Half a century later, philosopher Bertrand Russell (1935), in *In praise of idleness*, came to a similar conclusion to Lafargue: that people should work shorter days. Russell's approach was not so much informed by political economy (although he did observe some of the tensions in capitalist production), but by cultural objections to the work ethic and the virtue attached to it by the elite of society. For Russell, a shorter working day (four hours) would enable people to engage in activities that gave them pleasure. He suggested that the spread of such an approach across social classes was prevented by the organisation of labour markets and the moral indignation of the middle and upper classes. Wage work was deemed to be an expression of virtue, but a virtue, given the existence of a wealthy 'leisure class', that was only expected in, and of, particular social groups.

The work of Lafargue in particular is important because of its very clear exposition of the tensions for the working class of capitalist wage work. The problem, however, is that the critique of capitalist labour processes is not wholly developed. Lafargue and Russell merely argued for less wage work for individuals, not its abolition. The 'paradise of labour' (Abberley, 1996b, p 77) remains intact in its waged form. For Russell (1935, cited in Richards, 1983, pp 28-9), however, it would be spread, albeit more thinly, to more people: 'If the ordinary wage-earner worked for four hours a day, there would be enough for everybody, and no unemployment'.

In contrast, others (for example, Kropotkin, 1913; Gorz, 1982; Black, 2011) have argued that only when wage labour is abolished will the exploitation of capitalism be addressed. So, for example, Kropotkin (1913, p 2) argued that it is the wage system that prevents the 'equitable organisation of society'. And, given production is a social process – that the 'means of production and of satisfaction of all needs of society, having been created by the common efforts of all, must be at the disposal of all' (Kropotkin, 1913, p 2) – it was only through the abolition of the wage system that the needs of all would be met. For Kropotkin, such a situation could only occur in a society framed by Anarchist Communism, a society with economic and political freedom.

Similar arguments regarding the nature of wage work are made by Gorz (1982) and Black (2011). They both point to wage labour as a 'forced' activity and how because of this the freedom of the individual is limited. Gorz (1982), for example, argues that wage labour is concerned with the exchange of quantities of time and not an end in itself. In contrast, self-determined activity, such as aesthetic and artistic activity, are not only ends in themselves, but also their production is not concerned with the exchange of time. However, Gorz (1982, p 2) argues that the abolition of wage labour 'does not mean abolition of the need for effort, the desire for activity.... Instead, the abolition of work simply means the progressive, but never total suppression of the need to purchase the right to live ... by alienating our time and our lives'.

Black (2011) makes a similar point about the coercive nature of wage work. For Black (2011, p 2), work 'is production enforced by economic or political means, by the carrot or the stick'. He argues that any work enforced through rampant free markets or state communism is unacceptable. He makes no concessions to the number of hours to be worked (like Lafargue and Russell). For Black (2011, p 1), the alternative to wage labour is 'ludic conviviality, commensality, maybe even art'. Replacing labour with play will address what Black defines as the coercive nature − 'the totalitarian controls at the workplace − surveillance, rotework, imposed work tempos, production quotas, punching −in and −out etc' (Black, 2011, p 3) − of wage work. This is because play is 'always voluntary' (Black, 2011, p 4).

These approaches to challenging the way wage work is organised, at least at first glance, have much to offer disabled people. Approaches that demand the abolition of wage work and emphasise, in contrast, freely entered into and socially necessary activity (Kropotkin, 1913) and self-determined activity (Gorz, 1982; Black, 2011), are arguably consistent with the disabled people's movement's demand that disabled people should have greater choice in, and control over, their lives. Even the arguments for doing less wage labour associated with Lafargue (1883) and Russell (1935) would be consistent with such demands if it were flexible enough.

Such approaches to wage labour and disability located in various heterodox analyses, however, have their critics. Most notable is Abberley (1996a, 1996b). In many senses, Abberley's work would seem to have much in common with such analyses, for not only did he argue that disability is a historically specific social experience, he was also one of the few disability scholars in the 1990s arguing that wage labour for many disabled people would not address their oppression or result in their inclusion. However, he did not reach this position through heterodox economic analyses. Abberley was critical of Marx (1976, originally 1867) and later Communists, such as Wal Hannington (1937), for the use of disabled people for their 'propaganda value' to demonstrate the 'inhumanity and irrationality' of capitalism (1996a, p 7). Abberley (1996a, p 8) suggested that the logic of this aspect of Marxism was that 'impaired people would wither away in a society progressively abolishing the injurious consequences of production for profit'. This was problematic for Abberley because, first, even if it were possible to reduce socially produced impairment, it was inconceivable that it would ever be abolished altogether and, second, 'deeply grounded in Marxist notions of humanity' (1996a, p 8) was the marginality of disability.

Here, Abberley (1996a, 1996b) points to the importance of explanations of the way value is created in capitalist societies. What, for example, is important in the creation of use-value is the amount of the labour time socially necessary for its production. It is this use of labour time that becomes the norm of the human as worker. What is important for our purposes, is that Abberley (1996a, p 8) argues that disability in capitalist societies is conceptualised as being 'the negative of the normal worker'. While Marxism may provide an explanation for the oppression of disabled people, he argues that it does not provide a means of 'conceptualising a future for those impaired people unable to work' (1996a, p 8). This is because of way in which, as we have seen, Marx viewed the importance of labour (as opposed to the commodification of labour power [wage work]) that would be central to meeting individuals' needs, no matter how economically a society was organised. For instance, Abberley (1996a, p 10) cites Gouldner (1971) who notes: 'Marxism never really doubted the importance of being useful.... Its fundamental objection to capitalist society was to the dominating significance of exchange-value, not use-value. It objected to the transformation of men's labor into a commodity, but continued to emphasise the value and importance of work.'

Abberley, however, extends this critique to some of those heterodox approaches that demand the abolition of paid work. For instance, he criticises the argument we have seen of Gorz which suggests even after the abolition of wage labour that individuals will not have the right to 'rest more'. Abberley (1996b, p 70) argues that it is 'precisely' this 'kind of right that impaired people do demand, today and for the future'.

Abberley's views of the relationships between labour and disability are important because, first, they point to difficulties that we see in much empirical explanation of the receipt of income replacement disability benefits. These explanations which suggest that the relatively large number of people receiving such benefits is the consequence of a poorly operating (post-Keynesian) capitalism (Beatty and Fothergill, 2002, 2005, 2013; Beatty et al, 2000) suffer the same problems for which Abberley criticised earlier radical political economy. While Beatty and colleagues might not suggest that a more Keynesian-orientated economic approach (one focused on demand) would reduce levels of disability, they do argue that it would make it less visible by reducing the number of disability benefit claimants (by up to a million). For Beatty and colleagues, it is the ineffectiveness of a supply-side obsessed capitalism (and its institutions of governance), rather than its injuriousness nature, that is the problem. If late-modern capitalism could be organised more effectively, there would be more demand for the labour power of disabled people and they (or at least a million of them) would disappear from the disability benefit rolls.

Second, Abberley's approach suggests a need for a way forward that does not simply replace economic production with social production as the means by which the contribution of individuals is judged. An approach is needed that will allow for the observation that perhaps there are people who will, no matter how production is defined, never be as productive as others. In this space there must be room for an approach to be developed that allows for disabled people to legitimately not do wage work.

A right not to work

Disability activist, Sunny Taylor (2004, p 6), argues for a right not to work for disabled people:

> The right not to work is the right not to have your value determined by your productivity as a worker, by your employability or salary.... What I mean by the right not to work is perhaps as much a shift in ideology or consciousness as it is a material shift. It is about our [disabled people's] relation not only to labor but the significance of performing that labor, and to the idea that only through the performance of wage labor does the human being actually accrue value themselves. It is about cultivating a skeptical attitude regarding the significance of work, which should not be taken at face value as a sign of equality and enfranchisement, but should be analyzed more critically.

In many senses, Taylor, although coming from a heterodox political economic approach, reaches similar conclusions to those of Abberley (1996a, 1996b). Here, we can point to the way both Abberley and Taylor suggest that a major problem for disabled people is the centrality to cultural and economic life ascribed to wage work. Furthermore, both argue that many disabled people, because of their impairment and social reactions to it, may never be or may never be considered productive enough to be employed on the same basis as non-disabled people. They may, therefore, find it very difficult to compete in market-based economies. The main difference between Abberley and Taylor, however, is that the latter's analysis is located in a material analysis, while Abberley (1996b, p 77) argues that there is a need to develop 'theoretical perspectives which express the standpoint of disabled people, whose interests are not necessarily served by the standpoints of other social groups'. This involves looking beyond a 'paradise of labour' (Abberley, 1996b, p 77) of materialist and (some) feminist analyses.

Arguably, however, Abberley overstates the case. While, for instance, undoubtedly production remains central to the analysis, it is the case that analysts working within the social model tradition recognise the difficulties disabled people face in conforming to the demands of producing productive value in late-modern societies. For example, Oliver and Barnes (1998, p 96) note that:

> Expecting severely disabled people to be as productive as non-disabled people is one of the most oppressive aspects of capitalist society.... This will mean a reappraisal of the very meaning of work but this is something we must not shy away from. People could and should be rewarded for their contribution to the common good.

For Barnes and Roulstone (2005, p 322) there needs to be a reconfiguration of understandings of paid work that 'goes beyond the rigid confines of paid employment'. Barnes and Roulstone (2005) point to the work of Corbin and Strauss (1988) who identified three types of work:

- illness work – for instance, doing physiotherapy and organising medication;
- everyday work – household tasks;
- biographical work – for instance, activities by disabled people 'in order to incorporate impairment into their everyday lives' (Barnes

and Roulstone, 2005, p 323) – associated with 'illness management' (see also Chapter Fourteen, this volume).

This is a view of work – defined, for instance, as the 'application of physical or mental effort, skills, knowledge or other personal resources, [which] usually involves commitment over time, and has connotations of effort and a need to labour or exert oneself' (Waddell and Burton, 2006, p 4) – that goes well beyond economic production and wage work.

It is, however, the case that welfare 'reform' in Britain is concerned with wage work, rather than any other type of labour. While it might be argued that its definition should be extended to include labour other than the economically productive kind, it can equally be argued that the case should, as Taylor (2004) suggests, be made for a right not to work in a capitalist sense. Such an approach would help to bring an end to the material and psychosocial consequences of contemporary welfare regimes that are central to the proletarianisation of labour power. The mix of neoliberal economics and communitarian-based notions of obligation (see Chapter Two, this volume) that drive welfare 'reform' in Britain would, for example, be removed if it was recognised that people had a right not to work (Grover and Piggott, 2013a).

A moral philosophical approach to a right not to work

We have seen that the idea of the right to work is arguably limited in Britain to an acceptance that disabled people should not be discriminated against in opportunities for paid employment. This is a liberal approach through which the main claim is against the state to ensure that there is effective equal opportunities legislation in place. It makes few claims against other actors, most notably employers. However, while British governments have been unwilling to countenance much beyond this liberal notion of equality of access for disabled workers, it can be argued that in recent years, governments have moved towards an obligation to work (Secretary of State for Work and Pensions, 2008, chapter 2). Legally, disabled people cannot be made to work (that would be 'forced work' – see Grover and Piggott, 2013b), but the obligation to work is enforced through economic and social 'less eligibility' that puts wage workless people in a position where materially and culturally they have little choice but to work. Arguably, therefore, in Britain there is a disjuncture between a liberal approach to the right to work and a more authoritarian approach located in the obligation to work.

The liberal approach to the right to work, however, can equally be used to argue for a right not to work. Gorz (1999, p 96), for example, notes that the 'right to work and the right not to work are of equal importance and are indissociably linked. The former cannot coexist without the latter'. Meanwhile, Levine (2001, p 318) argues that liberals, or more specifically liberal egalitarians, need 'to radicalize their own conceptions of what equality requires'. It is within this context that Levine makes an argument for a right not to work. He acknowledges that this may feel counterintuitive, but he argues that such feelings are the consequence of a historical–institutional concern with those people often described as the 'undeserving poor' or 'shirkers and scroungers' in some contemporary discourses about disability (Garthwaite, 2011). For Levine (2001, p 321), the notion of a right not to work comes from a conjoining of the 'idea that states ought to be neutral with respect to competing conceptions of the good' and:

> the long-standing liberal commitment to tolerance with the moral philosophical conviction that equal respect for persons entails equal respect for their conceptions of good. The neutrality of the states in allowing various conceptions of the good to co-exist on an equal basis is particularly important for the argument for a right not to work.

If the view of individuals is that 'gainful employment is abhorrent or idleness esteemed' (Levine, 2001, p 321), then, according to liberal egalitarianism, that should be seen as being equally acceptable as the view that paid work is not abhorrent and that idleness should be rejected.

We are not suggesting that disabled people are any more or any less likely to reject paid employment than non-disabled people are (although note Abberley's, 1996a, 1996b, comments on the right of disabled people to rest more). What we are suggesting, however, is that given these arguments, a right not to work is as defensible for disabled people as a right to work. If the social model of disability suggests that disabled people should have an equal opportunity to labour, equally it should acknowledge that they should, along with non-disabled people, have the right not to work. To *not* have a right not to work means that wage work is privileged as an activity. Even if only a minority of disabled people do not countenance wage work as being a good, it should not be privileged over non-work-based notions of the good. The implication in employment terms is that if disabled people are to have choice, that choice must involve not being pressurised, as is currently the case, into preparing and competing for wage work.

Conclusion

In this chapter we have focused on debates about relationships between disabled people and wage work. Drawing on heterodox political economy and critiques of it, and philosophical approaches to the notion of the social good, we have argued that the case for a right not to work for disabled people can be made. Such an approach is consistent with Black's (2011, p 17) argument that: 'No one should ever work. Workers of the world ... *relax!*' Drawing on Abberley's (1996a, 1996b) work, we suggest that disabled people should be able to relax without having to live with the fear and immiseration that, certainly in Britain, attempts to commodify their labour power through welfare 'reform' are currently having. We are not suggesting policies that are supposed to support disabled people into wage work should be abolished (although we also acknowledge the deeply problematic nature of such policies – see Chapters Four and Five, this volume). What we are suggesting, though, is that disabled people should not be forced into engaging with these programmes on the threat of economic sanctioning and cultural censuring.

The danger is that such an approach could be interpreted as an argument for the othering of disabled people as not being able or capable of paid employment. Again, this is not what we are suggesting. In contrast, we are suggesting that a right not to work can be seen as a balance to the current emphasis – an obligation to work – in welfare 'reform' in Britain (and the arguments are applicable to other countries) for the vast majority of working-age disabled people. The problem is that the liberal acceptance of a right to work has, for disabled people and for their non-disabled peers, been usurped by state policies that emphasise paid work as being *the* means by which individuals can express their responsibilities as active citizens. Of course, many disabled people are happy to do this. But this means that those people who, for whatever reason, cannot do wage work are othered as being particularly problematic and burdensome. If, however, there was a recognised right not to work, the othering of workless disabled people would no longer be an issue. Such an approach would be consistent with the disabled people's movement's desire that disabled people should have control over, and choice in, their lives. This is because it would free disabled people from the authoritarian and disabling tendencies of current welfare and labour market policies, which starve disabled people of choice through increasingly linking benefit receipt to making efforts to prepare for, and securing, wage work.

Notes

[1] These payments are available to all low-paid workers, but there are additional premiums for disabled people, or those low-paid workers with disabled children.

[2] https://www.gov.uk/government/speeches/health-and-wellbeing

[3] www.un.org/en/documents/udhr/

[4] www.disabilityaction.org/centre-on-human-rights/resources/un-convention/

[5] See, for example, the websites of Mencap (www.mencap.org.uk/campaigns/what-we-campaign-about/employment-and-training) and the Muscular Dystrophy Campaign (www.muscular-dystrophy.org/get_involved/campaigns/campaign_news/6893_trailblazers_challenge_minister_about_access_to_work_scheme).

[6] See, for instance, the website of the Shaw Trust (www.shaw-trust.org.uk/).

References

Abberley, P. (1996a) 'The significance of work for the citizenship of disabled people', paper presented at University College Dublin, 15 April, http://disability-studies.leeds.ac.uk/files/library/Abberley-sigofwork.pdf

Abberley, P. (1996b) 'Work, utopia and impairment', in L. Barton (ed) *Disability and society: Emerging issues and insights*, London: Longman, pp 61-79.

Barnes, C. (1992) *Disability and employment*, Leeds: British Council of Organisations of Disabled People/Department of Sociology and Social Policy, Leeds University.

Barnes, C. and Roulstone, A. (2005) '"Work" is a four letter word: disability, work and welfare', in A. Roulstone and C. Barnes (eds) *Working futures? Disabled people, policy and social inclusion*, Bristol: Policy Press, pp 315-27.

Beatty, C. and Fothergill, S. (2002) 'Hidden unemployment among men: a case study', *Regional Studies*, 34(7), pp 617-30.

Beatty, C. and Fothergill, S. (2005) 'The diversion from "unemployment" to "sickness" across British regions and districts', *Regional Studies*, 39(7), pp 837-54.

Beatty, C. and Fothergill, S. (2013) 'Disability benefits in the UK: an issue of health or jobs?', in C. Lindsay and D. Houston (eds) *Disability benefits, welfare reform and employment policy*, Basingstoke: Palgrave Macmillan, pp 15-32.

Beatty, C., Fothergill, S. and Macmillan, R. (2000) 'A theory of employment, unemployment and sickness', *Regional Studies*, 34(7), pp 617-30.

Black, B. (2011) *The abolition of work*, London: The Anarchist Library.

Carter, P. and Jackson, N. (2005) 'Laziness', in C. Jones and D. O'Doherty (eds) *Manifestos for the business school of tomorrow*, Turku, Finland: Dvalin Books.

Carter, P. and Jackson, N. (2007) 'Workers of the world...relax! Introducing a philosophy of idleness to organisation studies', in C. Jones and R. Ten Bos (eds) *Philosophy and organization*, London: Routledge.

Clarke, J. (2004) *Changing welfare changing states: New directions in social policy*, London: Sage Publications.

Corbin, J. and Strauss, A. (1988) *Unending work and care: Managing chronic illness at home*, San Fransisco, CA: Jossey-Bass Publishers.

Darier, E. (1998) 'Time to be lazy. Work, the environment and modern subjectivities', *Time and Society*, 7(2), pp 193-208.

Finkelstein, V. (1980) *Attitudes and disabled people: Issues for discussion*, New York, NY: International Exchange of Information in Rehabilitation.

Garthwaite, K. (2011) '"The language of shirkers and scroungers?" Talking about illness, disability and coalition welfare reform', *Disability & Society*, 26(3), pp 369-72.

Gleeson, B. (1999) *Geographies of disability*, London: Routledge.

Gorz, A. (1982) *Farewell to the working class*, London: Pluto Press.

Gorz, A. (1999) *Reclaiming work: Beyond the wage-based society*, Cambridge: Polity Press.

Greaves, M. and Massie, B. (1979) *Work and disability 1977*, London: The Living Foundation.

Grover, C. and Piggott, L. (2005) 'Disabled people, the reserve army of labour and welfare reform', *Disability & Society*, 20(7), pp 707-19.

Grover, C. and Piggott, L. (2007) 'Social security, employment and Incapacity Benefit: critical reflections on *A new deal for welfare*', *Disability & Society*, 22(7), pp 733-46.

Grover, C. and Piggott, L. (2013a) 'A right not to work and disabled people', *Social and Public Policy Review*, 7(1), www.uppress.co.uk/SocialPublicPolicy2013/Grover.pdf

Grover, C. and Piggott, L. (2013b) 'A commentary on resistance to the UK's Work Experience programme: work, capitalism and exploitation', *Critical Social Policy*, 33(3), pp 554-63.

Hannington, W. (1937) *The problem of the distressed areas*, London: Gollancz/Left Book Club.

Hepple, B. (1981) 'A right to work', *Industrial Law Journal*, 10(1), pp 65-83.

Kropotkin, P. (1913) *Anarchist Communism: Its basis and principles*, London: Freedom Press.

Lafargue, P. (1883) *The right to be lazy*, Chicago, IL: Charles H. Kerr.

Levine, A. (2001) 'Fairness to idleness: is there a right not to work?', in K. Schaff (ed) *Philosophy and the problems of work*, Lanham, MD: Rowman & Littlefield, pp 317-36.

Marx, K. (1976) *Capital: A critique of political economy*, Volume 1, introduced by E. Mandel, London: Penguin Books.

Moore, W. (1998) 'The determinants and effects of right-to-work laws: a review of recent literature', *Journal of Labor Research*, XIX(3), pp 445-69.

Moore, W. and Newman, R. (1985) 'The effects of right to work laws: a review of the literature', *Industrial and Labor Relations Review*, 38(4), pp 571-85.

Offe, C. (1984) *Contradictions of the welfare state*, London: Hutchinson.

Oliver, M. (2009) *Understanding disability: From theory to practice* (2nd edn), Basingstoke: Palgrave Macmillan.

Oliver, M. and Barnes, C. (1998) *Disabled people and social policy: From exclusion to inclusion*, London: Longman.

Parker Harris, S. Owen, R. and Gould, R. (2012) 'Parity of participation in liberal welfare states: human rights, neoliberalism, disability and employment', *Disability & Society*, 27(6), pp 823-36.

Peck, J. (1996) *Work-place: The social regulation of labor markets*, New York, NY: Guilford Press.

Richards, V. (ed) (1983) *Why work? Arguments for a leisure society*, London: Freedom Press.

Russell, B. (1935) *In praise of idleness and other essays*, London: George Allen & Unwin.

Ryan J. and Thomas, F. (1987) *The politics of mental health* (revised edn), London: Free Association Books.

Sapey, B. (2000) 'Disablement in the informational age', *Disability & Society*, 15(4), pp 619-36.

Secretary of State for Work and Pensions (2008) *No one written off: Reforming welfare to reward responsibility*, Cm 7363, Norwich: The Stationery Office.

Taylor, S. (2004) 'The right not to work: power and disability', *Monthly Review*, 55(1), http://monthlyreview.org/2004/03/01/the-right-not-to-work-power-and-disability

Thompson, E. (1967) 'Time, work–discipline, and industrial capitalism', *Past and Present*, 38(1), pp 56-97.

UN (United Nations) (2006) *Convention on the rights of persons with disabilities*, New York, NY: UN.

UPIAS (Union of the Physically Impaired Against Segregation) (1976) *Fundamental principles of disability*, London: UPIAS.

Waddell, G. and Burton, K. (2006) *Is work good for your health and well-being?*, London: The Stationery Office.

Weber, H. (2006) 'Providing access to the internet for people with disabilities: short and medium term research demands', *Theoretical Issues in Ergonomics Science*, 7(5), pp 491-8.

FOURTEEN

Disability, work and welfare: the disappearance of the polymorphic productive landscape

Alan Roulstone

Introduction

The question of disabled people's productive contributions has been the 'spectre at the feast' in policy terms from early capitalist industrialisation in Britain (Barnes et al, 1999). The imperative to move formerly 'unproductive' disabled people, and those deemed 'faux' disabled people, away from welfare towards work represents a key challenge – intellectually, politically and economically. There are few more urgent themes identified in anti-welfare discourses developed since 1997 (DWP, 2003, 2008, 2011). The redoubling of efforts of Britain's coalition government to stop the 'wasted lives' of disabled people distanced from paid work and the perceived threat of overspending on the future economic health of the British economy suggest that this question is unlikely to become less pervasive in the coming years (HM Government and DWP, 2010). The current government position is that too many disabled people have been written off by disincentives to enter paid work and benefits that reinforce this 'perverse' incentive to remain out of work for often long or life-long periods (DWP, 2011).

In the interest of balance, these ideas can be seen to sit alongside anti-discrimination legislation (ADL) precepts that employers must be open to the employment of those previously excluded from the contemporary workplace (Government Equalities Office, 2010). Overall, however, the limited impact of an ADL approach and the continued growth in out-of-work benefits from 1.25 million people on Incapacity Benefit in Great Britain in 1980 to 2.5 million in 2006 (Anyadike-Danes and McVicar, 2008) arguably led to a hardening of rhetoric post the accession of the coalition government in 2010 (Lister and Bennett, 2010; Garthwaite, 2011; Grover and Piggott, 2013; Grover and Soldatic, 2013). Current debates and solutions to the disability employment problem are by their nature short term and attempts to reduce headline figures for disability and out-of-work benefits seem driven by rather febrile concerns to correct what are longstanding challenges overnight. The focus of this chapter is on the longer-run structural exclusion of disabled and 'non-standard' individuals. It is a strong contention of the chapter that a failure to reappraise these historical developments and a contemporary comprehension of diverse forms of productive activity will ensure policy failure and the continued stigmatisation of many disabled people (Prideaux et al, 2009).

This chapter aims to draw out the lens in exploring longer-run developments in the construction of valued and valorised contributions to advanced economies. It will be argued that paramount concerns with the transmission of individuals from welfare to work fails to unpack the increasingly narrow constructions of work at the heart of anti-welfarist debates. It will further argue that longer-run developments and economic constructions have led work to be seen as synonymous with paid employment (Warren, 2005). Disabled people, as with their non-disabled counterparts, were once involved in a much broader range of economically validated and productive work that included localised contractual, familial and kin obligation, reciprocal arrangements, promissory commitments, and feudal-bonded and forced activities (Humphries and Gordon, 1992; Gleeson, 1999). Although not all disabled people were viewed as capable of this array of activities, many were required to contribute to socially and communally determined activities as the absence of formal rational economic-productive systems beyond localised values and labour supply meant that cyclical and natural events often needed 'all hands to the pump' in dealing with bulges of physical activity (Gleeson, 1999). Despite the often very harsh relationship between humankind and the prevailing environment, the absence of production norms in pre-advanced industrial and agricultural capitalism (Abberley, 1999) and the often family-centred economy afforded greater particularistic interpretations of just who was sound enough to contribute to working activities. This diversity of economic activities and work forms is reflected in the continued mix of economic and cultural obligations and necessities in the Global South. As I have argued elsewhere (Roulstone, 2013, p 221):

> [M]uch of the majority world work is a broad spectrum of non-contractual economic activity which can range over (and be a mix of) barter, small commodity production, hawking, provisioning (from waste land & tips), begging and wider exchanges of labour which include goods, services

and promissory activity which are not based on contractual arrangements.

This is not to argue that pre-industrial or indeed current majority world alternatives to paid work are freely chosen, idyllic or romanticised, but rather that in the past and in many countries in the present, validated activities were, and are, broader in scope and more diverse in character. While we may risk fetishizing the key differences between agriculture, proto-capitalism and late capitalism, the growing emphasis on wage labour, impersonal exchanges of value and formal legal contractual employment spell both continuity and convergence. The rise of industrial capitalism, one whose apotheosis is symbolised in the factory system of the late 1800s, the attempts to control key aspects of work by disaggregation, deskilling and the calculation of constituent work elements all helped to forge the links between work and a corresponding monetary value (Taylor, 1911). Although not inherently inimical to all disabled people's specific productive capacity, many disabled people were in time essentially 'designed out' of productive activity where norms of effort, stamina, strength, awareness of danger (for example, good sight) and endurance became increasingly pervasive (Finkelstein, 1980; Gleeson, 1999).

Industrialisation and capitalisation were haphazard and never conformed neatly to industrial ideologies (Kirby, 2013). However, the 'negative serendipity' associated with the most pure interpretations of the factory system had a profound impact on those with 'non-standard' bodies/minds (Roulstone, 2002). These new systems of industry, ones tying together calculative and industrial logic, were not unique to capitalism. Both industrial capitalism and industrial communism were based on myths and idolisation of productive paragons in the shape of Schmidt in Taylorist writings (Doray and Macey, 1988) and Stakhanhov in Soviet mythology (Wren and Bedeian, 2004). Thus, we can say that polymorphic, or many faceted validations and valorisations of 'work', were eroded in both industrial capitalism and the developing communism of the 1930s.

Economic and structural barriers then were rooted in the developments of industrial capitalism of the 19th century and in time were systematised into 'scientific' production processes in both 20th-century capitalism and command communism. In this way, the often haphazard and localised cultural negativity towards disabled people gave way to wider and shared systems based on normal productive parameters, ensuring that disabled people would only begin to re-engage in a limited way with paid work following the welfare state settlement of the 1940s (Borsay, 2005; Roulstone and Prideaux, 2012) and the ADL of the 1990s (Gooding, 1995; Lawson and Gooding, 2005; Lawson, 2008). These positive developments of employee protections and aspirations can be seen as helpful systems. However, they do not challenge the assumptions that valued economic activity can only be accommodated in the carapace of paid work in the formal economy. The best way to sum up the paradox of limited positive developments is to describe ADL and reasonable adjustments as ameliorating, but not challenging, the paramount economic-social system that equates work with paid contractual employment (Stapleton and Burkhauser, 2003; Pope and Bambra, 2005).

The following explores the diversity of economic activity that preceded advanced economic systems (both capitalistic and communistic) and which could offer some clues as to how contemporary economic and social contributions could be opened up for scrutiny in a way that values and validates a broader range of activities. Put simply, there is a further paradox here; that an economic system having designed out 'non-standard' people now expends much energy in trying to design them back into the very system that excluded them. And this is attempted without challenging hegemonic constructions of productive value. I will end by exploring policy implications of the narrowing of valued economic activity in the context of employment scarcity and structural unemployment in Western societies (OECD, 2014).

Work and productive activity before 'advanced' economic systems

It is easy to forgive a preoccupation in disability, and employment and welfare policy, with the here and now. Troubles are experienced in a contemporary context that seem in their urgency to afford little 'slack' with which to engage with what might be seen as luxurious historical reflection. However, given that employment systems continue to assume a narrowly defined parameter for productive capacity – for example in working flexibly or building up hours – the continued search for solutions to the disability employment problem will likely limit any thoroughgoing response to the broader economic exclusion of disabled people. What then of historical insights that capture the diversity of social and economic life before advanced industrial systems?

McClelland (1961, p 26) is useful here in stating that 'traditional culture is characterized generally by norms of diffuseness, particularism, affectivity and ascription, whereas industrial culture leans heavily towards norms of specificity, universalism, neutrality and performance'.

Nothing here suggests that pre-industrial societies and economies were preferable or somehow less challenging. A general consensus among otherwise diverse commentators on disability is that disabled people have faced cultural and, at times, physical exclusion, ridicule and even violence (Barnes, 1991; Stiker, 1999; Borsay, 2005). However, the absence of predetermined and shared supra-communal productive norms and expectations does provide a context within which productive potential is locally calibrated and invoked. Work in pre-industrial society is both an economic and social contribution to socially approved activity, which variously makes the community more secure, integrated, protected or externally valued. It can take the form of productive activity such as harvesting food, securing territorial boundaries, enhancing the protection of a settlement and also cultural activity that sustains group cohesion (McClelland, 1961). In pre-capitalist society, although work could often be haphazard and at the whim of natural and seasonal forces, the equation of work with localised and community-specific value systems equated to polymorphic activities, contributions and valuations. Work was not constructed as an all-or-nothing formalised system with clear productive thresholds. The subsistence or petty commodity production characteristics of many pre-industrial societies did not require this formulation. Over time, work became synonymous with contracted, and often pre-calibrated, assumptions as to normal productivity parameters into which work and worker have to fit. Time itself is quantified and disciplined into set units of worth in this formulation (Thompson, 1967).

As work came to be associated increasingly with paid employment, unemployment emerges as its natural corollary. As the industrial sociologist Grint (1991, p 7; see also Joyce, 1987) notes: 'Unemployment is not a category that would be recognized outside of a very limited slice of space and time ... [and] tells us as much about the kind of society we inhabit as about a kind of individual stigmatised.' Here, Grint is making clear that the notion of being unemployed equates to the position of not being able to sustain paid employment in an increasingly harsh, unstable (with cyclical waves of economic recession) and calculative system. Although the absence of work was not unknown in pre-industrial society, it was often due to illness or sanctioned non-activity or crop failure. However, structural unemployment can be understood as the often socially stratified and structural absence of opportunities for growing numbers of sick and disabled people who could not conform to productivity and performativity standards in some productive contexts (Roulstone, 2002).

Hence, work can be understood in multifarious ways to include a range of economic and cultural activity. Work can variously be construed as 'transformative capacity' (Brown, 1992) as a means to realise our species being as in Marx's notion of *homo faber* or as Hegel (1807) notes in *Phenomenology of the spirit* as a reproduction of the self. Marx (1844, p 14) makes clear even in his earlier philosophical writings the freedom and yet constraint of *homo faber*:

> Man is directly a natural being. As a natural being and as a living natural being he is on the one hand endowed with natural powers, vital powers, he is an active natural being. These forces exist in him as tendencies and abilities – as instincts. On the other hand, as a natural, corporeal, sensuous objective being he is a suffering, conditioned and limited creature, like animals and plants. That is to say, the objects of his instincts exist outside him, as objects independent of him; yet these objects are objects that he needs, essential objects, indispensable to the manifestation and confirmation of his essential powers.

And yet, despite this very raw and real confrontation with nature, in productive terms (as an activity and affirmation), here lies the basis of the self-realisation of humans. This is because this work 'would have directly confirmed and realized my authentic nature.... Our production would be as many mirrors from which our natures would shine forth. This relation would be mutual: what applies to me would also apply to you' (Marx, 1992, pp 277-8). Here, Marx is making clear that work has not always been subject to an impersonal calculation and the means of work (for instance, machinery and workplaces) have not always been owned by others whose interests are at odds with workers. In this sense, work becomes something that is increasingly estranged from an individual as work begins to be constructed as paid employment.

Developments that link productive work with contractual, carefully delineated and timed exchanges can be traced to pre-industrial market developments. As Dumont (1977) notes, the ideas of Adam Smith and the 17th- and 18th-century mercantilists led to a merging of state/political and economic spheres. In this sense, although at first far from widespread constructions, in time political citizens become those who can be accommodated both in the new global marketplace and as welfare categories within state systems. Similarly, binary notions of the formal/informal economy grew out of this nascent market ideology. Prior to this point, local constructions of valid economic activity covered much that would later be placed either side of a legitimate binary. Hence, 'reciprocal arrangements not placed in the realm of official records suddenly became aberrant economic activities as citizenship and engagement with official strictures become intertwined-taxes, returns' (Harding and Jenkins, 1989, p 56). Finnegan et al (1985, p 461) make a similar point in stating it 'is somehow implicitly assumed that only jobs which are remunerated through the cash nexus as part of market place transactions and are counted and taxed by government agencies is real work'.

What, then, are the guiding principles of participation in these newly developed market economies? Udy (1970, p 40) is useful on this point, noting that: 'Participation in contractual work organizations is based on an explicit agreement to behave in a specified way for a specified time in the future.' The ability to conform to productive norms is key here. But market capacity also requires a more generally congruent market commitment and worldview. What McClelland (1961, p 16) dubs the 'industrial ethic' requires a future commitment and the 'need for achievement'. In a similar vein, Hagen (1962, p 11) highlights the indispensability of values conducive to the development of innovative 'entrepreneurial personalities'. In complex market and productive settings, a clear rule-bound and legal-rational structure is established that is transferable and replicable elsewhere. Hagen (1962, p 79) characterises this by noting that: 'Manpower, authority structure and rationality are among the most important dimensions of complex organization.'

Such calculative, impersonal and monetarily based organisations of work, however, are not universal. In pre-advanced industry, obligations were often to family/kin. So, for example, in Malinowski's (1922) famous study of Trobriand Islanders he asserted that economic and social ties were inextricably linked in the cognitive, ritual and economic structures of everyday life. This assertion is still present in writings that are concerned with kinship and markets, and traditional and modern trading systems such as many South Asian economies (Fukuyama, 2011). Commitments to economic goals are here synonymous with commitments to wider social mores. In this sense, the terms 'work', 'leisure' and 'rest' are all highly relative and arguably meaningless categories where they are so closely bound together.

Many ritual practices grew out of physical activities, risks and challenges. Productive cosmology was subordinate to a wider cosmology of the kin and spirit network. Likewise, Ivens' (1930, p 35) depiction of Solomon Islanders established that: 'In general, each family works its own plot through various kinds of communal and sharing arrangements that are not possible without kindred. At periods of peak workload families reciprocate with each other as well as families in their kindred'. The anthropologist Marshall Sahlins (1972) asserted that much pre-industrial economic activity did not conform to the notion of working and fixed constructions of hours and days of work at the heart of modern organisation, as is still the case in some peasant societies (Bourdieu, 1977). This notion of a reluctant proletariat is deliciously conveyed in E.P. Thompson's (1967) 'Time, work discipline and industrial capitalism' where he notes that pre-industrial virtues had to be erased from the industrial proletariat if they were to undertake a full working week. Here, the particularistic nature of familial/kin organisations suffer from 'intrinsic manpower limitations, since they are by nature restricted to a given network of kin relations and subsistence values. This situation poses routine problems in the face of heavy seasonal workloads in agriculture' (Udy, 1970, p 66). We know, of course, that economy, society and belief systems intersected in aiding or limiting 'advanced' industrial society's development (Weber, 1905).

The notion of waged work being the basis of a *good society* connects otherwise disparate writings. For example, Saint Simon and Thomas Carlyle were both very much against the prescriptions of ancient society that equated hard work with very low social status (Held, 1987). Even during the 19th century, some commentators constructed the necessity to undertake paid work as the antithesis of gentlemanly and conspicuous living (Veblen, 1899). While early capitalism struggled with what it viewed as recalcitrant and refractory people unsuited to the world of work (Lafargue, 1883; Thompson, 1967), the logic of industrial capitalism and a more narrowly defined notion of work-ability (as the ability to sustain paid labour) began to spread as the default assumption. As disabled people often occupied lower social positions, the benefits of paid work and a leisured life each became out of reach for many disabled people. In a more philosophical vein, Lafargue (1883, p 4; see also Chapter Thirteen, this volume) argued for the 'right to be lazy', noting:

> Capitalist ethics, a pitiful parody on Christian ethics, strikes with its anathema the flesh of the labourer; its ideal is to reduce the producer to the smallest number of needs, to suppress his joys and his passions and to condemn him to play the part of a machine turning out work without respite and without thanks.

Thus, for Lafargue (1883, p 29), 'laziness' (what essentially meant a shorter working day of no more than three hours) would enable creative escape from, and the transcending of, capitalist work precepts and effects by allowing 'the rest of the day and night for leisure and feasting'. Bertrand Russell (1935) explored similar ideas in *In praise of idleness*. While recognising the importance of the way labour markets were organised, Russell's arguments were more focused on the cultural importance of paid work, in particular the way in which earning money, rather than spending it, was held to be virtuous for working people. However, for Russell (1935, p 2) it was consumption that helped to maintain demand:

> [W]hat a man earns he usually spends, and in spending he gives employment. As long as a man spends his income, he puts just as much bread into people's mouths in spending as he takes out of other people's mouths in earning. The real villain, from this point of view, is the man who saves.

For Russell (1935), a shorter working day (he suggested four hours) would allow more people to do paid work because not only would it require more people to do the same amount of work, but also it would allow working people to consume, but also to engage in activities that, once again, for the majority were beyond the expectations of capitalism (for instance, by allowing working people to develop their interests in science, the arts and politics), but: 'Above all, there will be happiness and joy of life, instead of frayed nerves, weariness, and dyspepsia' (Russell, 1935, p 14).

More recently, Gorz (1985), following the early philosophical works of Karl Marx, suggests that idleness is not the answer, but scope for heterogeneous productive capacities to afford better realisations of the self. Marx, of course, wrote extensively about alienated and unalienated labour (Marx, 1844). Of note here, Marx also had a very expansive notion of economic production and a refusal to see such contributions as simply deriving from paid work. For example, he provides what might be seen as a somewhat 'tongue in cheek' appraisal of a social category (prisoners) that some might see as the least productive of all social members:

> The criminal produces not only crime but also criminal justice, he produces the professor who delivers lectures on criminal law, and even the inevitable textbook in which the professor presents his lecture as a commodity for sale to

the market. There results an increase in material wealth....
Further the criminal produces the whole apparatus of the
police and criminal justice [system]. (Cited in Bottomore
and Rubel, 1963, p 167)

This is an extreme, but useful, example of how social accounting of
value or productivity is delineated crudely and exclusively in most
advanced industrial societies. This formulation by Marx makes clear
that there are many forms of value created by individuals that are
more or less valued and rewarded even in advanced economies and
that the calculative nature of capitalism is highly selective in just what
it sanctions as worthy of reward.

Gender, household and the disappearing worker

When looking at how productive selves through history are constructed
to be more narrowly defined in terms of paramount market principles,
a good example, and one that parallels the exclusion of many disabled
people's lives from the badge of the productive, is the gradual historic
redefinition of domestic labour as non-productive. With the rise of
public, dislocated and contractual work in the 18th and 19th centuries,
an opposition was established between valorised and non-valorised
work. As Maynard (1985, p 130) notes: 'Nevertheless, housework is an
important and necessary element in the maintenance of the daily life
for husbands and children, whilst also contributing indirect benefits to
the economy and wider society ... the family is now regarded not as
productive but as a unit of consumption of goods produced elsewhere.'
  Economy qua productive value, begins to be associated with
market as opposed to family/kin-based activity, while productive
activity becomes, in turn, dislocated from the local, domestic and
self-provisioned character of work. What might be called the formal
market economy begins to be defined as a sphere autonomous from
the family in Britain by the 19th century. In a seminal article, Tilly and
Scott (1978, p 227) make clear the anomalous and arbitrary nature of
the distinction between productive and reproductive work: 'If work is
defined as "productive activity for household use or exchange" then it
is clear that ... domestic, productive and reproductive labour is work,
since it has economic value both for the family and society.' This reflects
the broader concerns of the domestic labour debate, which hinge on
the issue of why women have a disproportionate unpaid role in the
domestic sphere and the value (and unrecognised cost savings) that
such domestic work provides (Himmelweit, 1998).

In the same way as women were designed out of the paramount definition of paid work, a process heavily imbued with gender assumptions about biology, the categorical disassociation between 'non-standard' bodies and productive work-ableness had been cemented by the 20th century. This is especially true in terms of barriers to accessing the paid labour market, less so to retention once an impairment emerges (Kirby, 2013).

Only in times of war did necessity challenge these assumptions about productive capacity and help to redefine formerly excluded bodies back into the legitimate employment category (Barnes, 1991; Humphries and Gordon, 1992). Somewhat ironically, of course, during World War Two, Nazism reached its own apotheosis of productive logic, which deemed some disabled people, especially learning disabled people, '*unnütze esser*' or useless eaters. For the Nazis and the Tiergartenstrasse 4 project, a project that exterminated people with intellectual disability, disabled people were degenerates who were able to consume without a corresponding productive contribution to the economic system (Burleigh, 1994). Biologically essentialist ideologies have clearly underpinned each of the above systems of sexism and disablism in establishing industrial ideologies.

Disabled people and contemporary polymorphic productive contributions

Not only are very different constructions and realities of work evident throughout our own island history, but even a brief foray into the contemporary diversity of work in the majority and second world suggests that paid employment is a minority pursuit (Brau and Woller, 2004; Coleridge, 2005). Many activities in the majority world can be construed as economic, whether in the sense of bare survival or through the myriad and portfolio ways in which people 'make out', for example, through barter, small commodity production, foraging, hustling, reciprocal (non-monetary) arrangements, forced labour and contractual employment (Roulstone, 2012). Disabled people, except those with the most profound impairments, sustain roles in many of these activities. Many beg or hustle to ensure a living. Are such activities not work in the broadest sense of efforts to realise goods or money to aid survival and social reproduction? Although invariably in harsh conditions, this minority construction of work as paid employment challenges the assumed binaries of being 'able' or 'not able' to work. The irregularity of economic opportunity and activity perhaps ironically sits better with people who may have partial or intermittent scope to influence productive activity. The absence of authority, legal contract and production norms serves inadvertently to accommodate difference, partial capacity and inclusion, no matter how harsh for those who would be unlikely to reach thresholds of performativity and aesthetic acceptability in 'advanced economies'. It is noteworthy, however, that continued particularistic influence of family and kin can help to assist disabled people in a small number of paid employments in the cities of the majority world. The charitable sector particularly has taken an important role in sponsoring innovative projects that connect disabled people with a range of quasi-market opportunities, such as not-for-profit and cooperative ventures (Coleridge, 2005).

The above observations point to a questioning of paramount Western economic and policy assumptions about the shape and boundaries of work *as* paid employment. Even a passing historical and comparative gaze at 'work' suggests that it takes many forms and that it is possible, and perhaps reasonable, to challenge this assumption of synonymity of work as contracted employment. What it says to contemporary policy analysis is that a revisiting of just what counts as economic contributions is central to any meaningful appraisal of individual and group social worth. This may seem like an exercise in nostalgia or an ill-fated attempt to reverse unidirectional historical and 'linear' processes. However, as the following suggests, even a cursory glance at contemporary activities undertaken by disabled people could be reframed as productive economic activity, the benefits of which accrue to the wider society and community (Prideaux et al, 2009).

Discussion and conclusion: towards an inclusive construction of work

It would be easy to describe the 60% of working-age disabled people not in paid work as economically inactive and unproductive (see HM Government and DWP, 2010). Wider research points to a very different picture. For instance, if interpreted broadly as adding value to communities, stimulating economic activity, aiding environmental improvements and improving a social skill set, then the array of direct payments employment (of personal assistants [PAs]), involvement in access groups, civic contributions and unpaid voluntary work all contribute in a way that, although difficult to monetise, is clearly adding value to the community, economy and wider workforce skillset. For example, disabled people are as likely as their non-disabled counterparts to take part in formal volunteering and civic roles (Williams et al, 2008). Disabled people who are direct payments recipients may employ up to six PAs per week and complete payroll activities, and deal with human resource and health and safety functions. This new form of work and workplace helps to challenge the shifts outlined above towards the binary separation of work and welfare, and also the notion of the increasingly dislocated workplace. Employers are seen as the acme of the economic and social system of capitalist society. Being a disabled employer, administering National Insurance, developing and using knowledge of employment law and enhancing PA skills remain firmly within a cash transfer and welfare paradigm; however, far from the culturally elevated state of 'real' employer. To this extent, our understanding and validations have not kept pace with service models and philosophies. Indeed, the question of who services whom and who is the recipient and who the economic producer is blurred in these new social transactions. However, these are likely to remain the minority economic activity where contractual employment for many remains based on a clear hierarchy of worth and formalised valorisation.

There is a clear need in the absence of enabling and sustained paid work to reflect again on the economic contributions of disabled people, for example, the multiplier effect of their spending, their contribution to the development of a skill set (for themselves as employers and for PAs), and in their voluntary work the contributions that they make in the absence of paid work. Disabled people are also, of course, frequently spousal carers and may be involved in their share of the domestic economy. We need further critical evaluation of the value of disabled people's activities outside of paid work if we are to develop an equitable policy platform fit for the 21st century. Rather than praise idleness or search for a future life without work, it would be better to reframe our understanding of work and welfare to recognise the full economic and social contributions that many disabled people make in contemporary society. Disability policy is both a long-term and immediate activity and responds to both levels of concerns. Unless one takes a Panglossian view that full employment is possible, that the definition of economic activity can formally be widened, then it can be argued that the policy agenda in Britain and other advanced economies is doomed to fail.

The continued framing of disability employment policy success as gaining paid employment would not simply have to solve the immediate goal of engaging more disabled people with paid employment, but would have to square up to the centuries' long shift to contractual work and the decline of kinship. This is not to argue for a kind of policy fatalism that cuts disabled loose from the work–welfare challenge.

Indeed, this is just as abhorrent as a belief in the power of all disabled people to engage in full-time contracted work.

Alongside a failure to dramatically improve the number of disabled people in paid work is a squeamishness in policy terms to have a searching debate about who should be expected to work, who is able to work and who is not. The recent and rather damaging review of out-of-work benefits (Incapacity Benefit and latterly Employment and Support Allowance) for sick and disabled people was not evidence based, nor grounded in humane disability-led assessments (Harrington, 2012). In this way, we still know very little as to where the boundary sits for work ability in a global market. We simply know who is likely to change their behaviour in response to severe welfare and work policy reforms. A cynic might argue that the latter will do, that if it gets more sick and disabled people into paid work then it is good regardless of an evidence base. However, the absence of historical memory in disability employment policy means that much analysis remains abstracted and epiphenomenal. Material surpluses and redistributive welfare systems have shown us the way to a humane society. A humane society has to acknowledge diversity in all its forms, to review its value systems and foster a critique of narrowly defined systems that value certain forms of work and productivity. The right to be supported where work is not possible is also important. History points to the erstwhile polymorphic landscape and its humane possibilities.

References

Abberley, P. (1999) 'The significance of work for the citizenship of disabled people', paper presented at University College Dublin, 15 April.

Anyadike-Danes, M. and McVicar, D. (2008) 'Has the boom in Incapacity Benefit claimant numbers passed its peak?', *Fiscal Studies*, 29(4), pp 415-34.

Barnes, C. (1991) *Disabled people in Britain and discrimination: A case for anti-discrimination legislation*, London: Hurst & Company.

Barnes, C., Mercer, G. and Shakespeare, T. (1999) *Exploring disability: A sociological introduction*, Cambridge: Polity Press.

Bourdieu, P. (1977) *Algeria 1960*, Cambridge: Cambridge University Press; Paris: Éditions de la Maison des Sciences de l'Homme, 1979.

Borsay, A. (2005) *Disability and social policy in Britain since 1750: A history of exclusion*, Basingstoke: Macmillan.

Bottomore, T. and Rubel, T. (1963) *Karl Marx: Selected writings in sociology and social philosophy*, Harmondsworth: Pelican.

Brau, J. and Woller, G. (2004) 'Microfinance: a comprehensive review of the existing literature', *Journal of Entrepreneurial Finance and Business Venture*, 9, pp 1-26.

Brown, R. (1992) *Understanding industrial organisations: Theoretical perspectives in industrial society*, London: Routledge.

Burleigh, M. (1994) *Death and deliverance: 'Euthanasia' in Germany, c.1900 to 1945*, Cambridge: Cambridge University Press.

Coleridge, P. (2005) 'Disabled people and "employment" in the majority world: policies & realities', in A. Roulstone and C. Barnes (eds) *Working futures? Disabled people and social inclusion*, Bristol: Policy Press.

Doray, B. and Macey, D. (1988) *From Taylorism to Fordism: A rational madness*, London: Free Association Books.

Dumont, L. (1977) *From Mandeville to Marx*, Chicago, IL: University of Chicago Press.

DWP (Department for Work and Pensions) (2003) *Pathways to Work: Green Paper*, London: The Stationery Office.

DWP (2008) *No one written off: Reforming welfare to reward responsibility*, London: The Stationery Office.

DWP (2011) *21st century welfare*, London: The Stationery Office.

Finkelstein, V. (1980) *Attitudes and disabled people*, New York, NY: World Rehabilitation Fund Monograph.

Finnegan, R., Roberts, B. and Gallie, D. (1985) *New approaches to economic life*, Manchester: Manchester University Press.

Fukuyama, F. (2011) *The origins of the political order: From prehuman times to the French revolution*, London: Profile Books.

Garthwaite, K. (2011) '"The language of shirkers and scroungers?" Talking about illness, disability and coalition welfare reform', *Disability & Society*, 26, pp 369-72.

Gleeson, B. (1999) *Geographies of disability*, London: Routledge.

Gooding, C. (1995) *Disabling laws, enabling Acts*, London: Pluto.

Gorz, A. (1985) *Paths to paradise: The liberation from paid work*, London: Malcolm Imrie.

Government Equalities Office (2010) *Equality Act 2010: Detailed Guidance*, www.gov.uk/equality-act-2010-guidance

Grint, K. (1991) *Sociology of work: An introduction*, Cambridge: Polity Press.

Grover, C. and Piggott, L. (2013) 'Disability and social (in)security: emotions, contradictions of "inclusion" and Employment and Support Allowance', *Social Policy and Society*, 12(3), pp 369-80.

Grover, C. and Soldatic, K. (2013) 'Neoliberal restructuring, disabled people and social (in)security in Australia and Britain', *Scandinavian Journal of Disability Research*, 15(3), pp 216-32.

Hagen E. (1962) *On the theory of social change: How economic growth begins*, Homewood, IL: Dorsey Press.

Harding, P. and Jenkins, R. (1989) *The myth of the hidden economy*, Milton Keynes: Open University Press.

Harrington, M (2012) *An independent review of the Work Capability Assessment – year three*, London: DWP.

Hegel, G. (1807) *Phänomenologie des Geistes* [Phenomenology of the spirit], Oxford: Oxford University Press, 1976.

Held, D. (1987) *Models of democracy: From Athenian democracy to Marx*, Stanford, CA: Stanford University Press.

Himmelweit, S. (1998) 'Accounting for caring', *Radical Statistics*, winter, pp 1-8.

HM Government and DWP (Department for Work and Pensions) (2010) *The coalition: Our programme for government*, London: HM Government and DWP.

Humphries, S. and Gordon, P. (1992) *Out of sight: The experience of disability 1900-1950*, Plymouth: Northcote.

Ivens, W. (1930) *The Island Builders of the Pacific*, London: Seeley Service.

Joyce, P. (1987) *The historical meanings of work*, Cambridge: Cambridge University Press.

Kirby, P. (2013) 'The body and the industrial workplace, 1780-1850', invited lecture, Northumbria University, 15 May.

Lafargue, P. (1883) *The right to be lazy*, Chicago, IL: Charles H. Kerr.

Lawson, A. (2008) *Disability and equality law in Britain: The role of reasonable adjustments*, Oxford: Hart Publishing.

Lawson, A. and Gooding, C. (eds) (2005) *Disability rights in Europe: From theory to practice*, Oxford: Hart Publishing.

Lister, R. and Bennett, F. (2010) 'The new "champion of progressive ideals"? Cameron's Conservative Party: poverty, family policy and welfare reform', *Renewal*, 18(1), pp 84-109.

McClelland, D. (1961) *The achieving society*, London: Martino Books.

Malinowski, B. (1922) 'Argonauts of the Western Pacific: an account of native enterprise and adventure in the Archipelagoes of Melanesian New Guinea', *Studies in Economics and Political Science*, no. 65, London: Routledge & Kegan Paul, 1984.

Marx, K. (1844) *Economic and philosophic manuscripts*, London: Wilder, 2011.

Marx, K. (1992) *Early writings*, New York, NY: Penguin.

Maynard, M. (1985) 'Houseworkers and their work', in R. Deem and G. Salaman (eds) *Work, culture and society*, Milton Keynes: Open University Press.

OECD (Organisation for Economic Co-operation and Development (2014) *Structural unemployment: The OECD economic outlook: Sources and methods*, Washington, DC: OECD.

Pope, D. and Bambra, C. (2005) 'Has the Disability Discrimination Act closed the employment gap?', *Disability and Rehabilitation*, 27, pp 1261-6.

Prideaux, S., Roulstone, A., Harris, J. and Barnes, C. (2009) 'Disabled people and self-directed support schemes: re-conceptualising work and welfare in the 21st century', *Disability & Society*, special edition, 24(5), pp 557-69.

Roulstone, A. (2002) 'Disabling pasts, enabling futures? How does the changing nature of capitalism impact on the disabled worker and jobseeker?', *Disability & Society*, 17(6), pp 627-42.

Roulstone, A. (2012) 'Disabled people, work and employment: a global perspective', in N. Watson, A. Roulstone, and C. Thomas *Routledge handbook of disability studies*, London: Routledge.

Roulstone, A. (2013) 'Disabled people, work and employment: a global perspective', in N. Watson, A. Roulstone and C. Thomas (eds) *Routledge handbook of disability studies*, London: Routledge.

Roulstone, A. and Prideaux, S. (2012) *Understanding disability policy*, Bristol: Policy Press.

Russell, B. (1935) *In praise of idleness: And other essays*, London: Routledge.

Sahlins, M. (1972) *Stone Age economics*, New York, NY: Aldine Atherton.

Stapleton, D. and Burkhauser, R. (eds) (2003) *The decline in employment of people with disabilities: A policy puzzle*, Kalamazoo, MI: W.E. Upjohn Institute for Employment Research.

Stiker, H. (1999) *History of disability*, Ann Arbor, MI: Michigan University Press.

Taylor, F. (1911) *Scientific management, comprising shop management: The principles of scientific management and testimony before the Special House Committee*, New York, NY: Harper & Row.

Thompson, E.P. (1967) 'Time, work-discipline and industrial capitalism', *Past & Present*, 38(1), pp 56-97.

Tilly, L. and Scott, J. (1978) *Women, work, and family*, London: Routledge.

Udy, S. (1970) *Work in traditional and modern society*, New York, NY: Prentice Hall.

Veblen, T. (1899) *The theory of the leisure class*, New York, NY: Start Publishing.

Warren, J. (2005) 'Disabled people, the state and employment: historical lessons and welfare policy', in A. Roulstone, and C. Barnes (eds), *Working futures: Disabled people, policy and social inclusion*, Bristol: Policy Press.

Weber, M. (1905) *The Protestant ethic and the spirit of capitalism*, London: Unwin Hyman.

Williams, B., Copestake, B., Eversley, J. and Stafford, B. (2008) *Experiences and expectations of disabled people*, London: Office for Disability Issues.

Wren, D. and Bedeian, A. (2004) 'The Taylorization of Lenin: rhetoric or reality?', *International Journal of Social Economics*, 31(3), pp 287-99.

Part Five
Conclusion

FIFTEEN

Conclusion: themes in *Disabled people, work and welfare*

Chris Grover and Linda Piggott

Disabled people, work and welfare has focused on various aspects of relationships between work and income replacement social welfare benefits for disabled people. In various ways, the chapters critically engage with the idea that 'work is the best form of welfare' for disabled people, which is visible in Britain and many of the other countries that the book has focused on. There are several themes that can be drawn from the chapters of the book. These include:

- the nature of wage work as a process;
- difficulties for disabled people that arise from the desire to commodify their labour power;
- difficulties that there are in making the claim that wage work provides for disabled people both a secure and above-poverty-level income.

While these themes are in practice inextricably linked, for analytical purposes we look at them separately below.

Wage work as a socially embedded process

We see, for example, that as it is dependent on the productive value of individual workers, the labour process under capitalist forms of accumulation is something that inherently acts against the employment of disabled people. Competitive individualism and the extraction of profit from the work of employees means that at a fundamental level disabled people are disadvantaged in labour markets. This is because, depending on who one reads, even within disability studies, they are perceived by employers as being less productive than other, non-disabled workers or because of their impairment, they are less productive as they are unable to labour within the temporal and rhythmic demands of wage work and/or its intensity. There have, of course, been various attempts to address such issues, for example, the payment of subsidies to employers so that essentially it becomes profitable to employ them; the retraining and rehabilitation of disabled workers; work experience and tasters that are not only supposed to help (re)attach workless disabled people to labour markets, but also to demonstrate their potential to employers. Such interventions, though, are only required because of the characteristics, such as competitive individualism and economic productivity, that underpin capitalist notions of wage work and other employment activity.

It is within this context that Chapters Twelve to Fourteen discussed aspects of alternatives to wage work as being the activity through which disabled people are valued. Drawing on examples from Britain and Canada, Chapter Twelve discussed the value of work outside of that necessarily concerned with productive value and profit maximisation. For Hall and Wilton, employment within social enterprises and participation in volunteering and the creative arts can have individual and social benefits for disabled people that are outside of those provided by the experience of wage work.

Meanwhile, Chapter Fourteen highlighted the loss of what Roulstone describes as polymorphic landscapes of work to a presumption that it is wage work — and it alone — that should define the potential contribution of disabled people. Such an approach is problematic not only because of the barriers that disabled people face in accessing wage work, but also because it is selective in the contribution that disabled people make in contemporary societies. While it was argued in Chapter Fourteen that such alternatives to wage work do not present a case for withdrawing policies for supporting into wage work disabled people who want to do it, Chapter Thirteen argued that rather than focusing on a 'right to work' for disabled people (along with non-disabled people), there should be a focus upon 'right not to work'. Once again, this would not mean that there would be no employment support for disabled people, but that by not privileging wage work, there would be no need for the state to force disabled people through the imposition of economic and social 'less eligibility' to engage with employment 'support' services. Not only would this remove the more pernicious policies at the intersection of welfare and work in Britain, it also would help to fulfil one of the aims of the disabled people's movement — to enable disabled people choice and control over their lives.

Social policy and the commodification of disabled people's labour

A second theme that emerges from *Disabled people, work and welfare* relates to attempts to commodify the labour power of disabled people. The commodification of labour power essentially involves attempts to get people to sell their labour power as if it were the same as any other commodity. We have seen throughout the chapters of this book that there are various ways of doing this; for example, keeping benefits for disabled people low, even in those countries (such as Poland and the United States [US] – see Chapters Six and Seven respectively) that do not have compulsory work-related activity governed through conditionality as, for instance, Britain does. Such conditionality is a second main way in which governments in various countries, but most notably in Britain and Australia, have attempted to commodify the labour power of disabled people.

There are various problems with policy interventions aimed at commodifying disabled people's labour power. Chapter Fourteen, for instance, pointed to the way that changes to disability benefits in Britain in recent years have been inhumane in the way that they have assessed disability. Furthermore, in different ways, Chapters Four and Five highlighted some of the difficulties in Britain with attempts to commodify the labour power of disabled people. They demonstrated, for instance, the economic and political pressures that act against successful attempts to do this. Despite government discourse that constructs various communitarian and paternalistic concerns with disabled people being excluded from wage work, such people have been pushed to the back of the employment support queue by the marketisation of employment services and by changing political priorities. In the case of marketised services, there is little profit for contractors in delivering employment services to disabled people because they tend to be further away from labour markets. Hence, they tend to be 'parked' in a state of wage worklessness, an observation also made in Chapter Seven on employment services in the US and in Chapter Eight in regard to fears about the provision of services to support disabled people into wage work in Denmark. With regard to changing political priorities, the increase in the number of people registered as unemployed have led to non-disabled workless people being afforded greater political and policy priority than disabled people who do not have a job. The consequence is that those disabled people who are keen to (re)enter wage work, and therefore are willing to have their labour power commodified, are often poorly served by those services that are supposed to support them.

In addition, Chapter Eleven demonstrated that it is often not enough just to deal with the employment issues of disabled people as a means of supporting them into and keeping wage work. In contrast, disabled people often need support with a range of issues that many non-disabled people face (for instance, in balancing work–life demands, debt and short-term financial emergencies) in addition to the barriers and discrimination disabled people face. Furthermore, Chapters Nine and Ten demonstrated the complexities of work–welfare relationships. Chapter Nine, for instance, reminded us that disabled people must not be taken as a homogenous group. Some disabled people, learning disabled people in the case of Chapter Ten, are more disadvantaged in labour markets than others, while Chapter Nine demonstrated that disability intersects with other social structures to reproduce advantage and disadvantage. It showed, for example, the importance of social capital in helping young people who are deaf or hard of hearing in accessing well-paid employment with enterprises that are likely to accommodate their impairments. Taken alongside the other chapters of *Disabled people, work and welfare*, the study discussed in Chapter Nine suggested that the development of more effective employment policies (and, given the findings and analysis in Chapters Four and Five, there surely need to be more effective policies) will not be enough to address the employment disadvantage of all disabled people, for they, at least as they are currently shaped, do not address the social disadvantages faced by the poorest disabled people.

Work, poverty and disability

A third theme that emerges from the chapters in *Disabled people, work and welfare* is the material hardship, the poverty, that disabled people face. There are several reasons for this, and they relate to both wage work as a process and the commodification of disabled people's labour power.

We see this most starkly in the conditionality regimes that frame disability benefits. The focus in Chapter Three on Newstart in Australia demonstrated the dangers for disabled people of welfare regimes that are intent on defining as many disabled people as possible as being fit for work. The consequence of shifting increased numbers of people from income replacement disability benefits to unemployment-related benefits (such as Newstart in Australia and Jobseeker's Allowance in Britain) is that it increases poverty and the further disadvantages – for instance, poor housing, social isolation, and increasing and/or exacerbated mental and physical health problems – that this brings. The ratcheting up of benefit sanctions – so now, for example, in Britain a person adjudged to not be adequately fulfilling the conditions for their receipt of Employment and Support Allowance (ESA) can have it reduced until they do what is demanded of them – will undoubtedly exacerbate the poverty of disabled people in Britain.[1]

Chapters Two and Three demonstrated the fundamental problems with such an approach. Drawing on Stuart White's notion of a 'civic minimum', Chapter Two examined the philosophical difficulties in unilaterally changing the demands made of claimants (that is, increasing their responsibilities) while making it more difficult to claim more generous disability benefits (that is, retrenching their social rights). Moreover, Chapter Three demonstrated in the Australian context the consequence of such retrenchment – a life of 'hard yakka', of having to manage the grind of everyday poverty. As we have seen, though, not all countries have increased the conditionality attached to the receipt of disability benefits. However, we have seen in the case of Poland (Chapter Six) and the US (Chapter Seven) that disabled people in such countries still face severe hardship, for instance, benefits in Poland that equate to less than the minimum wage and which in the US provide an income at or below the poverty level.

At risk of creating spurious spatial hierarchies of disadvantage, it might be argued, however, that the situation in contemporary Britain is particularly difficult for disabled people. This is because the rolling out of ESA, which makes it more difficult for disabled people to claim income replacement benefits on the grounds of disability, has since 2010 been accompanied by austerity measures that have affected not only other benefits paid just to disabled people (for, example, the main additional cost benefit, Disability Living Allowance is being replaced by Personal Independence Payments, with the aim of reducing the caseload by 20% and expenditure by £1 billion per year by 2014/15), but also benefits that are payable to all people because they are either universal or they are means-tested and available to all people providing their income is low enough. In the case of the latter, for example, we can point to the effect of the 'spare room subsidy' (or 'bedroom tax') on disabled people (Cross, 2013). It reduces the amount of Housing Benefit that people living in social housing can receive if they are deemed to be living in a property that has too many bedrooms for their needs. The policy has been condemned as 'causing severe financial hardship and distress to people with disabilities' (Work and Pensions Committee, 2014, para 77). This is because reductions in benefit caused by the implementation of the 'bedroom tax' take no account of 'spare' bedrooms that disabled people require as a consequence of a need to store equipment related to their disability and the difficulty that disabled people face in moving to smaller accommodation that is suitably adapted to their needs.

The consequence of the combination of changes to income replacement benefits for disabled people and austerity-driven welfare 'reform' measures is that disabled people in Britain are facing precarious economic futures as their income, often for the same reasons – a desire on the part of governments to save money and to reinforce the financial incentive to take (low paid) waged work – is eroded from various directions. Perhaps the greatest problem, however, with the approach to address the disadvantage of disabled people through paid work is that such an approach does not particularly offer protection against poverty. In Britain, for example, the issue of in-work poverty is as problematic as that of out-of-work poverty. It has been argued for many years in Britain that 'work [is] the best route out of poverty' (Secretary of State for Work and Pensions, 2010, para 5). If this was ever the case – and evidence suggests that for many people it has not been (see, for example, Abel-Smith and Townsend, 1965) – it certainly no longer is. As Britain's Social Mobility and Child Poverty Commission (2013, pp 5-6) has recently noted, paid work:

> ... is not a cure for poverty. Today child poverty is overwhelmingly a problem facing working families, not just the workless. Two thirds of Britain's poor children – compared to less than half in 1997 – are now in families where an adult works. The available data suggest that in three quarters of those, someone already works full-time.

It is the case, therefore, that even if there is an enforcement of less eligibility to commodify the labour power of more disabled people and to allow more disabled people to access paid work, it is unlikely to address the poverty that they face. The danger is that out-of-work poverty will be replaced by in-work poverty. Overall, what *Disabled people, work and welfare* demonstrates is that the relationship between wage work and welfare is difficult and complex. While the British (and other liberal) welfare regime continues to be rooted in concerns with access to social welfare benefits being particularly discouraging of wage work, disabled people face a future of economic precariousness, of greater poverty, even when in such work.

Note

[1] There have been 86,083 'adverse' sanction decisions made in Britain (that is, those that withhold the payment of at least some benefit) related to Employment and Support Allowance, where it was recorded whether the person had a disability or not. The majority (69.1%, or 59,444) of these decisions involved a person self-declaring a disability (https://sw.stat-xplore.dwp.gov.uk/webapi/jsf/tableView/customiseTable. xhtml).

References

Abel-Smith, B. and Townsend, P. (1965) *The poor and the poorest: A new analysis of the Ministry's of Labour's 'Family Expenditure Surveys' of 1953–54 and 1960*, London: Bell.

Cross, M. (2013) 'Demonised, impoverished and now forced into isolation: the fate of disabled people under austerity', *Disability & Society*, 28(5), pp 719-23.

Secretary of State for Work and Pensions (2010) *Universal Credit: Welfare that works*, Cm 7957, Norwich: The Stationery Office.

Social Mobility and Child Poverty Commission (2013) *State of the nation 2013: Social mobility and child poverty in Great Britain*, London: Social Mobility and Child Poverty Commission.

Work and Pensions Committee (2014) *Support for housing costs in the reformed welfare system*, 4th report of Session 2013-14, HC 720, London: The Stationery Office.

Index

Note: Page numbers in italics refer to tables and figures, and page numbers followed by "n" refer to end of chapter notes